July: Larry and the Love of Oranges

August: Peak Experience

September: Double Duck

October: Gizzards and Grapes

November: Piemonte on Piedmont

December: Chef's Holiday

BAY WOLF
RESTAURANT COOKBOOK

BayWolf
Restaurant Cookbook

Michael Wild

Lauren Lyle

G. Earl Darny   Adele Novelli Crady

Photography by Laurie Smith

TEN SPEED PRESS
Berkeley / Toronto

🔟

Ten Speed Press
Box 7123
Berkeley, California 94707
www.tenspeed.com

Distributed in Australia by Simon & Schuster Australia, in Canada by Ten Speed Press Canada, in New Zealand by Southern Publishers Group, in South Africa by Real Books, in Southeast Asia by Berkeley Books, and in the United Kingdom and Europe by Airlift Book Company.

Cover and book design: Nancy Austin
Copyediting: Rebecca Pepper
Food and prop styling: Wesley Martin and Lauren Lyle

Front and back jacket artwork by Rupert Garcia, reprinted with permission of BayWolf Restaurant; Rena Bransten Gallery, San Francisco; and Galerie Claude Samuel, Paris.

Library of Congress Cataloging-in-Publication Data

BayWolf Restaurant cookbook / Michael Wild ... [et al.] ; photography by Laurie Smith.
    p. cm.
Includes index.
  ISBN 1-58008-260-2
  1. Cookery, American--California style. 2. BayWolf Restaurant. 3. Cookery, International. I. Wild, Michael, 1940–
TX715.2.C34 B39 2001
  641.59794--dc21

                                    2001000926

Printed in Hong Kong

First printing, 2001

1 2 3 4 5 6 7 8 9 10 - 06 05 04 03 02 01

To my family: Felice, Jill, Babu, Avram, and David

Writing a book and running a restaurant share at least one vital distinguishing characteristic: they both require the concerted effort of a group of people working toward a common goal. Thus I want to extend my profound thanks to those whose work has made this book possible and BayWolf a success.

First and foremost, to my partners Larry Goldman and Michael Phelps, who have been with me every step of the way, and to Michael Brown, our former partner, who helped us get started.

To Lauren Lyle, whose passion, skill, and unerring good taste inform every aspect of her work.

To Earl Darny, whose work is indeed a sweet treat and who never misses a beat.

To Adele Crady, amanuensis extraordinaire, who has eaten at BayWolf weekly since we opened and who often knew what I wanted to say better than I did.

To Phil Wood for the proposition, and to Lorena Jones, Nancy Austin, Laurie Smith, and Wesley Martin for the fulfillment and for making us look so good.

In the kitchen, especial thanks to Nathan Peterson for mentoring and maintaining, and to Louis LeGassic for keeping everything together and letting us work around him.

To the kitchen crew present and past: Robert Dorsey, Eugenio Soriano, Steven Alamo, David Tanis, Jene LaRue, Rick Hackett, Carol Brendlinger (for many memorable meals), Steven Brendlinger, Chris Hanson, Lee Colman, Hilary Maxworthy, Mil Apostle, Joe Nouhan, Maggie Pond, Bryar Brown, and Rebecca Carter.

To our former pastry chefs: Anna de Leon, Carly Stillman, Kate Dowling, Cydne Posner, and Karen Nielsen.

To the front crew past and present: Mark McLeod, Dan Robinson, Deborah Stampfli, John Doyle, Eric Ipsen, Kyria Ramey, Gretchen Forsgard-Worthington, Jacinta Bouwkamp, and Jon Carroll (emeritus).

To our devoted and longtime staff: Aaron Turner, Michele Simon, and Jose Barragan.

To the designers, creators, and builders: Randy Wilson, Rick Demarest, Paul Discoe, Janice Weingrod, and Constance Scott.

To my wine mentors and friends: Jim Clendenen, whose passion, skill, good taste, and modesty inspire us all; and Tony Cartlidge, Bob Lindquist, Randall Grahm, Steve Edmunds, Dick and Nancy Ponzi, Gerald Asher, Kermit Lynch, and Becky Wasserman.

To our peerless purveyors: Jim Reichardt, Paul Johnson, Tom Worthington, Bill Fujimoto, Bruce Aidells, Hobbs Shure, The Cheese Board, Steve Sullivan, and George Vukasin.

To the creators of commemorative menus: Will Powers, Cheryl Miller, Robin Cherin, Wesley Tanner, Christine Taylor, and Clay Doyle.

To the community of artists: Rupert Garcia, a great friend to me and the restaurant; and Raymond Saunders, Dewey Crumpler, Archana Horsting, Devorah Nussenbaum, Kaoru Kitigawa, Donna Allman, and Kinde Nebeker.

And special thanks to all of those not listed who have helped the restaurant in numerous ways, large and small, that have not gone unnoticed and unappreciated.

ACKNOWLEDGMENTS

CONTENTS

April: In Paris

May: When Northern
Italy Took Hold

June: Wine Matters

July: Larry and the Love of Oranges

August: Peak Experience

September: Double Duck

October: Gizzards and Grapes

November: Piemonte on Piedmont

December: Chef's Holiday

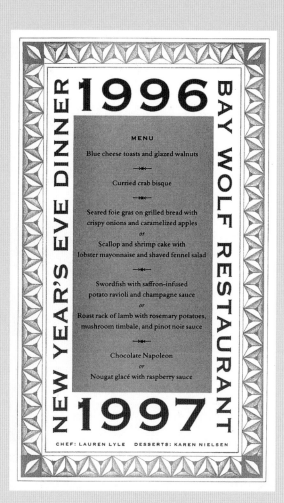

NEW YEAR'S EVE DINNER

BAY WOLF RESTAURANT

1996

1997

MENU

Blue cheese toasts and glazed walnuts

Curried crab bisque

Seared foie gras on grilled bread with
crispy onions and caramelized apples
or
Scallop and shrimp cake with
lobster mayonnaise and shaved fennel salad

Swordfish with saffron-infused
potato ravioli and champagne sauce
or
Roast rack of lamb with rosemary potatoes,
mushroom timbale, and pinot noir sauce

Chocolate Napoleon
or
Nougat glacé with raspberry sauce

CHEF: LAUREN LYLE   DESSERTS: KAREN NIELSEN

MENU BY CHRISTINE TAYLOR

When we opened the doors to BayWolf for lunch on the vernal equinox in 1975, a square-block enclave in North Berkeley hadn't yet been christened the Gourmet Ghetto. Bruce Aidells hadn't found his way into the kitchen of Le Poulet, American Charcuterie was still science fiction in Omaha, and Chez Panisse had barely begun serving its $4.95 prix fixe meals. Unknown to all of us, however, a new generation of intrepid youthful travelers, Eurail passes in hand, was returning home with visions of boulangeries and a longing for Italian street markets.

I'd been teaching English and world literature at San Francisco State, enjoying the privileged status of being one of the youngest faculty members. My childhood friend, Larry Goldman, had decamped from dental school. We'd spent our young adult years hanging out, often together, in all the beatnik, poet, home-style Italian, pasta-eating, and espresso-drinking meccas of the hipster artistes in North Beach. We'd stand outside the Blackhawk, too poor to go in, and listen to Thelonious Monk or John Coltrane or sometimes outside the Jazz Workshop, wishing we could slip inside to hear Charlie Mingus.

Our model restaurant was the old Little Joe's on Broadway, where we'd invest in the revolving daily specials. Maybe tripe on Mondays, braised chicken with green olives ladled over polenta on Tuesdays, sausage and chard on Wednesdays, and, on beloved Fridays, the melismatic fish stew, *cacciucco*. I tried to eat once a week at Vanessi's. I'd sit at the counter and watch them cook something on the old oak grill. I was more interested in the cooking and the taste of the food than in the concept of styling. I was attracted to friendly, wholesome food.

I had grown up around people who took food seriously without drawing any attention to it or connecting any virtue to it. Our family's idea of Saturday entertainment in the 1950s was to drive out to the San Fernando Valley and visit the chicken farms, buy fresh produce, and go to farmer's markets. So, although I had always loved to shop, cook, and eat, for too long I considered it beneath me to waste my skills as writer, poet, artist, and teacher on the lowly job of cooking.

We knew that we had an aptitude for eating and some combined skill for cooking, but it wasn't our plan actually to run the restaurant. We thought we'd start it up, get it running smoothly, and then slide into the next midlife crisis. Our launch was serendipitous. I took Larry out in a boat on Lake Merritt and said, "I have this proposition. I'm thinking about opening up a little business modeled on the Cheese Board. The people who work there will own it and be part of it. Do you want to do this or not? You've got to answer before we get back to shore." I think he said yes. Two other friends, Michael Brown and Michael Phelps, also said yes and became our partners.

INTRODUCTION

Virtually everyone we talked to advised us not to do it: "You're undercapitalized, you're inexperienced, far more restaurants fail than succeed, don't even think about it." We rose to the challenge. We started with $20,000, a month-to-month verbal rental agreement, and more experience in eating than in managing and serving. When our carefully chosen selection of international cheeses fell prey to mice in the basement, we moved into our next unplanned incarnation as a homey little lunch spot, serving omelets and hamburgers in our Victorian house, likened by an early reviewer to "a small-town boardinghouse."

We were naive. It didn't occur to us that, for the first three years, we'd be working full time, double time, all the time. That we'd spend nine months painfully remodeling the building, that our other partners would be as inexperienced in every practical and useful detail as we were. Michael Brown had worked briefly in the old upstairs bar at Chez Panisse, but his most recent work experience had been with the road-show production of *Hair*. The rest of us had never worked in a restaurant or been in a business. Given our beatnik intellectual anti-aspirations, the idea of becoming businessmen was neither attractive nor interesting. We had disdain for it.

We were known as "what was the name of that place where we ate?" until our lawyer persuaded us that a name was essential. Our midlife crises had brought us to this building and to this work, and so we called our corporation Ananke, for the Greek concept of divine necessity. In a wild session of free association, we began to focus on a name that would clearly identify us with the San Francisco Bay Area, with a little aside to a former North Oakland inhabitant, Jack London, and his story of the Sea Wolf. Stirring in my affection and affinity for the old English saga of Beowulf, we had our name. Beowulf's weird—his destiny and his adversary—was the monster Grendel. Our weird was our reluctant initiation into corporate America.

The restaurant is a source of joy to us now, a quarter-century later, but for the first three years we were the last people to get paid. The money part was the hardest part, and we learned the hardest way. We were always demoralizingly in debt. We were the dishwashers and the janitors. We had no long-term plan, no underpinning business model. For me, the first three years were the equivalent of getting a doctoral degree in food and wine.

Miraculously, we were also able to buy the building. I'd been cooking in the restaurant, a little reluctantly, a little resentfully, for a few years. In 1977 I traveled in France with my godparents. They introduced me to three-star restaurants. I was welcomed by Roger Vergé at Moulins de Mougins and treated as a social equal and a colleague. I was given the run of the restaurant. I was astounded to discover that the chef-owner-proprietor was an exalted being in France, revered as an equal of artists and painters and poets.

PHOTO BY JACINTA BOUWKAMP

I studied the menus, the restaurant graphics, the wine shops, bakeries, épiceries, fromageries, and charcuteries—no museums, no sights, no castles. I embarked on an intensive self-driven march through the entire French canon, reading, cooking, and drinking my way through *Larousse Gastronomique.* In a country where chefs are royalty and food is an art, I had my epiphany. When I returned, I proclaimed, "This is worthy of my ego. This is what we're going to do, and we're going to do it well."

I came home from France with incredible energy and renewed verve. In my absence, Lily LeCoq and David Tanis (later to become a principal chef for Chez Panisse's upstairs cafe and downstairs restaurant) had come to work for us. They had simplified and clarified the menu, directing and focusing it along traditional French lines. We began, little by little, to see the path ahead. We saw that we'd be able to make changes and maybe even bank salaries. After five years we were able to redesign the restaurant, add a second dining room and a grill, and expand our seating capacity from forty or fifty to our current hundred. The restaurant changed, our commitment deepened, and our aspirations began to evolve.

PHOTO BY LIZ HAFALIA

My parents were Russian and German. We had lived in France, I'd traveled in Italy, and I had been exposed to an enormous range of good home and ethnic cooking. This background gave me a head start. I knew what all of the dishes that I'd rediscovered in France were, what they consisted of, and how they should taste. I could remember and reproduce them. I'd never invested this gift with any particular significance—it was just part of my birthright—but I used it to good advantage in the restaurant.

Slowly we realized that we were poised to be part of a cultural phenomenon. Suddenly chefs and restaurants were on the cover of *Time* magazine, in the newspapers as tastemakers, evolving into cultural icons on television. Individuals were changing the way they perceived food and their personal, emotional, and historical relationships to it. There was tremendous interest in all things edible. Being a chef was no longer a lowly profession in America. This suited me just fine. I enjoy the processes of shopping and cooking. Like drawing and painting and writing, they involve a great element of showing off. It feeds my ego when I get people to notice me, get a response, get them to notice how interesting and tasty I can be. I'd rather make something and blow your mind than make something and blow my mind. When I'm by myself, I never cook.

We have always cooked from the marketplace, not because it's fashionable but because it's the right thing to do. Whether at home or at work, I go to the market, see what looks great, and let it dictate what I'm going to serve. In the early years I'd go every morning to Allied Poultry, C&M Meats, Monterey Market, and Spengers. I had to go, and we had to pay cash; we had no credit. Now the meat, the fish, our bounty of Reichardt ducks are all delivered, but I still go to Monterey Market most days and examine the produce for myself to see what Bill Fujimoto has been encouraging his growers to produce. If Bill tells you something is organic, it's because he knows what his growers do to their soil, what they do and don't put on their plants. He's very principled, and his standards are high. I enjoy every aspect of the market.

I've adjusted my views on the virtues of "organic" food in the years since organic meant hideous, gnarly carrots at the Berkeley Co-op. For a long time I didn't care; I thought what you *did* mattered more than what you did it to. I thought I'd rather have something not perfect cooked by someone who knew how to cook than something perfect cooked by someone who was inept. Ultimately it's better to have something perfect cooked by someone who knows how to cook.

At BayWolf, we try to take the best ingredients and the traditions that are most appropriate to them and imbue them with some fun, put our own creative spin on them. There's no reason to emulate the classics note for note, but from them we can learn a great deal about techniques and combinations.

Recipes are a point of departure, and then you play with your food and make it your own. Cook it, push it, finesse it, figure out how to improve the flavor with a little of this, less of that. Never assume that a recipe is the definitive version of something. A good cook needs to trust and refine and fine-tune according to his or her own sensibilities, to learn the difference between something that's good and something that's very good.

LAUREN AT WORK.

A few individuals can hear a piece of music and reproduce it from memory. A few chefs can taste a dish and know how to reproduce it, know the technique and ingredients, and maybe even identify who cooked it.

Our menus are outlined monthly around themes that we've refined over the years. The themes derive from our obsessions, talents, preferences, and affections. In January we prepare the sort of heartwarming, nurturing, robust dishes that would get anyone through a gloomy winter. In February, we introduce the romance of Venice and prepare an annual Valentine menu. With March, we launch into the opening rites of spring, remembering various eating trips and the ideas we carried home. April in Paris is apt: I was born in Paris, in April. In April the Bay Area marketplace is filled with tiny spring vegetables, very much like the marketplaces in Paris. For May we move to northern Italy because we love the food and the consonance of the marketplace with our own. The month of June celebrates wines and their counties and countries. July and August are months of all-American local produce exuberance. In the late summer we have an abundance of local tomatoes, peppers, figs, the produce that bespeaks Spain.

We opened the doors for dinner on the autumnal equinox in 1975 and so September signals our anniversary, a time to celebrate our purveyors and our fabulous ducks and proprietary wines. October hovers around felicitous fall combinations of vegetables and fruits. November speaks directly to the foods of the Piemonte: glorious foraged mushrooms, tiny grilled birds, powerfully infused polentas, and the Concord grapes grown in abundance in the Napa Valley. In December we host dozens of individual family and office parties, prepare batches of duck confit for the new year, and celebrate in our own ways with our family and friends.

Working with our executive chefs over the years, integrating their experiences and preferences with my own, tasting and incorporating newly available varieties of locally grown produce, we perpetually reevaluate and redefine our monthly concepts. We know the overall structure a year in advance, but the refinements and embellishments rely on the marketplace and the largesse and inventiveness of chef Lauren Lyle.

I hired Lauren the day she walked through the door. It wasn't her résumé that convinced me; it was her enthusiasm and obvious passion. She started on the bottom rung as a pastry chef's assistant and propelled herself into chef de cuisine. You'd show her once and she could do it exactly the way you had shown her, and then the next time she'd improve on it. No one I've ever known can extract as much flavor from or introduce as much flavor into things as Lauren can. My style was a lusty one, and Lauren was a match for it. There's *stuff* to it: even when it's completely delicate, it still has this internal power. Richness isn't the same as substance.

Pastry chef Earl Darny came to us from Stars (in its prime). An ideal pastry chef is, like Earl, infused with enthusiasm for the challenge of bringing exotic and familiar, delicate and homey, rich and refined favorites, discoveries, and inventions to our devoted and dessert-loving clientele.

Little things make a large difference in a small restaurant. We agonize about these small details and play with them endlessly, tweaking as we go, discussing the niceties of the particulars inherent in "getting it right." It's essential that the entrance be spotlessly clean,

Bay Wolf
1999 Pinot Dinner

Amusements en passant

1991 Au Bon Climat Sparkling Pinot Noir-et-Blanc
1995 Handley Sparkling Brut Rosé

Double duck plate

1997 Au Bon Climat Pinot Blanc "Reserve"
1997 Handley Pinot Gris
1998 Ponzi Pinot Gris
1997 WillaKenzie Pinot Blanc

Seared king salmon with pancetta

1997 Au Bon Climat Pinot Noir "Sanford & Benedict"
1997 Handley Pinot Meunier
1997 Ponzi Pinot Noir
1997 WillaKenzie Pinot Meunier

Duck braised in Pinot Noir

1997 Au Bon Climat Pinot Noir "Isabelle"
1996 Handley Pinot Noir "Estate/Reserve"
1996 Ponzi Pinot Noir "Reserve"
1996 WillaKenzie Pinot Noir "Pierre Leon"

1997 Au Bon Climat Pinot Noir "Isabelle"
1996 Handley Pinot Noir "Estate/Reserve"
1996 Ponzi Pinot Noir "Reserve"
1996 WillaKenzie Pinot Noir "Pierre Leon"

Golden raisin ricotta tart

1997 Cold Heaven "Late Harvest" Viognier

CHEF: Lauren Lyle
SWEETS: Earl Darny
WINEMAKERS: Jim Clendenen, Mila Handley, Laurent Montalieu, Dick and Nancy Ponzi

MENU BY CHRISTINE TAYLOR

be inviting, and have a warm glow to it. Equally essential is that the bar person is smiling and that everyone on the staff greets everyone who walks in.

We aren't a deep-pocket restaurant; we weren't made perfectly at birth. Every year we experience some kind of wonderful, small improvement in terms of the physical place. If you do it all yourself, you can constantly improve it. The restaurant looks nothing today like it did twenty years ago. The level of style and sophistication has grown with age and relative prosperity, as we've gotten older and learned to value these things more. We have more resources to bring to the question of what we can do to make the restaurant look and feel more comfortable, to more keenly mirror our sensibilities, to enhance the ease and pleasure of dining here, to refine the look and the service. We have more experience and greater clarity about our objectives now. We want our restaurant to be our own first restaurant of choice for its spirited, elegant ambience; its imaginative, tasty food; and its flawlessly friendly, entirely professional service.

The restaurants that have staffs with the greatest longevity are motivated by something other than money. They value the family thing, the quality thing, and feeling good about their workplace. In the beginning we were four partners. Three of us, myself, Larry Goldman, and Michael Phelps, have stayed the course for twenty-five years. This fact brings stability and focus to the restaurant, a committed family with common interests and a common interest in maintaining standards of excellence, vitality, and credibility.

We have long been under the spell of the sensibility articulated by Elizabeth David. Her books are pressed on every one of our kitchen staff. We expect them to embrace her injunction to cook "with care and skill, regard for the quality of the materials, without extravagance or pretension." We have few traditions at BayWolf, but we bring to our endeavor due regard for quality, joy for the labor, and respect for the traditions we find most felicitous.

As a friend of the restaurant and its proprietress, I'm treated like a pasha at Chez Panisse. The ideal BayWolf would be a place in which every individual coming through our doors would feel the comfortable ease and privilege of the insider, would be treated with the respect accorded the rich and famous or the fearsome food critic. We've grown to believe that our restaurant can be a meeting place for friends and strangers, a hangout for artists, a festive space in which to celebrate birthdays and anniversaries, New Year's Eve and Christmas Eve, a home away from home. We want to provide some mortar of soulfulness between the courses. If we don't have uncompromisingly high standards, it's just a job and we've misjudged our calling.

BAY WOLF

RESTAURANT COOKBOOK

The Wolf at the Door

For the American cook on a culinary pilgrimage to France, the ingesting of cassoulet in all its variety is a soulful rite of passage. I've eaten many singularly unhealthy meals while indulging my craving for cassoulet. It was a dish that was rarely encountered here in the early 1980s, and so I was compelled to eat it wherever and whenever I could. With its evocations of ancient pots simmering in rustic fireplaces all winter long, cassoulet is quintessentially French. It's the perfect winter meal, as magical as its mystique. What could be finer on a cold winter's eve than a pot of childhood-infused pork and beans with the amendment of crisp crumbs folded and refolded into the mix, absorbing the grease and intensifying the astounding layers of flavors and textures, the long, slow cooking producing a tantalizing mist of aromas?

Cassoulet derives its name from the *cassole,* the covered pot in which it's brewed and served. It was once unique to the duck- and goose-fat-rich region of southwestern France. Every town and every cook has their own version, made with local duck and goose rillettes or confit, some legendary mythical bean from grandmother's apocryphal garden, and coarse local sausages of duck, goose, lamb, or pork.

French and Italian charcuteries relate to pork the way Eskimos relate to snow and Bedouins to sand: in it they see infinite variety, with countless nuances, and descriptive variables. You'll see ten kinds of bacon from different parts of the pig: one for lardons, one for soup or cassoulet, and maybe a few for breakfast. The degree of smokiness and the balance or imbalance of fat to lean seem infinitely variable and endlessly appetizing.

I love the pig, particularly in those places where the people and the culture love it and know what to do with it: France, Italy, Germany, and China. When I travel, I zero in on the local pig products. From my first visits to Europe as a child, I learned the pleasures of starting every meal with ham. It was easy for a kid to eat, and it was familiar yet different everywhere. Every region has its own, and it's my self-appointed task to seek out the local ham wherever I am.

I've eaten many memorable cassoulets, but the greatest ones I've eaten have been here, in the BayWolf kitchen. Our variations, refinements, and departures are based on the traditional form, reinvented each winter for ourselves and our fellow feeders. The cooking style and the inspiration derive from France, but the product itself has become local. Our ducks are drinking the same water as our Sonoma grapes. We use ham hocks from local artisan Hobbs Shure because not only are they local, but they're also some of the best on earth. He cuts the front end of little prosciutti, and then cures and smokes them like miniature hams.

Bill Fujimoto of Monterey Market encourages a farmer near Dixon to grow heirloom beans. We use one type of bean per cassoulet but a variety of beans during our brief cassoulet season: little and big lima beans (freshly dried), scarlet runners, Barlottis that look like rugby balls and have a texture resembling bean butter, and the most popular bean in France, the flageolet.

Hearty winter dishes perfectly showcase Lauren's ability to create the ever-varying, always wonderful substance we call goo. It's an unlovely word for a refinement of essences. If we were in France they might call this substance rillette or acknowledge its lineage from confit. It isn't a sauce. Instead, it's a celebration of her ability to reduce meat stuffs, particularly duck, not to the point of bitterness or over-reduction but to their most intensely concentrated form. It's inexplicable and ineffable. It externalizes her concept of taste and the relevance of richly balanced layers of flavor. You could spread it on bread or take it home and have it for breakfast or slather it on your body. It embodies all the generous joy of the thing itself. You can't stop eating it.

Eating my way through France, I've marveled at the number of people there, especially from an older generation, who return routinely to their traditional restaurant to get the traditional dish prepared in precisely the same way it's been prepared for hundreds of years. At BayWolf, we're the opposite. We want our food to taste marvelous, we want to mine the past for jewels, but absolutely everything we do is an adaptation, an improvisation.

With your cassoulet, drink a rustic wine with enough acidity to keep things moving and your palate as clear as it's likely to be under the circumstances. It isn't an occasion for a really good bottle of wine but a perfect opportunity for a Beaujolais that rinses your teeth, a quaffing wine. The more complexly flavored a dish is, the simpler the wine you should serve. The more singular the flavors, the more complex the wine.

CHIOGGIA BEET AND TANGERINE SALAD *with Celery, Walnuts, and Citrus Vinaigrette*

Baby Chioggia beets, striped pink, orange, red, or white, are gorgeous little gems to look at and to eat. They also have a more delicate texture than the baseball-sized beets that may be more available. Seek them out at farmer's markets, or take a shot at growing them. The vinaigrette for this salad is based on a citrus reduction that intensifies the fruit flavor. If your vinaigrette seems too thick, just whisk in the juice of another tangerine to loosen it.

CITRUS VINAIGRETTE
Zest and juice of 4 seedless tangerines
2 tablespoons white wine vinegar
2 teaspoons sugar
Juice of 2 small Meyer or Eureka lemons
Salt and freshly ground black pepper
1/2 cup extra virgin olive oil

BEETS
2 bunches baby Chioggia beets
Salt

4 seedless tangerines
1/2 cup sliced celery, almost paper-thin
1/2 cup walnuts, toasted and coarsely chopped
1/2 cup pomegranate seeds
4 small handfuls red lettuces such as red oak leaf or red romaine
Salt and freshly ground pepper

TO PREPARE THE VINAIGRETTE:

Finely chop the tangerine zest, and place it in a saucepan with the juice, vinegar, and sugar. Bring to a boil, then lower the heat and reduce until only a couple of tablespoons remain and the liquid has become a glaze. Pour into a small bowl and cool. Squeeze in the lemon juice, season with salt and pepper, and finish by whisking in the olive oil.

TO PREPARE THE BEETS:

Preheat the oven to 375°. Trim the beet greens and save for another purpose. Wash the beets thoroughly and bake in a single layer, covered, in a pan with a little water. The beets are ready when their skins slip off easily. Baby beets will take 20 to 30 minutes, larger beets may need to cook up to 1 1/2 hours. Cool the beets, remove the skins, and cut into rounds and quarters randomly. Sprinkle with salt and marinate in a little vinaigrette until ready to serve.

TO ASSEMBLE THE SALAD:

Peel the remaining 4 tangerines with a knife and cut into rounds. Toss the beets, celery, walnuts, tangerine rounds, and pomegranate seeds in some of the vinaigrette. Dress the lettuces lightly and carefully with the vinaigrette and season with salt and pepper.

SERVES 4

4

WARM DUCK LIVER SALAD
with Apples, Bacon, Sherry, and Dandelion

Duck liver exists to accompany sweet apples and bitter greens. The caramelized apples work best if sautéed over medium-high heat. This means you must tend to them. Using tongs to turn the apples has the unfortunate result of squishing them. Instead, practice flipping them over in the pan with a flick of your wrist or turning them gently with a spatula.

RENDERED DUCK FAT
2 cups water
6 to 8 cups duck fat

VINAIGRETTE
1 shallot, minced
1 thyme sprig
1 garlic clove, smashed
1/4 cup sherry vinegar
4 ounces bacon, sliced
1/2 cup virgin olive oil
Salt and freshly ground black pepper

SALAD
2 green apples, unpeeled, cut into chunks
1 tablespoon butter

2 tablespoons sugar
Splash of sherry
1 cup tiny baguette or levain cubes
Salt and freshly ground black pepper
2 bunches dandelion greens
8 duck livers, bile sacks and veins removed

TO RENDER THE DUCK FAT:

Put the water and duck fat in a heavy saucepan and bring to a boil. Lower the heat and simmer until the water has boiled out and the remaining fat is clear and golden. Strain. You will have about 6 cups. Unused rendered duck fat may be stored in a covered glass jar in the refrigerator or freezer indefinitely.

TO PREPARE THE VINAIGRETTE:

Soak the shallot, thyme, and garlic in the vinegar for 20 minutes. Cook the bacon until it is done but not too crispy. Cut it into small pieces and set aside in a large stainless steel bowl. Pour any rendered bacon fat into the vinegar mixture, and finish with oil, salt, and pepper.

TO PREPARE THE SALAD:

Sauté the apples in the butter and sugar until caramelized. When golden, deglaze the pan with a splash of sherry. Set aside. Preheat the oven to 350°. Toss the bread with 2 tablespoons of the duck fat or olive oil, sprinkle with salt and pepper, and toast on a baking sheet for 10 to 15 minutes, until golden and crispy.

Wash the greens and trim the stems. Just before serving, dry the livers before cooking (they shoot hot fat everywhere if wet). Season them with salt and pepper and sauté them in 2 tablespoons of the duck fat or olive oil over medium-high heat. Do not overcook; they should still be pink inside. They continue to cook after being removed from the pan, so try cooking them a bit less than you would think. Cool the livers briefly and cut into thirds.

TO ASSEMBLE THE SALAD:

Pour some of the vinaigrette over the reserved bacon. Place the bowl over low heat. If you have an electric stove, do not put the bowl directly on the burner. Toss the greens with the bacon and vinaigrette until wilted, then add the apples, bread cubes, and livers. Add more vinaigrette if necessary, and serve.

SERVES 4

MUSHROOM BARLEY SOUP

The deep, earthy flavors of this soup emerge best if the onions and mushrooms are well browned and a very flavorful stock is used. Let the soup rest in the refrigerator overnight for optimum flavor.

1/2 cup barley

1 onion, diced

2 tablespoons butter, or as needed

1 tablespoon olive oil

1 pound fresh domestic mushrooms, very finely diced

Salt

2 garlic cloves, minced

Splash of sherry

1 dried porcini mushroom, soaked, cleaned, and finely chopped

2 thyme sprigs, chopped

8 cups poultry stock, heated

Sherry vinegar

Finely chopped Italian parsley

TO MAKE THE SOUP:

Cook the barley in rapidly boiling water for 45 minutes to 1 hour, or until it is tender. Drain and set aside. Cook the onion in the butter and oil until translucent. Add the diced mushrooms and cook over medium heat until quite brown. Add more butter if necessary to prevent sticking. Season with salt. Add the garlic and deglaze with a splash of sherry. Add the dried mushroom, thyme, barley, and hot stock. Simmer gently for 20 minutes, skimming as necessary.

TO SERVE THE SOUP:

Adjust the seasoning with sherry vinegar and garnish with parsley.

SERVES 6 TO 8

BRAISED BEEF *with Salsa Verde*

Salsa verde is delicious with any fish, meat, or vegetable. When preparing this sauce, it is very important to chop all of the ingredients by hand; using a food processor will destroy its texture. Look for a well-marbled beef for this dish. Lean meat will tend to be dry and stringy. As with any braise, it is extremely important to cook the meat slowly and at a moderate temperature, not exceeding 350°. Cooked too hot or too quickly, the meat will dry out. This is one of the reasons I like to start meat braises two or three days in advance and let them take their time. Serve with horseradish-flavored mashed potatoes (page 88), or keep the potatoes plain and stir in a little beef bone marrow in place of some butter.

BEEF
- 3 pounds rolled beef chuck
- Salt and freshly ground black pepper
- 2 carrots, peeled and diced
- 2 celery stalks, diced
- 1 onion, diced
- 4 tablespoons olive oil
- 4 cups beef stock, heated
- 6 peeled garlic cloves
- 2 allspice berries
- 1 whole clove
- 2 juniper berries
- 2 bay leaves
- A few Italian parsley stems
- 4 thyme sprigs

SAUCE
- 2 shallots, sliced
- Reserved beef trimmings
- 1 tablespoon reserved beef fat or olive oil
- 6 cups beef stock
- 1 thyme sprig
- 6 black peppercorns
- 1/2 bay leaf

SALSA VERDE
- Finely chopped zest and juice of 2 lemons
- 2 shallots, minced
- 2 to 4 tablespoons extra virgin olive oil
- Salt and freshly ground black pepper
- Finely chopped leaves of 1 thyme sprig
- 2 tablespoons finely chopped Italian parsley
- 1 tablespoon capers, rinsed and finely chopped
- 3 tablespoons finely chopped cornichons

TO PREPARE THE BEEF:

Two days before serving, cut the beef into 1 1/2- by 2-inch pieces. Season with salt and pepper and refrigerate overnight. Save any meaty trim for the sauce.

The next day, preheat the oven to 325°. Sauté the carrot, celery, and onion in 2 tablespoons of the oil. Transfer to the bottom of an oven-proof pan that will just hold the beef comfortably. In the sauté pan, brown the beef in the remaining 2 tablespoons oil. Place the beef on top of the vegetables. Pour off and reserve the fat from the browning pan. Deglaze the pan with 1 cup of the beef stock and add it to the beef. Add the garlic, allspice, clove, juniper, berries, bay leaves, parley stems, and thyme and the remaining 3 cups beef stock to the pan. Cover it with parchment paper and then tightly with foil. Braise in the oven for 2 hours, then check for doneness. The meat should be fork-tender. Cool it, uncovered, in the pan. Refrigerate overnight or until serving.

TO PREPARE THE BEEF SAUCE:

Brown the shallots and beef trim in the fat. Add 2 cups of the stock, thyme, peppercorns, and bay leaf. Simmer gently and skim the scum fastidiously. When reduced by half, add 2 more cups of stock. Continue in this fashion until all of the stock is incorporated. Reduce the sauce to a spoon-coating consistency, and then strain it through a chinois or fine strainer. Rewarm when ready to serve.

TO PREPARE THE SALSA VERDE:

Put the lemon zest in a small bowl with the lemon juice and shallots. Macerate for 20 minutes, then finish with oil, salt, and pepper. Just before serving, stir in the thyme, parsley, capers, and cornichons.

TO SERVE:

If you serve the beef on individual plates, instead of family style, spoon the salsa verde directly onto the meat and after you plate the beef sauce. Otherwise, you'll find oil drops floating in the beef sauce.

SERVES 4

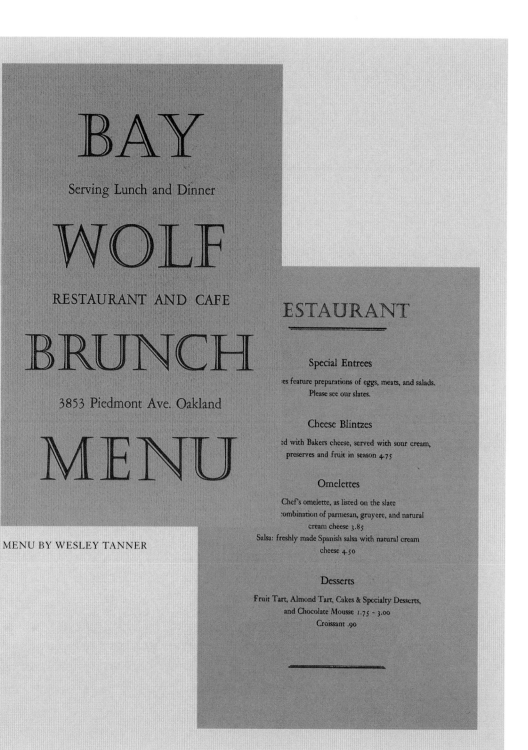

BAY

Serving Lunch and Dinner

WOLF

RESTAURANT AND CAFE

BRUNCH

3853 Piedmont Ave. Oakland

MENU

MENU BY WESLEY TANNER

ESTAURANT

Special Entrees

es feature preparations of eggs, meats, and salads.
Please see our slates.

Cheese Blintzes

:d with Bakers cheese, served with sour cream,
preserves and fruit in season 4.75

Omelettes

Chef's omelette, as listed on the slate
:ombination of parmesan, gruyere, and natural
cream cheese 3.85
Salsa: freshly made Spanish salsa with natural cream
cheese 4.50

Desserts

Fruit Tart, Almond Tart, Cakes & Specialty Desserts,
and Chocolate Mousse 1.75 - 3.00
Croissant .90

STEELHEAD SALMON
with Capers, Currants, Couscous, and Cauliflower

Properly steamed couscous is a revelation, and once you've tasted it, especially if you make it yourself, you will never go back to the instant method. This preparation is based on Paula Wolfert's technique. One steams, wets, and rests the couscous several times to produce light and fully puffed grains. Couscous is typically steamed in a couscoussière, which can be found occasionally at Middle Eastern markets. You can improvise one by placing a steamer basket on top of a pot. Wrap wet linen around the pot rim and edges of the steamer to prevent steam from escaping through the sides.

COUSCOUS
1 tablespoon olive oil

3 cups couscous (not the instant variety)

Salt

3 tablespoons butter

Lemon juice

VINAIGRETTE
1 shallot, minced

3 tablespoons white wine vinegar

3 tablespoons freshly squeezed lemon juice

3 tablespoons dried currants

A few tablespoons white wine

$1/2$ to $3/4$ cup extra virgin olive oil

2 tablespoons capers, rinsed and chopped

$1/4$ cup finely diced celery

Pinch of sugar

Pinch of saffron threads

2 tablespoons minced chives

Salt and freshly ground black pepper

CAULIFLOWER
1 small head cauliflower, separated
   into florets

$1/4$ cup peanut or olive oil

Salt and freshly ground black pepper

SALMON
$1^{1}/2$ pounds steelhead salmon fillets, skinned,
   and cut into 6-ounce portions

Salt and freshly ground black pepper

Olive oil

TO STEAM THE COUSCOUS:
Fill the bottom of a couscoussière three-quarters full of water. Add the oil. The oil will alert you if the pan is out of water, since you won't be able to see inside easily. You will hear the sizzling of the oil before the pot begins to smoke. Smoked couscous is indeed a tragedy, and if it's going to occur, it usually does so near the end of the process when you're moments away from completion.

Bring the water to a boil, then lower the flame to maintain a gentle boil. Place the couscous in a large bowl and wet it with 2 cups of water. Let it sit for a few minutes, and then use your palms and fingertips to break up the grains. The goal is for all of the grains to be separate. The more fastidious you are about dividing the grains now, the easier the couscous will be to handle later. Brush the inside of the steamer with olive oil or butter to prevent sticking. Add the couscous and steam for 15 minutes, or until the top of the couscous is hot.

Return the couscous to a clean bowl and sprinkle with $1^{1}/2$ cups ice water. Break up the couscous as before and let rest for 15 minutes, or until cool. Always make sure that the bowl or steamer is free of old couscous grains before adding the new grains. Steam the couscous again for 15 minutes, wet with 1 cup cold water, rake the grains, and let rest. Steam again for 15 minutes, transfer to the bowl and taste. It may not need any more water, and if it does, it may need only a light sprinkling of a couple of tablespoons. Season with salt, let sit for 15 minutes, and then check the salt again. Like legumes, couscous absorbs a lot of salt. At this point you can hold the couscous in the steamer to keep it warm. Melt in the butter and squeeze a little lemon juice over it.

TO PREPARE THE VINAIGRETTE:

While the couscous steams, soak the shallot in the vinegar and lemon juice and the currants in the wine for 20 minutes. Drain the currants and add to the shallots. Whisk in the oil and add the capers, celery, sugar, saffron, and chives. Season with salt and pepper.

TO PREPARE THE CAULIFLOWER:

In a sauté pan, lightly brown the cauliflower over high heat in the oil. Season with salt and pepper and taste a floret. If you prefer it more tender, continue to cook it in a 350° oven for a few minutes.

TO PREPARE THE SALMON:

Season the salmon with salt and pepper and sauté it in oil until medium-rare. Start it on high heat, and then turn it down just a little. This will give the fish a more even gold crust with no burned edges. Sauté for 5 to 8 minutes, depending on the thickness of the fish.

TO SERVE:

Place a mound of couscous on a plate and top with a portion of fish, some cauliflower, and some vinaigrette.

SERVES 4

E*veryone in this restaurant knows the Mediterranean vernacular in his or her bones—from many trips, many cookbooks, many classes, many years in the kitchen. There are no conceptual missteps. The food is lovely and balanced, showing off the good ingredients so widely available now.*

— PATRICIA UNTERMAN

CASSOULET

Like all sausages, the ones in this cassoulet benefit from a couple of days' hanging in the refrigerator. Start making the sausage at least the day before you intend to use it, but preferably two or three days in advance. If you plan to hold the sausages longer than a few days, add a pinch of saltpeter to your meat. Use kitchen string and paper clips to hang the sausages from a vacant rack in your refrigerator. When making any kind of sausage, be sure that your meats and, if possible, equipment are very cold. This will facilitate the passage of the meat through the grinder.

SAUSAGES

1¹/₂ pounds pork butt, cut into thin strips

Kosher salt

¹/₄ teaspoon ground white pepper

¹/₄ teaspoon freshly ground black pepper

¹/₄ teaspoon ground green peppercorns

1¹/₄ teaspoons ground bay leaf

Pinch of dried thyme

Grating of nutmeg

1 garlic clove, finely chopped

Pinch of ground cayenne pepper

Pinch of ground allspice

1 ounce salt pork, well rinsed and
   cut into cubes

2 ounces pork fatback, cut into cubes

6 feet hog casings, rinsed

BEANS

6 cups cannellini or Great Northern beans

3 carrots, peeled and cut into large pieces

3 celery stalks, cut into large pieces

2 onions, cut into large pieces

2 bay leaves

6 thyme sprigs

6 savory sprigs

A few parsley stems

A few black peppercorns

3 pancetta slices

12 cups duck or chicken stock

CASSOULET

Rendered duck fat (page 6)

1 bunch thyme

5 legs duck confit, meat removed
   from 2 and 3 legs left whole (page 160)

1 pound braised lamb (page 86)

3 cups fresh or dried levain breadcrumbs

TO PREPARE THE SAUSAGES:

Up to 3 days before serving, sprinkle the pork butt lightly with salt and seasonings. Distribute evenly and refrigerate overnight.

The next day, put the pork butt, salt pork, and fatback through the largest holes of your grinder. Make sure that the blade is sharp or the meat will tend to emulsify and back up in your machine. Push out the meat that is left behind in the tube, mix it with the remaining meat, and knead well. Fry up a little patty to test for salt and spice. Keep in mind when you season that salt and other flavors will intensify over the next 24 to 48 hours, especially the garlic. Don't go crazy.

Refrigerate the meat for several hours, until it is thoroughly cold, then stuff it into the well-rinsed hog casings. Don't forget to rinse the inside of the casing as well. To form links, pinch down 5 inches from one end of the sausage, avoiding air pockets, and twist it several times away from yourself. Next pinch down 5 inches farther and twist toward yourself. Continue in this fashion, alternating backward and forward twists the length of the

(continued)

sausage, and then hang them in the refrigerator until you're ready to use them. You should have 6 to 8 sausages.

TO PREPARE THE BEANS:

The day before serving, sort through the beans and remove any rocks or chunks of dirt, then cover with water and soak overnight. The next day, drain and rinse the beans, then put them in a large pot with the carrots, celery, and onions. Tie the herbs and peppercorns in cheesecloth and add to the pot with the pancetta and the stock. Do not add any salt. Slowly bring to a boil, then reduce the heat to a gentle simmer. Add the sausages to the beans and simmer for 8 minutes, until they are just cooked, then remove them from the pot. Sausages should never boil hard or their fat will melt out. Depending on the size of the bean, cooking will range from 1 to 1½ hours. Make sure the beans don't burst open. When

the beans are tender, drain them and reserve the cooking liquid. Remove the vegetables, pancetta, and herb bundle and discard. Taste the cooking liquid. Do not add any salt to anything yet. The salt content in pancetta varies dramatically; if the salt content is high, it may not be necessary to add any more salt to the beans. Reduce the bean cooking liquid by half and add it back to the beans. If the liquid needs more salt, add it now. Let the beans sit in the hot liquid and absorb the salt until you're ready to assemble the cassoulet.

TO ASSEMBLE THE CASSOULET:

Preheat the oven to 275° or 300°. Brown the sausages in some duck fat, cool, slice on an angle, and set aside. Ladle a layer of beans into the bottom of a deep ceramic or glass baking dish. Lay down a couple of sprigs of thyme, then some of the duck meat, sausage, and lamb. Continue with more beans, thyme, and meat. Top with the 3 whole duck legs. Pour the bean cooking liquid into the dish so that it reaches just below the top layer of beans. Mix the breadcrumbs with some duck fat and spread some of them in a generous layer over the top. Reserve the remaining breadcrumbs and bean liquid. Bake for 4 hours. Add more breadcrumbs as those on the top brown. Check the liquid level periodically, so it doesn't dry out too much. Serve the cassoulet from the vessel in which you cook it.

SERVES 12 TO 15

CHOCOLATE MOUSSE–FILLED ALMOND CAKE *with Crème Anglaise*

Crème anglaise, a classic custard sauce, provides the perfect, delicate counterpoint to the natural pairing of the rich chocolate mousse filling and the full-textured, deeply almond-flavored cake. The cake can be made up to a day in advance.

CAKE

7 ounces almond paste (available at specialty food stores)

2 egg whites

6 whole eggs, separated

2/3 cup granulated sugar

6 tablespoons sifted cake flour

Powdered sugar for dusting top of cake

CHOCOLATE MOUSSE

7 ounces bittersweet chocolate

1/2 cup sugar

2/3 cup water

5 egg yolks

1 1/2 cups heavy cream, whipped until stiff

CRÈME ANGLAISE

1 cup whole milk

2 teaspoons vanilla extract

1/4 cup sugar

5 egg yolks

TO PREPARE THE CAKE:

Preheat the oven to 350°. Beat the almond paste in an electric mixer with the 2 egg whites until smooth. Set aside. In the mixer, whip the 6 egg yolks with 1/3 cup of the granulated sugar until light and fluffy. Beat in the almond paste. Fold the flour into the yolk mixture, a little at a time. Whip the remaining 3 egg whites with the remaining 1/3 cup sugar until stiff. Fold into the yolk mixture. Pour into a parchment-lined 10-inch round cake pan. Bake for 40 to 45 minutes, or until a toothpick inserted into the center comes out clean. Let cool in the pan, then remove from the pan, trim the top to even it, and cut horizontally into equal layers.

TO PREPARE THE MOUSSE:

Melt the chocolate in a stainless steel bowl over warm water and set aside. Place the sugar and water in a pan and bring to a boil. In a medium stainless steel bowl, beat the sugar mixture into the egg yolks. Fill a separate, larger bowl with ice water and set aside. Place the egg yolk bowl over a pot of boiling water and whip until doubled in volume. Place it in a larger bowl filled with ice water and continue whipping until the mixture is the same temperature as the melted chocolate. Add the chocolate to the yolk mixture and mix well. Fold in the whipped cream. Refrigerate until set, about 1 hour. Spread the mousse between the cake layers and dust the assembled cake with powdered sugar. Refrigerate until serving.

TO PREPARE THE CRÈME ANGLAISE:

Heat the milk with the vanilla and sugar. Bring to a boil. Add a little milk mixture to the yolks to warm them before adding the remaining milk. Place this mixture back in the pan and cook over low heat for 10 to 15 minutes, or until it thickens. Strain through a fine strainer into a clean stainless steel bowl. Place atop a bowl of ice and gently stir the custard until cool. Cover with plastic wrap and refrigerate.

TO SERVE:

Cut the cake with a serrated knife, wiping it clean after each cut. Place a slice of cake in the center of each plate, and pour the crème anglaise around it.

MAKES ONE 10-INCH CAKE

BABAS AU RHUM

with Lime Cream and Caramelized Pineapple

Easily my most memorable dessert experience is a baba au rhum acquired from an old pâtisserie on Boulevard St. Germain in 1966. I knew, without having any real frame of reference, that this was the real thing, the essential baba. It brought tears to my eyes. The only hard liquor my father really liked was St. James rum. He'd bring it home, with some bottles of true Cointreau, from trips to Paris in the 1950s, and I remember acquiring a taste for it. When you add a little sugar and some kitchen alchemy to the mix of highly flavored rum and the ineffable aroma of wild yeast, you have a dessert after my own heart. This version is enhanced with caramelized pineapple and a delicate lime cream. The orange flower water is well worth seeking out in specialty food or Middle Eastern food stores.

BABAS

1/4 cup whole milk

1 teaspoon active dry yeast

3 whole eggs

1/4 teaspoon vanilla extract

1/2 teaspoon orange flower water

1/4 cup plus 2 tablespoons cake flour

1/4 cup plus 2 tablespoons all-purpose flour

2 teaspoons sugar

1/4 teaspoon salt

4 tablespoons sweet, unsalted butter, at room temperature

1/2 cup raisins

DIPPING SYRUP

2/3 cup water

1 cup sugar

1/4 teaspoon vanilla extract

1/4 teaspoon orange flower water

1/2 cup dark rum

LIME CREAM

Zest of 1 lime, removed in strips

1/2 cup freshly squeezed lime juice

1/2 cup sugar

4 egg yolks

2 whole eggs

1 cup heavy whipping cream

CARAMELIZED PINEAPPLE

2 cups cubed fresh or canned pineapple, in its own juice

1 cup sugar

Generous splash of dark rum

2 tablespoons sweet, unsalted butter

TO PREPARE THE BABAS:

Preheat the oven to 375°. Warm the milk in a small saucepan until it is about body temperature. Add the yeast and let it proof until bubbly. Add the eggs, vanilla, and orange flower water to the yeast mixture. Pour into the bowl of an electric mixer fitted with a paddle attachment. Sift the flours with the sugar and salt. Add the flour mixture to the yeast mixture and mix on low. When the dough comes together, start adding the butter, a tablespoon at a time, mixing until all of the butter is well incorporated. Beat in the raisins. The dough will be sticky and soft.

Scoop the dough into 8 buttered 3-ounce molds, filling them about three-quarters full. Let rise in a warm place until the dough comes over the top of the molds. Preheat the oven to

375º and bake the babas for 20 to 30 minutes, or until light golden brown. Remove from the molds while hot and let cool on a rack.

TO PREPARE THE DIPPING SYRUP:

Bring the water and sugar to a boil in a heavy-bottomed saucepan. Remove from the heat and add the vanilla, orange flower water, and rum. While the syrup is hot, dip each baba into this syrup and place the babas in a large, shallow bowl. Pour the leftover syrup over them and leave them to absorb the extra liquid.

TO PREPARE THE LIME CREAM:

Combine the lime zest, juice, sugar, egg yolks, and whole eggs in the top of a double boiler and cook, stirring for 15 to 20 minutes, or until thick. Strain into a bowl through a fine strainer. Cover with plastic wrap and chill until cold. Whip the cream until stiff and fold it into the cold curd. Use immediately or refrigerate until serving.

TO PREPARE THE CARAMELIZED PINEAPPLE:

Heat a nonstick sauté pan until very hot. Add the pineapple and cook, using the heat of the pan to caramelize the natural sugars in the pineapple. When the pineapple is colored, add the sugar and continue to cook until the pineapple exudes some of its liquid. Remove from the heat and add the rum. Return to the heat and add the butter. Cook until the butter is melted. Use immediately.

TO SERVE:

Place a baba in the center of each serving plate. Top with a dollop of lime cream, and surround with pineapple.

MAKES 8 BABAS

BRIOCHE BREAD PUDDING
with Brandied Cherry Sauce

This sauce is the perfect justification for brandying cherries in the summer. Good brandied cherries are available in fine food stores and delicatessens nationwide and can be substituted. You can also substitute purchased brioche instead of making your own, but do try the brandying and the brioche making at least once in your lifetime. Playing with fresh cherries and basking in the aroma of fresh yeast are irreplaceable delights.

BRIOCHE

1 1/2 teaspoons active dry yeast

1/2 cup plus 2 tablespoons warm water

5 whole eggs

2 tablespoons sugar

4 1/2 cups all-purpose flour

1 3/4 teaspoons salt

1 1/2 cups sweet, unsalted butter,
    at room temperature

CUSTARD

5 large egg yolks

2 large whole eggs

3/4 cup sugar

Pinch of salt

1 1/4 cups heavy whipping cream

2 cups whole milk

1/2 vanilla bean, or 1 tablespoon vanilla extract

BRANDIED CHERRY SAUCE

3 tablespoons water

1/2 cup sugar

1 cup pitted brandied cherries, coarsely
    chopped (recipe follows)

1 cup liquid from brandied cherries

3 tablespoons unsalted butter

TO MAKE THE BRIOCHE:

Dissolve the yeast in the warm water. Add the eggs and sugar and mix well. Pour into the bowl of an electric mixer fitted with a paddle attachment, add the flour and salt, and mix on low speed until the dough pulls away from the sides of the bowl. Switch to the hook attachment and continue to knead on low speed, adding the butter, a tablespoon at a time, until it is all incorporated into the dough. The dough will be sticky. Transfer to a well-buttered bowl, cover with plastic wrap, and refrigerate for 1 hour or overnight. It is more important for the dough to be firm than for it to double in size.

Roll the dough out on a floured surface into a 9 by 10-inch rectangle. Use as little flour as possible so that the dough remains tender. Roll the dough, jelly-roll style, into a log. Place in a buttered 9 by 5-inch loaf pan. Mist the top with a spray bottle, or gently brush with water. Cover loosely with plastic wrap and place in a warm spot to rise. Let rise for 45 minutes to 1 1/2 hours, or until doubled in size.

Preheat the oven to 400°. Bake for 20 minutes, or until the top starts turning golden brown. Reduce the oven temperature to 350° and continue baking for another 20 minutes, or until the loaf sounds hollow when tapped on the bottom. Remove from the pan and place on a cooling rack to cool.

(continued)

TO PREPARE THE CUSTARD:

Mix together the egg yolks, whole eggs, sugar, and salt. Heat the cream together with the milk, split open the vanilla bean, and scrape the pulp into the milk mixture. Bring to a boil. Pour a little (no more than $1/4$ cup) of this hot mixture into the egg mixture to warm the eggs. Mix well, and then add the rest of the hot milk mixture. Strain through a fine sieve.

TO MAKE THE BREAD PUDDING:

Preheat the oven to 350°. Cut off the crusts of the cooled brioche and slice it $3/4$ inch thick. Cut each slice in half. Butter an 8-inch square pan. Lay the pieces of brioche in the pan, letting them overlap one another. Pour half of the custard mixture over the slices. Let sit for about 5 minutes, and then pour the rest of the custard over the top. Set the pan into a larger, deeper pan and fill the larger pan half full of hot water to make a water bath. Bake for about 45 minutes, or until the custard is just set. Remove from the water bath.

TO MAKE THE CHERRY SAUCE:

While the bread pudding is baking, bring the water and sugar to a boil. Add the cherries, turn off the flame, and add the brandy. Add the butter, return to the heat, and bring to a boil.

TO SERVE:

Cut the bread pudding into squares. Place the squares on individual serving plates. Pour the hot cherry sauce over the top and serve.

MAKES ONE 8-INCH PUDDING

Brandied Cherries

2 pints sour or Bing cherries (do not pit)
1 cup sugar
$1/2$ cup water
2 cups good brandy
2 tablespoons light corn syrup

Wash and sterilize a 3-quart glass jar with a sealable lid by placing it mouth down in boiling water for 15 minutes. Place the cherries in hot water to warm, but do not cook them. Pack the cherries into the jar. Place the sugar and water in a pan and bring to a boil. Add the brandy and pour over the cherries. Place the lid on the jar and refrigerate for 1 month. After a month, add the corn syrup. Reseal and invert. Refrigerate for 1 more month before using. These cherries will keep for up to 4 months in the refrigerator.

TANGERINE AND POMEGRANATE SORBETS

Tangerines are the jewels of the citrus world. Their fragrant scent and sweet flesh make them ideal dessert ingredients, alone and unadorned or in combination with complementary fruits such as the ruby pomegranate in this simple dessert. Juicing tangerines is easy: just cut them in half and juice them as you would an orange.

TANGERINE SORBET

   4 cups tangerine freshly squeezed juice

   3/4 cup sugar, more if needed

POMEGRANATE SORBET

   4 cups pomegranate juice
      (4 to 6 pomegranates)

   1 cup sugar, more if needed

TO PREPARE THE TANGERINE SORBET:

Mix the juice and sugar. Taste and add more sugar if necessary. When tasting the sorbet bases, remember that they should be a little sweeter than the finished product. When frozen, the sorbet will taste less sweet. Pour into an ice cream freezer and freeze according to the manufacturer's instructions.

TO PREPARE THE POMEGRANATE SORBET:

Remove all of the seedpods from the pith. Use rubber gloves to protect your hands from becoming a lovely color. Place the seeds in a food processor or blender and crush them at low speed. Place in a fine strainer and strain the juice from the seed mass. You should have 4 cups of juice.

Mix the juice and sugar and taste to see if the base is sweet enough. If the pomegranates are tart, add a little more sugar. Place in an ice cream freezer and freeze according to the manufacturer's instructions.

TO SERVE:

Place 1 scoop of each sorbet in a glass dish or goblet.

MAKES 1 QUART OF EACH SORBET

February

Venice and Mardi Gras

Two of the most spectacular and storied parties in the world take place late in the winter in the melancholy city of Venice and the raffish environs of New Orleans. Two dynamic cities, two bizarre incarnations for carnival and that launching-of-Lent bacchanal that brings out the weird and the wild in these equally exotic but disparate locales. Mardi gras is French for "fat Tuesday," the day before Ash Wednesday, the day on which revelry is exchanged for fasting and those chewy beignets, the delectable Creole cousin of the doughnut, are foregone for the requisite forty days and nights of Lent.

Arriving in Venice in winter, you can easily visualize brightly dressed, vividly masked and plumed revelers darting in and out of medieval doorways in the mists. In Venice you're awed by your first vision of the Grand Canal, what Goethe reverentially referred to as "the most beautiful street in the world." In New Orleans you prowl the French Quarter as the scents of thyme and garlic and shellfish bisque mingle with riffs from Bourbon Street.

These are melting-pot cities that excel in the invention and preparation of melting-pot dishes: creamy polenta and southern-style grits, *arancini* and hush puppies, the fish stews of Venice and the gumbos of New Orleans. Flavored with sassafras, the gumbos are gold tinted and enriched by saffron. Sassafras is the leaf of a tree of the laurel family. Once sold in French markets in New Orleans for teas and tisanes, it is now most recognized as an essential agent in the thickening and flavoring of gumbos. Saffron is the dried and powdered orange-red stigmas and styles of a purple crocus, a jewel in the Venetian spice merchant's crown and the world's most expensive spice. Both cities once stood at the crossroads of commerce, and both are famous as much for their anomalous aesthetic and architectural styles as for their distinctive cuisines and their historically rich traditions for embarking on the Christian season of anti-eating, Lent.

In the early 1980s we were delighted to be caught up in the emerging vogue for Cajun and Creole cuisine. Through Bruce Aidells, we enjoy a relationship with Paul Prudhomme and other New Orleans restaurateurs. It was exciting food, fun to cook and eat, and uniquely American. There was great charm to it. We incorporated it into our menus for several years. Over time, however, we reluctantly conceded that it wasn't appropriate for the restaurant. Diners would call for reservations and be unsettled by the sound of gumbo or jambalaya or shrimp rémoulade on the menu; it just didn't fit the evolving identity. The food hasn't lost its delight. We'll squeak in an homage to Mardi Gras with a dish that features red beans and rice or a gumbo soup, but our focus has solidified in other directions.

The food of Venice is easier to integrate into the Bay-Wolf repertoire, with the possible exception of one of the greatest Venetian entrées, *fegato alla veneziana*, sliced, well-peppered calf's liver sautéed with onions. What many consider a coarse or plebeian dish elsewhere is the most profound delicacy in the sauté pans of the Venetians. I had to eat it when I first visited Venice because it was one of the dishes my father really loved and actually cooked once in a great while. He'd go to a German butcher in Los Angeles for the calf's liver and have it sliced very thin. This he would cook for a few seconds on each side with some sliced onions and a little vinegar. Liver is not forgiving; it has to be perfectly cooked and must be served and eaten quickly, but my father had loved it in Venice and mastered it in Hollywood.

Venice is not an environment in which to drink a dark, red, brooding wine. The sparkling Prosecco is the ideal, ebullient antidote to the gloom of the haunted winter canals, much as beer is the force that stands up to all entrées New Orleanais.

Valentine Dinner

Valentine soup ♥ hearts and flowers

~

Bay Wolf Caesar salad
Grilled artichokes and blood oranges ♥ hazelnut dressing
Scallop and shrimp cake ♥ salmon caviar
Smoked duck breast ♥ French lentils and mango

~

Seared swordfish ♥ couscous and date-mint sauce
Duck à l'orange ♥ baby turnips and their greens
Beef filet mignon ♥ truffled mashed potatoes and celery hearts
Polenta hearts ♥ roast vegetables and parsley sauce

~

Italian sweet cream ♥ raspberries and strawberries
Chocolate almond heart cake ♥ chocolate sauce
Tangerine and blood orange sherbet ♥ lavender shortbread

CHEF: Louis Le Gassic ~ DESSERTS: Earl Darny

Sixty-eight dollars, excluding beverages, tax, and gratuity
Corkage $18

2000
bay wolf restaurant

MENU BY MELISSA EHN

BLACK OLIVE TAPENADE CROUTONS

For this tapenade, I use a food processor, which makes it very smooth. If you don't have one, or if you prefer a chunkier-style tapenade, chop everything by hand. Either way, it is worthwhile to make a large amount, since it holds well for a long time. In fact it's best to make it a couple of days before you intend to serve it so the flavors can marry. As for the ingredient ratios, you want to keep in mind that you're working with several salty ingredients. Do not add any salt until the very end. Start by processing the olives and some chopped herbs and nuts. Add the other ingredients to taste. If your tapenade is too acidic or salty, you can fix it by adding more olives or nuts.

3 cups kalamata, niçoise, or oil-cured black olives, pitted (do not use any prepitted or lye-cured canned olives)

1 to 2 tablespoons capers, rinsed

1 to 2 salt-packed anchovies, filleted and rinsed

1 large garlic clove

1/2 cup toasted pine nuts, hazelnuts (skinned), or walnuts, finely chopped or ground

1 tablespoon chopped Italian parsley and/or basil or oregano

Virgin olive oil

Pinch of ground cayenne pepper

Grilled or toasted bread

Put the ingredients, except the bread, into a processor and purée until smooth. Taste and adjust seasoning. Remember, you need to adjust the seasoning according to how the tapenade tastes on the toast and not just how it tastes out of the bowl. Serve on the grilled or toasted bread.

MAKES ABOUT 2 CUPS TAPENADE AND 12 TO 16 CROUTONS

VALENTINE DINNER

BAY WOLF 1999

Amuse bouches

Bay Wolf Caesar salad
Oysters on the half shell with champagne mignonette
Celery root ravioli pillows with wild mushrooms
Prawns with almonds and Meyer lemon

Lasagna with mushrooms and ricotta salata cheese
Fennel-crusted swordfish with French lentils and preserved lemon vinaigrette
Spanish-style Liberty Ranch duck with red wine and hazelnut picada
Slow-cooked beef ragout with potato purée and salsa verde

Chocolate heart cake
Italian sweet cream with berries
Earl's Valentine sweets

CHEF: LAUREN LYLE   DESSERTS: G. EARL DARNY

MENU BY CHRISTINE TAYLOR

CAULIFLOWER SOUP
with Black Olive Tapenade Croutons

This is a clear, light, almost translucent essence of cauliflower. Unlike the majority of our winter soups, this is not prepared by caramelizing the vegetables to achieve depth of flavor. The key is to avoid browning the vegetables and to use a light chicken stock made from unroasted bones, or water.

SOUP

1/4 cup butter

1 large yellow onion, diced

1 head cauliflower, coarsely chopped

1 thyme sprig

5 cups light chicken stock or water, heated

Salt and freshly ground white pepper

1 cup heavy whipping cream

Freshly squeezed lemon juice (optional)

Black Olive Tapenade Croutons (opposite)

TO PREPARE THE SOUP:

Melt the butter in a large, heavy-bottomed pot. Add the onion and cook until soft and translucent. Do not brown. Add the cauliflower and thyme and cook, covered, over low heat for 10 minutes more. Add the stock and cook, uncovered, for 20 to 30 minutes, or until the cauliflower is completely tender. Season with salt and white pepper.

Purée in a blender with the cream, and then strain through a medium strainer. Adjust the seasoning. Add a little lemon juice just before serving, if desired. Serve hot with the croutons on the side .

SERVES 4

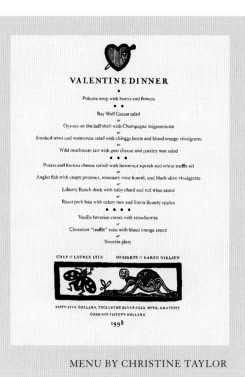

VALENTINE DINNER

Polenta soup with hearts and flowers

Bay Wolf Caesar salad

Oysters on the half shell with Champagne mignonnette
or
Smoked trout and watercress salad with chiogga beets and blood orange vinaigrette
or
Wild mushroom tart with goat cheese and parsley root salad

Potato and fontina cheese ravioli with butternut squash and white truffle oil
or
Angler fish with crispy potatoes, rosemary roast fennel, and black olive vinaigrette
or
Liberty Ranch duck with baby chard and red wine sauce
or
Roast pork loin with celery root and Sierra Beauty apples

Vanilla bavarian cream with strawberries
or
Chocolate "truffle" cake with blood orange sauce
or
Sweetie plate

CHEF // LAUREN LYLE   DESSERTS // KAREN NIELLSEN

FIFTY-FIVE DOLLARS, EXCLUDING BEVERAGES, WINE, GRATUITY
CORKAGE FIFTEEN DOLLARS

1998

MENU BY CHRISTINE TAYLOR

CRAB CAKES

Crab cakes are not merely delicious, they're fun, they're funky, they're homey and stylish, they're creamy and crispy, they're evocative of some otherworldly locale we've never visited. The trick to making these cakes is to find the perfect balance of wetness and dryness. This varies depending on the wetness of your crabmeat and the thickness of your mayonnaise. Serve these crab cakes alone as an appetizer or with some finely shredded coleslaw and black-eyed peas as a main course.

1 pound cooked crabmeat, picked over

4 green onions, white and light green parts only, minced

1/2 cup fresh breadcrumbs, more if needed

1 cup thick mayonnaise, more if needed

2 small celery stalks, minced

1/4 fennel bulb, minced

Finely chopped zest and juice of 3 lemons

1 tablespoon chopped Italian parsley

Salt

Ground cayenne pepper

Paprika

1 egg, beaten, if needed

1/4 cup butter, clarified

Lemon wedges

A dollop of mayonnaise

Mix the crabmeat with the green onions, breadcrumbs, mayonnaise, minced vegetables, lemon zest, and parsley. Season to taste with salt, cayenne, paprika, and lemon juice. Form the crab mixture into little patties. If the mixture is too dry, they will not hold together. If necessary, add more mayonnaise or a beaten egg. If the mixture is too wet, add some breadcrumbs. Fry the patties in the clarified butter until golden brown on both sides, about 3 minutes per side.

Serve with lemon wedges and additional mayonnaise.

SERVES 4

GRILLED ARTICHOKES
with Blood Orange Vinaigrette

These artichokes can be served hot off the grill or at room temperature after they have marinated for a while. If you marinate the artichokes for any length of time, make sure that they are not swimming in vinaigrette, or they will become oil logged. This dish can be made with other types of oranges, but make sure they have good acidity to balance the smoke from the grill.

VINAIGRETTE

Finely chopped zest and juice of
   3 blood oranges
1 tablespoon sugar
1 teaspoon freshly squeezed lemon juice
$1/2$ to $3/4$ cup virgin olive oil
Salt and freshly ground black pepper

ARTICHOKES

4 artichokes
Juice of $1/2$ lemon
Salt and freshly ground black pepper
Olive oil

2 or 3 blood oranges
1 small head frisée, rinsed, dried, and torn
   into bite-sized pieces
A few niçoise olives

TO PREPARE THE VINAIGRETTE:

Put the zest and juice in a small saucepan with the sugar. Reduce over medium heat until only 3 tablespoons remain. Pour into a small bowl, cool, and add the lemon juice. Whisk in the olive oil, salt, and pepper.

TO PREPARE THE ARTICHOKES:

Trim the tough outer leaves from the artichokes. Cut off the top half of the flowering end, then put the artichokes directly into a pot with the lemon juice and cold water to cover. Bring to a boil, then lower the heat to a sim-mer. Cook the artichokes for 25 to 30 minutes, or until they are just tender. The leaves will detach when pulled. If they come off too easily, they are probably overcooked. Drain the artichokes. When they are cool enough to handle, trim any inedible parts and any fibers along the stem. Cut the artichokes in half lengthwise and remove the choke. Season with salt and pepper and toss in a little olive oil.

Grill the artichokes over a hot fire. Mark them well on all sides. The artichokes are already cooked, but it's best if they can get some color and smoky flavor. When the artichokes are ready, immediately toss them in some of the orange vinaigrette.

TO SERVE:

Trim the oranges with a knife, then cut into thin rounds. Dress the frisée, olives, and orange slices in the remaining vinaigrette. Serve with the grilled artichokes.

SERVES 4

OXTAIL SOUP

Oxtails are sublime because their meat is juicier and more gelatinous than that of many other cuts of beef. Although this preparation comes in the form of a soup, it is most appropriate as a main course rather than an appetizer. Here, we pull the meat from the bones for ease in eating. But if you and your guests can really get into your food, it's more fun to leave the meat on the bone and savor it "manually."

5 pounds oxtails

Salt and freshly ground black pepper

6 tablespoons olive oil

1 carrot, peeled and diced

1 celery stalk, diced

1 onion, diced

5 to 7 cups rich poultry or veal stock, heated

5 garlic cloves

2 bay leaves, crumbled

5 thyme sprigs

A few black peppercorns

1 dried porcini mushroom

1 large handful fresh shiitake mushrooms, stemmed and cut into thin julienne

1 small handful fresh oyster mushrooms, stemmed and cut into thin julienne

2 tablespoons butter

1 celery root, peeled and diced

1 tablespoon chopped Italian parsley

Sherry vinegar

The day before serving, season the oxtails well with salt and pepper.

The next day, preheat the oven to 350°. Brown the oxtails in 4 tablespoons of the oil. Transfer to a deep, ovenproof pan that will just hold them comfortably. Pour off some of the rendered oxtail fat and then caramelize the carrot, celery, and onion in the same pan in which you browned the oxtails. Remove the vegetables from the pan, and deglaze the pan with 1 cup of the stock, scraping up any browned bits. Pour this liquid into the pan containing the oxtails. Add the caramelized vegetables, garlic, bay leaves, thyme, peppercorns, dried mushroom, and 4 cups stock. Cover the pan tightly with a layer of parchment and then a layer of foil. Braise in the oven until the meat starts to fall from the bone, about 2 1/2 hours. Cool to room temperature.

Pick the meat off the bones. Reserve the bones for another purpose. Strain the braising liquid into a clean pot and add the meat. If the braising liquid is a bit salty, add 2 cups of clean stock to it.

Sauté the mushrooms in the butter and remaining 2 tablespoons oil, and then add to the soup. In the same pan, heat a little more fat and cook the celery root until tender. Add to the soup with the parsley and a few drops of vinegar. Serve hot.

SERVES 4 TO 6

29

BIG RICOTTA CHEESE RAVIOLI
with Rapini, Meyer Lemon, and Pine Nuts

To create delicate little pillows of pasta, make your pasta sheets very thin for this dish. You should be able to see your counter or table through the sheets. This will eliminate those thick, chewy edges characteristic of less fortunate ravioli. We use rapini, the more refined and milder relative of broccoli rabe, for this dish, but you can substitute baby dandelion greens or any other bitter green. We buy Belwether Farms's ricotta for this dish. It's a clean, fresh, deliciously superior product from a small-production artisan.

PASTA DOUGH

2 whole eggs

Salt

1½ cups all-purpose flour

1 egg yolk

1 tablespoon olive oil

RICOTTA FILLING

1 pound Belwether Farms ricotta cheese

2 tablespoons chopped chives

Salt to taste

Rice flour or semolina for dusting

SAUCE

3 tablespoons olive oil

1 red onion, minced

Salt and freshly ground black pepper

1 bunch rapini greens, thick stems trimmed

2 large garlic cloves, minced

Pinch of dried red chile flakes

1 salt-packed anchovy, filleted, rinsed, and minced

1½ cups chicken stock

Finely chopped zest and juice of 2 Meyer lemons

1 to 2 tablespoons butter

1 tablespoon chopped Italian parsley

¼ cup pine nuts, toasted

TO PREPARE THE PASTA DOUGH:

Whisk 1 of the eggs in a small bowl with a pinch of salt and set aside. Mound the flour on the table and make a well in the center. Place the remaining egg and the yolk in the well. Add another pinch of salt and the oil. Whisk the eggs and oil with a fork, gradually incorporating the flour. Keep a little water nearby in case you need more liquid. Pasta for ravioli should be a bit wetter than for noodles so that the dough will stick to itself and won't dry and crack during assembly. Bring the dough together and knead for a few minutes. Put the dough in a plastic bag and let rest for 20 to 30 minutes at room temperature.

TO PREPARE THE FILLING:

Gently mix the ricotta with the chives and salt to taste. Refrigerate until ready to use.

TO ASSEMBLE RAVIOLI:

Divide the pasta dough into 4 equal pieces. Cover 3 pieces in plastic wrap and roll the remaining piece into a thin, wide sheet, either

(continued)

using a hand-turned pasta machine or rolling out on a lightly floured work surface. Repeat with the other 3 pieces of dough. Brush 2 of the sheets with the egg wash. Divide the cheese into 8 portions and distribute in mounds over the pasta. Leave 2 inches between each cheese mound. Cover with the reserved pasta sheets, pressing out any air pockets. Cut the ravioli into large squares, circles, or diamonds with a pastry cutter or a knife. If you use a knife, seal the edges with fork tines. Transfer the ravioli to a baking sheet dusted with rice flour or semolina.

Cover with a napkin dusted with rice flour and set aside until ready to use.

TO PREPARE THE SAUCE:

Ten minutes before you're ready to serve, heat the olive oil in a large sauté pan or divide the ingredients between 2 standard-size sauté pans. Add the onion, season with salt and pepper, and cook over high heat until lightly browned. Add the rapini and wilt into the onions. Add the garlic, chile flakes, and anchovy. Cook briefly, then add the chicken stock and lemon zest. Reduce by two-thirds, then adjust the seasoning and add lemon juice to taste. Swirl in the butter, parsley, and pine nuts.

TO COOK AND SERVE THE RAVIOLI:

Cook the ravioli in a generous amount of salted, boiling water. This will take 40 to 60 seconds, depending on the thickness of your pasta. Drain and distribute among 4 warmed plates. Pour the sauce over the ravioli and serve.

SERVES 4

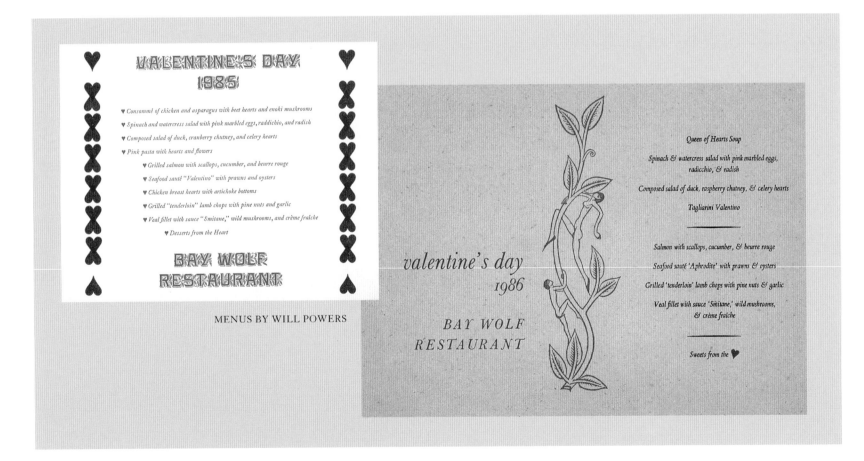

VALENTINE'S DAY
1985

♥ Consommé of chicken and asparagus with beet hearts and enoki mushrooms
♥ Spinach and watercress salad with pink marbled eggs, raddichio, and radish
♥ Composed salad of duck, cranberry chutney, and celery hearts
♥ Pink pasta with hearts and flowers
♥ Grilled salmon with scallops, cucumber, and beurre rouge
♥ Seafood sauté "Valentino" with prawns and oysters
♥ Chicken breast hearts with artichoke bottoms
♥ Grilled "tenderloin" lamb chops with pine nuts and garlic
♥ Veal fillet with sauce "Smitane," wild mushrooms, and crème fraîche
♥ Desserts from the Heart

BAY WOLF
RESTAURANT

MENUS BY WILL POWERS

valentine's day
1986

BAY WOLF
RESTAURANT

Queen of Hearts Soup

Spinach & watercress salad with pink marbled eggs, radicchio, & radish

Composed salad of duck, raspberry chutney, & celery hearts

Tagliarini Valentino

Salmon with scallops, cucumber, & beurre rouge

Seafood sauté 'Aphrodite' with prawns & oysters

Grilled 'tenderloin' lamb chops with pine nuts & garlic

Veal fillet with sauce 'Smitane,' wild mushrooms, & crème fraîche

Sweets from the ♥

BLACK SEAFOOD RISOTTO
with Squid, Mussels, and Vermouth

This is a classic celebration of squid. Once you've eaten it in Venice or its environs, it's impossible not to be interested in it. Its goodness derives from the special quality imparted to the rice by the infusion of squid ink. Squid ink is really, really, flavorful: very specific, very fine. The more you know this dish, the more you like it.

1¹/₂ pounds squid

3 tablespoons butter

1 tablespoon olive oil

1 yellow onion, diced

1 small fennel bulb, diced

2¹/₂ cups Arborio rice

2 cups dry white wine, heated

8 cups fish stock, heated

Salt and freshly ground black pepper

1 tablespoon toasted and ground fennel seed

¹/₂ cup dry vermouth

1¹/₂ pounds mussels

2 heaping tablespoons freshly grated Parmesan cheese

1 tablespoon chopped Italian parsley

Clean the squid by removing the beaks from the tentacles and the guts from the rest of the body. Discard the eyes portion of the head. Save the tiny, silver-colored ink sacs in a small bowl. Cut the bodies into smaller pieces.

Heat the butter and oil in a large saucepan. When bubbly, add the onion and fennel and sweat gently for 5 to 8 minutes, or until tender and translucent. Do not brown. Add the rice and fry for a bit, stirring constantly. Add the white wine and a cup of the stock, and lower the heat to a simmer. Break up the ink sacs with a fork, add a little fish stock to them, and strain into the pot. Stir occasionally. When the rice has absorbed most of the liquid, add a few more cups of stock. Continue in this manner until the rice is almost cooked. The whole process can take up to 40 minutes. Season well with salt, pepper, and ground fennel seed. Add the vermouth, calamari, and mussels. Cover the pan and cook until the mussels open. Check the seasoning just before serving, then stir in a little grated Parmesan and chopped parsley.

SERVES 6 TO 8

CHOUCROUTE GARNIE

Choucroute *is the French word for sauer-kraut. The traditional Alsatian dish consists of sauerkraut served, or "garnished," with potatoes, ham, sausages, and goose. We prefer to braise the cabbage rather than prepare the fermented kind. As I've found from personal experience, home fermenting can leave a most undesirable odor in its wake. If you have a clay oven, use it for this dish. It works a magic that I cannot explain. The one time I love to drink beer is with choucroute. A pilsner, not a stout—something rich and lively that jumps on your tongue. The juniper in choucroute and the hops in beer are a flavor connection that achieves a good marriage. Note that the duck confit needs to "cure" for at least two weeks before it can be used.*

SAUSAGES

1 pound pork butt, cut into strips

5 ounces pork fatback, cut into strips

3 ounces bacon

Salt and freshly ground black pepper

2 garlic cloves, minced

4 bay leaves, ground

Ground nutmeg

1/2 teaspoon sugar

1 1/2 teaspoons coriander seed, toasted and ground

1/2 cup dry marsala, reduced by half

5 feet hog casings, rinsed

CHOUCROUTE

4 tablespoons rendered duck fat (page 6)

6 bacon slices, julienned

2 onions, julienned

2 heads savoy cabbage, julienned

Salt and freshly ground black pepper

1/2 bunch thyme, tied

6 garlic cloves, finely chopped

2 bay leaves

A few black peppercorns

5 juniper berries

3 cups poultry stock, heated

2 cups dry white wine, heated

White wine vinegar

3 legs Duck Confit (page 160)

Mustard

Cornichons

TO PREPARE THE SAUSAGE:

Up to 3 days before serving, season the meats generously with salt and pepper. Mix with the garlic, bay leaf, nutmeg, sugar, and coriander.

The next day, grind the meat and knead in the marsala. Fry up a little patty, taste it, and adjust the seasoning as necessary. Remember that the flavors will intensify the longer the sausages hang in the refrigerator. Unless you intend to eat them right away, season a little on the light side. However, it will be much more worthwhile to let them hang for a few days. Refrigerate the meat for several hours, until it is thoroughly cold, then stuff it into the well-rinsed hog casings. Don't forget to rinse the inside of the casing as well. To form links, pinch down 5 inches from one end of the sausage, avoiding air pockets, and twist it several times away from yourself. Next pinch down 5 inches farther and twist toward yourself. Continue in this fashion, alternating backward and forward twists the length of the sausage, and then hang them in the refrigerator until you're ready to use them. You should have 8 sausages.

TO PREPARE THE CHOUCROUTE:

In a large, nonreactive pot, heat 2 tablespoons of the duck fat and the bacon. Cook until the bacon is soft but cooked through. Add the onions and brown. Add the cabbage and continue browning. Season with salt and pepper. Add the thyme and garlic. Wrap the bay leaves, peppercorns, and juniper berries in cheesecloth and add to the pot. When the cabbage is just starting to brown, but still quite hard, add stock and wine. Bring to a boil, and then reduce the heat to a simmer. Poach the sausages in this braise for about 10 minutes, and then set them aside until ready to serve. Continue to simmer the cabbage for 30 to 45 minutes, until it is just tender. Strain off most of the liquid and reduce by half, then return it to the cabbage. Remove the thyme and spices. Adjust the seasoning with salt, pepper, duck fat, and vinegar.

TO SERVE:

Brown the sausages and 3 of the duck legs in the remaining 2 tablespoons duck fat, then add to the cabbage. Serve each person some of both meats and the cabbage. Make certain each person gets some juice. Serve with mustard, cornichons, and boiled little new potatoes.

SERVES 6 TO 8

3 THE THREEMENU REVIEW

23 FEBRUARY 1986

THE TABLE & ITS CONTENTS

"Preface"
Jill Kjómpedahl

"An Italian Salad in Oakland"
Kristen Dolph

"Salmon in the Grass, Creole style"
Carol Brendlinger

"Veal Loin and Wild Mushrooms"
Lee Colman

"Lemon Ice Cream and Spring Cookies"
Kate Dowling

the third annual
Threepenny Review
benefit dinner
at Bay Wolf

MENU BY WILL POWERS

ORANGE-SCENTED RICE PUDDING
with Oranges and Golden Raisin Compote

When Earl first suggested including rice pudding on the dessert menu, Larry's response was, "Who eats rice pudding?" There were six children in Earl's family, and rice pudding was a huge treat to them, greedily consumed by the gallon. Earl's instincts were right: this is always a hit.

RICE PUDDING

2 tablespoons sweet, unsalted butter

1 cup Arborio rice

Finely chopped zest of 1 large orange (approximately 2 tablespoons)

1/2 vanilla bean, split, or 1 tablespoon vanilla extract

3 cups whole milk

3/4 cup sugar

2 cups heavy whipping cream, whipped until stiff

COMPOTE

1 cup golden raisins

1 1/2 cups freshly squeezed orange juice

1/4 cup sugar

1 large orange (use the orange that you zested for the rice pudding)

TO PREPARE THE PUDDING:

Melt the butter in a medium, heavy-bottomed saucepan. Add the rice, zest, and scraped vanilla seeds or extract. Cook, stirring constantly, for a few minutes. Add the milk all at once. Stir constantly over a low flame. It will take about 30 minutes for the rice to absorb all of the liquid. When the rice is soft and all of the liquid has been absorbed, add the sugar and mix well. Pour into a shallow pan. Cover with plastic wrap and refrigerate to cool. When cold, fold in a few tablespoons of whipped cream to break up the mixture. Then fold in the remaining whipped cream.

TO PREPARE THE COMPOTE:

Place the raisins, juice, and sugar in a saucepan over low heat. Cook for 20 to 30 minutes, or until all of the liquid is absorbed. Let cool. Cut the skin off the orange, using a sharp knife. Cut between the membranes and gently pull out the clean wedges of orange. Add the wedges to the cooled raisins.

To serve, top each serving of rice pudding with some of the compote.

SERVES 6 TO 8

BLOOD ORANGE AND MEYER LEMON SHERBETS *with Lime Shortbread*

The vivid and beautiful blood orange was once quite exotic and expensive. Now grown commercially in the United States, they can often be found in large grocery stores. Meyer lemons are available only in the winter. They have soft skins and a more pronounced fragrance than the more common, thicker-skinned Eurekas. The acid content of Meyers is lower and the sugar content usually higher than other lemons. Sherbets are fruit ices with the addition of milk or cream, preferably cream.

BLOOD ORANGE SHERBET

4 cups freshly squeezed blood orange juice

1¹/₂ cups sugar

¹/₄ cup heavy whipping cream

MEYER LEMON SHERBET

2 cups freshly squeezed Meyer lemon juice

2 cups sugar

1³/₄ cups water

¹/₄ cup heavy whipping cream

LIME SHORTBREAD

¹/₂ cup sweet, unsalted butter

¹/₄ cup sugar

1 cup all-purpose flour

Finely chopped zest of 1 lime

1 teaspoon vanilla extract

TO PREPARE THE SHERBERTS:

Mix together the ingredients for each sherbert and freeze each separately in an ice cream freezer according to the manufacturer's instructions.

TO PREPARE THE SHORTBREAD:

Preheat the oven to 300°. Cut the butter into small pieces into the bowl of an electric mixer fitted with the paddle attachment. Add the sugar, flour, zest, and vanilla. Mix on low speed for about 10 to 15 minutes, or until the dough comes together. Roll the dough out to ¹/₂-inch thickness and cut it into desired shapes. Place on parchment-lined baking sheets and bake for 20 minutes, or until light golden brown.

TO SERVE:

Place 1 scoop of each sherbert in each serving bowl and insert a piece (or two) of shortbread.

MAKES ABOUT 1 QUART OF EACH SHERBERT AND 2 DOZEN COOKIES

WINTER FRUIT TART

In recent years, more and more glamorous and enticing dried fruits have come onto the market: persimmons, cranberries, many varieties of cherries, delicately preserved apricots, peaches, and pears. When fruits are dried, their flavor condenses and intensifies. This is a wonderful combination: the lightly cooked fruits retain their individual essences, the spices enhance them, and the wine and port inspire them.

FILLING

1 large apple, peeled and chopped
1/2 cup chopped dried apricots
1/2 cup dried cherries
1/2 cup golden raisins
1/2 cup chopped dates
Finely chopped zest and juice of 1 orange
1 cup red wine
1/4 cup ruby port
1/8 teaspoon ground cinnamon
1/8 teaspoon ground ginger
Pinch of freshly ground black pepper
1 cup brown sugar

DOUGH

1/2 cup sweet, unsalted butter
1 1/2 cups all-purpose flour
Pinch of salt
Pinch of sugar
1/4 cup ice water, more if needed

Egg wash of 1 egg, pinch of salt, and
    2 tablespoons heavy whiping cream
Sugar for sprinkling
Sweetened whipped cream

TO PREPARE THE FILLING:

Place the filling ingredients in a medium saucepan. Heat over a low flame until the fruit absorbs the liquid. Spread the mixture on a baking sheet and let cool.

TO PREPARE THE DOUGH:

Cut the butter into small pieces into a mixing bowl. Mix the flour with the salt and sugar. Work the flour and butter together with your fingers until the butter is the size of peas. Add the water, a little at time, folding and collecting the dough. Try not to knead it. You may need a few more tablespoons of water, depending on the dryness of the flour. Divide the dough in half and form into flat rounds. Wrap the rounds separately in plastic wrap and let rest in the refrigerator for about 15 minutes.

TO ASSEMBLE AND BAKE THE TART:

Preheat the oven to 400°. Roll each round of dough into a 1/4-inch-thick circle. Line the bottom of a 10-inch tart pan with 1 round and fill with the fruit filling. Lay the second round and over the filling, pressing the edges of the dough together. Brush the egg wash on top. Cut decorative holes in the surface. Sprinkle with sugar. Refrigerate until firm.

Bake for about 45 minutes. The tart should be golden brown and the filling should bubble through the holes. Let cool.

TO SERVE:

Cut the tart into 8 slices. Serve with sweetened whipped cream.

MAKES ONE 9-INCH TART

March

Spring in Lyon

I'd approached Lyon from the north, east, south, and west for years and always believed that the idea was to get in and out as quickly as possible. I'd known that Lyon was widely regarded as a gastronomic mecca, but it was not a destination for me until my son Avram took up residence there in the early 1990s. It's easy to be enthusiastic about Lyon, though. I've never been in a place as dedicated to food. The winters are gray and interminable. Compared to an international city such as Paris, Lyon is culturally insignificant, and so they've evolved wonderful little home-style spots that serve warm, friendly, less expensive food and the finest sausage outside Alsace and Germany. The Lyonnaise seem to have found ways to use all of the parts of the pig left over after the Parisians have acquired the more elegant cuts. Justly famous for the large, lightly cured, and liberally truffled sausage known as *cervelas,* Lyon is well situated near the Dauphiné for potatoes, Charolais for beef, Bresse for poultry, the Auvergne for lamb, Savoie for mushrooms, watercress from the Auzon Valley, and cherries and apricots from Vienne and Ampuis.

Lyon is the apotheosis of bourgeois cooking. It is possessed of an abundance of *boites* and *bouchons*, forty- or fifty-seat restaurants richly endowed with the sort of well-worn hospitality, the eating and drinking atmospherics that are so central to their comfort. These are not decorator restaurants but quiet evolutions of their owners' personalities. Each is a little different, but most share the characteristics of solid comfort and a well-larded menu of sausages and wines. The waiters don't have attitudes and the decor isn't chic; the Lyonnaise are devoted to food and down to earth. Even the rushing hustle-bustle is low-key. These neighborhood dining experiences are an integral part of Lyonnaise culture.

Lyon is a very manageable city, its good, old heart being twelve blocks by twenty blocks and populated with hundreds of restaurants. We discovered Chez Lea, drawn by its familiarly seductive smell of serious food. We became frequenters; I took my son's friends and my good friend Tomas there for the river light and the genuine and affordable Lyonnaise specialties. We ate broiled lobster and wild boar ragout, incredible chicken in a sauce that was finished with one of the local ancient vinegars and crème fraîche.

The food purveyor shops are like jewel boxes, the butchers and charcuteries are earnest and stimulating, their wares irresistibly pure. In California we invent spring. In Lyon it's a movement, from the perfection of the winter foods such as deep-fried pig ears and sausage and lentils, into the spring delicacies: asparagus and strawberries, new carrots, tiny peas, spring lamb, wild salmon, the end of citrus, the last of the shellfish. Things have been very clean and cold. The richness of oysters and other shellfish marries well with the smallness of the produce. Dainty, delicate shellfish goes with dainty and delicate things.

I'd start every meal with a dandelion salad. The perfect simplicity of a classic *salade Lyonnaise* is not to be disdained. So naturally made in its native habitat with wild bitter greens, a delicately voluptuous poached egg, little pieces of rich, smoky bacon, and one of the good, homemade vinegars that draw their essence from the vinous bounty of neighboring Côtes du Rhône, Mâcon, and Beaujolais. It's what one eats in Lyon, and I love it immoderately. If the balance is right, it makes you hungry in the way that lean wines such as the Loire wines, Sauvignon Blanc– or Chenin Blanc–based wines, and crisp Italian wines make you salivate, tickle the gumline, and create a tension that stimulates the appetite.

It's been said that Lyon is situated on three rivers—the Rhône, the Saône, and the Beaujolais—and that the food is more hearty than graceful. It's a heartiness that I find amenable and infused with its own companionable grace.

Second Annual
THREEPENNY REVIEW Benefit Dinner

RE:JOYCE MENU
BLACK VELVET
FINNEGAN'S HADDIE
CORNED DUCK & CABBAGE
LAMB ARABY
IRISH MISTS

BAY WOLF RESTAURANT
18 March 1984

MENU BY ROBIN CHERIN AND CHERYL MILLER

41

DANDELION SALAD
with Bacon, Egg, and Garlic Croutons

This is the essence of Lyon on a single salad plate and an occasion for finding and using a high-quality smoky, streaky bacon such as Hobbs. Fans of bitter greens will applaud you. Make the vinaigrette a bit on the acidic side, to cut through the richness of the egg and bacon.

2 bunches dandelion green

$1/4$ cup red wine vinegar

$1/2$ cup dry red wine

2 garlic cloves, smashed

1 thyme sprig

2 shallots, minced

Salt and freshly ground black pepper

4 bacon slices

2 eggs

Extra virgin olive oil

$1/4$ loaf levain, crusts removed and cut into small cubes

Trim off the long stems from the dandelion greens. Put the vinegar, wine, 1 of the garlic cloves, and thyme in a small saucepan and reduce to $1/3$ cup. Pour into a bowl over the shallots. Season with salt and pepper and let macerate for 25 minutes.

Meanwhile, cook the bacon (not too crispy) and save the fat for the vinaigrette. Break the bacon into smaller pieces and set aside. Bring the eggs to a boil, remove from the heat, and let stand, covered, for 6 minutes. Drain the eggs, peel, and cut in half lengthwise.

Preheat the oven to 375°. Warm a little olive oil in a pan along with the other garlic clove. When the oil is very garlicky, add some salt and pepper and then toss the bread cubes in it. Bake until golden and crispy.

Finish the vinaigrette by whisking in the reserved bacon fat. If the vinaigrette is still too acidic, whisk in olive oil.

To assemble the salad, remove garlic and thyme from the vinaigrette, heat a large stainless steel bowl directly over a burner, and add some of the vinaigrette, the bacon, and the greens. When the greens are wilted, add the croutons and adjust the seasoning. Add more vinaigrette if necessary. Serve warm, topped with the halved eggs.

SERVES 4

LAMB TONGUE SALAD
with Capers, Egg, and Mustard Vinaigrette

Lamb tongue is a very delicately flavored and textured meat. It needs lightly acidic, pickled garnishing and plenty of salt in the braising liquid.

TONGUE

6 cups water

1 cup dry white wine

1/2 cup white wine vinegar

1 cup salt

2 bay leaves

4 thyme sprigs

2 allspice berries

1 juniper berry, crushed

A few black peppercorns

A few toasted coriander seeds (optional)

6 garlic cloves, crushed

1 tarragon sprig

4 lamb tongues

VINAIGRETTE

1/2 cup dry white wine

1/3 cup white wine vinegar

1 tarragon sprig

2 shallots, minced

1/4 cup Dijon mustard

Salt and freshly ground black pepper

3/4 cup extra virgin olive oil

3 eggs

3 tablespoons capers, rinsed

Minced Italian parsley

Minced chives

2 heads Belgian endive, julienned

TO PREPARE THE TONGUES:

Place the water, wine, vinegar, salt, bay leaves, thyme, allspice, juniper, peppercorns, coriander, garlic, and tarragon in a medium saucepan and bring to a boil. Add the tongues and simmer gently for 1 1/2 to 2 hours, or until the outer skin is loose and the meat feels tender. Remove the tongues from the liquid and set the liquid aside. Peel off the outer skin and discard it. Store the tongues in the braising liquid until ready to serve.

TO PREPARE THE VINAIGRETTE:

Reduce the wine and vinegar with the tarragon to 1/4 cup. Cool, remove the tarragon, and pour into a bowl over the shallots. Let macerate for 20 minutes. Add the mustard, season with salt and pepper, and then whisk in the olive oil.

TO FINISH THE SALAD:

Bring the eggs to a boil, remove from the heat, and let stand, covered, for 6 minutes. Drain and refresh with cold water. Peel. Separate the yolks from the whites and press each separately through a fine-mesh strainer.

Slice the tongues thinly across the grain and dress with the vinaigrette. Sprinkle with the capers, eggs, and herbs. Dress the julienned endive and serve it alongside. Make sure there are shallots from the vinaigrette on the tongue.

SERVES 4

CELERY ROOT AND CELERY HEART SALAD
with Blue Cheese and Glazed Walnuts

This salad is best prepared with young celery and small celery roots. Large celery roots tend to hollow out in the center and be tough on the outside. Celery, in each manifestation, is a clean, fresh vehicle for the richness of the cheese and the sweet crunch of the walnuts.

VINAIGRETTE

1 shallot, minced

3 tablespoons sherry vinegar

Leaves from 1 thyme sprig, finely chopped

Salt and freshly ground black pepper

1/2 cup plus 1 tablespoon walnut oil

SALAD

2 pounds celery root, peeled and cut into thin triangles

4 small heads celery

1 tablespoon olive oil

1 cup walnuts

1 1/2 tablespoons sugar

4 small handfuls Italian parsley leaves

Salt and freshly ground black pepper

7 ounces blue cheese, crumbled

TO PREPARE THE VINAIGRETTE:

Soak the shallot in the vinegar with the thyme, salt, and pepper for 25 minutes. Whisk in the walnut oil.

TO PREPARE THE SALAD:

Blanch the celery root until tender, then refresh in ice water. Drain and pat it dry with a towel. Trim the celery 1 inch from the base. If the hearts are large, quarter and then blanch them as you did with the root. Marinate the roots and hearts in some of the vinaigrette.

Take 4 of the celery stalks you just trimmed, and slice them thinly on an angle. Be sure to remove any fibrous strings. Heat the olive oil in a sauté pan, add the walnuts and sugar, and cook over medium heat until the sugar begins to caramelize. Do not let the nuts burn. Transfer to a plate to harden and cool.

TO SERVE:

Add the walnuts, sliced celery, and parsley to the marinating roots and hearts. Season with salt and pepper, add a little more vinaigrette, and toss well. Garnish individual servings with the cheese.

SERVES 4

BRAISED PORK LEG
with Potato and Artichoke Gratin

A whole pork leg is a thing of beauty. It is the same beautiful joint from which ham is derived. At the restaurant we separate the whole leg into its main muscles, bard it with its own fat, and cook each muscle, very slowly, so that the fat sinks back into the meat. We cook it, muscle by muscle, throughout the night. It is perfectly clear meat with a more interesting, deeper succulence and a better flavor than the loin. This preparation yields enough meat for about ten servings. Store it in its braising juices and enjoy it over several days. It is a glorious leftover.

BRAISED PORK LEG

   4 pounds boneless pork leg meat, skin on

   2 garlic cloves, sliced

   Salt and freshly ground black pepper

   1/4 cup plus 2 tablespoons olive oil

   A few savory sprigs

   1 carrot, peeled and diced

   1 celery stalk, diced

   1 yellow onion, diced

   2 black peppercorns

   1 bay leaf

   2 cups pork or veal stock

POTATO AND ARTICHOKE GRATIN

   1 1/4 cups heavy whipping cream

   1/2 cup chicken, beef, or pork stock

   2 lemon zest strips

   Small chunk onion

   4 artichokes

   Lemon wedge

   2 russet potatoes

   Salt and ground white pepper

   1 cup dried breadcrumbs, tossed in
      2 tablespoons melted butter

   Handful of thinly sliced onion

SAUCE

   1 shallot, sliced

   1 thyme sprig

   2 black peppercorns

   A tiny bit of bay leaf

   8 1/2 cups pork and/or poultry stock, heated

   1 lemon zest strip

   1 tablespoon chopped Italian parsley

TO PREPARE THE PORK:

The day before serving, peel back the skin on the pork leg, using a very sharp knife. Make sure that the fat remains on the skin side. Leave one end of the skin attached. Trim a small chunk of meat and save it for your sauce. Make tiny incisions in the meat and insert the garlic slices. Season the meat generously with salt and pepper, rub it with 1/4 cup of the olive oil, and pack some savory sprigs firmly against it. Replace the skin, wrap tightly in plastic wrap and refrigerate overnight.

The next day, start the pork about 5 hours 45 minutes before you plan to serve it. While the pork is cooking for the last hour, assemble the gratin so it can go in the oven as the pork comes out (unless, of course, you have two ovens).

Preheat the oven to 250°. Sauté the carrot, celery, and onion in the remaining 2 tablespoons olive oil and put them in an ovenproof pot that will just hold the pork. Discard whatever juices have come from the pork and place the meat on

(continued)

45

top of the sautéed vegetables. Add the peppercorns, bay leaf, and stock. Fit a piece of parchment over the pork and cover with foil or the pot lid. Place in the oven and cook for 3 to 4 hours. The meat will be obviously tender when it is done. Cool in the pan still tented with foil. To serve, remove the pork from the broth and cut it in thin slices across the grain.

TO PREPARE THE GRATIN:

You can assemble the gratin in one 8 by 10-inch pan or in 4 individual molds. Butter the inside of the pan or molds. Heat the cream with ¹/₂ cup stock, lemon zest (no pith), and onion. Let steep for at least 15 minutes.

Preheat the oven to 375°. Remove the artichoke leaves until you reach the yellow part, then cut the remaining leaves off at the top of the choke, and discard them. Run a small knife around the inner rim of the choke to loosen the fuzz, then scrape it out with a spoon. Trim the stem end and a thin layer of the stem and base, any part that is dark green. Rub with a lemon wedge and drop into acidulated water while you prepare the remaining artichokes.

Peel the potatoes and slice thinly with a knife or mandoline. Arrange a single layer in the bottom of the buttered pan. Slice the artichokes and arrange them in a single layer over the potatoes. Season with salt and white pepper as you go. Continue making layers with the rest of the potatoes and artichokes.

Strain the cream mixture into the pan. It should not quite cover the vegetables. Scatter the onion slices over the gratin. Cover the pan and bake for 20 minutes. Remove the cover and continue to bake for another 20 minutes, or until the liquid is almost totally reduced. Cover the gratin with buttered breadcrumbs for the last 10 minutes of baking; or add them at the end and brown quickly under the broiler. The gratin can rest for an hour and be reheated just before serving without compromising its quality in the slightest.

TO PREPARE THE SAUCE:

With this or any other reduction sauce, it is important to avoid boiling the sauce hard. Boiling causes any fat and impurities to be emulsified into the sauce. Skim any froth or scum from the surface of the sauce as it cooks. Continue to skim, skim, skim. This will give you a very clean and clear sauce. It is equally important to add the stock gradually, 2 cups at a time, not all at once. The sauce will have more depth this way.

Ladle a bit of rendered fat from the pork braise into a saucepan, and brown the reserved pork chunk and shallot. Add the thyme, peppercorns, bay leaf, and 2 cups of the hot stock. Reduce the heat to a simmer. Add the remaining stock gradually as the mixture reduces.

Add the lemon zest when you add the last 2 cups of stock; any earlier and the sauce may become too lemony or bitter. Reduce the sauce until it is spoon-coating consistency. It should not be thick or sticky. Strain through a chinois or fine strainer. Just before serving, add the parsley.

TO SERVE:

Cut slices of the pork and plate with generous wedges of gratin. Drizzle pork with the sauce.

SERVES 4

BOUILLABAISSE *with*
Aioli- and Roasted Red Pepper–Smeared Toasts

I love bouillabaisse in general and this one, drawn from Lauren's perfect conception and delicious execution, in particular. The colors are gorgeous and the flavors bright and clean. Traditionally, bouilla-baisse is served with rouille, *a paste made with breadcrumbs, red peppers, and sometimes monkfish livers. Here we pair it with toasts smeared with aioli and roasted red peppers. Crunch with color.*

AIOLI

2 egg yolks, at room temperature

2 teaspoons tepid water

1 garlic clove, minced

1 1/2 cups olive oil

Salt

Lemon juice

3 carrots, peeled and diced

2 celery stalks, diced

1 onion, diced

1/2 fennel bulb, diced

3 leeks, diced

3 tablespoons olive oil

3 garlic cloves, chopped

6 thyme sprigs

1 bay leaf

3 tablespoons tomato paste

Finely chopped zest and juice of 2 oranges

2 cups dry white wine

6 cups fish stock

1/2 cup Pernod or other anise liqueur

2 tomatoes, roasted, puréed, and strained

4 ounces mussels, soaked and debearded

4 ounces clams, soaked

8 ounces monkfish or rock cod

8 ounces shrimp

4 ounces scallops

20 basil leaves, torn

1 tablespoon chopped Italian parsley

Lemon juice

6 tablespoons virgin olive oil

Rounds of levain or baguette, toasted

1 red bell pepper, roasted and finely chopped

TO PREPARE THE AIOLI:

Whisk together the egg yolks, water, and garlic. Whisk in the olive oil one drop at a time until the sauce emulsifies, then gradually whisk in the remaining oil. To make the sauce in a food processor, slowly add drops of oil to the egg yolk, water, and garlic while pulsing the processor on and off. Season with the salt and lemon juice. If the sauce breaks, in a separate bowl, whisk the broken aioli drop by drop into another egg yolk.

TO PREPARE THE BOUILLABAISSE:

In a large, nonreactive pot, lightly caramelize the carrot, celery, onion, fennel, and leeks in the oil. Add the garlic, thyme, bay leaf, tomato paste, orange zest and juice, wine, fish stock, Pernod, and tomato purée. Season well and simmer for 20 minutes.

A few minutes before serving, add the mussels and clams and simmer for a couple of minutes, then add the rest of the fish and shellfish. If your monkfish is particularly fat, put it in with the mussels. Simmer gently until everything is just cooked. If the shrimp, scallops, and monkfish are ready and the mussels and clams have not yet opened, transfer the unopened ones to a sauté pan with a little of the bouillabaisse base and cook over high heat to open. Adjust the seasoning to open and stir in the basil and parsley. Add lemon juice if it needs acid.

Ladle into warmed bowls. Drizzle a little virgin olive oil over each bowl. Pass toasts smeared with aioli and peppers.

SERVES 6 TO 8

Cockles & Mussels: Prawn, scallop, and mussel salad with sorrel sauce

Filet Mignon 'pickled' in Irish Whiskey with horseradish cream

'Boxty LaRue': Potato pancakes with cheddar cheese and bacon

Baby Lettuces with a spiced mead vinaigrette

Emerald Isle Soup: puree of potato and leek soup with watercress cream

Saint Patrick's Day

Fried trout rolled in oatmeal with Black Velvet Sabayon

Finegan's Haddie: salmon with smoked fish mousse and an Irish Whiskey beurre blanc

Corned Duck and Cabbage with sage-onion colcannon

Black pepper pasta with wild mushrooms, Irish Whiskey, and cream

Pork Pie with fresh peas, artichokes, and pickled onions

Ulysses Irish Lamb Stew with pickled red cabbage and soda bread

Bay Wolf   March 17, 1987

Kate's Fair Sweets

MENU BY WILL POWERS AND CHERYL MILLER

DUCK À L'ORANGE
with Turnips and Their Greens

Think of a duck waddling under an orange tree chomping on turnip greens. Classic duck à l'orange is made with bitter Seville oranges. If these are unavailable, any other high-acid orange will work. We learned quite by accident that over-reduced orange juice takes on the bitter-sweet quality of the Seville orange. Adding a bit of good marmalade to your sauce will give it a similar punch. Basmati rice, with a handful of wild rice mixed in, is a nice accompaniment.

DUCK

  4 duck legs

  Salt and freshly ground black pepper

  Finely chopped zest and juice of 4 large
    oranges, preferably Seville

  2 tablespoons sugar

  1 teaspoon dried thyme

  1 bay leaf, crumbled

  10 cups duck or chicken stock

  2 orange zest strips

SAUCE

  1 shallot, minced

  Duck hearts and gizzards (optional)

  1 thyme sprig

  1 small bay leaf, crumbled

  2 black peppercorns

  1 orange zest strip

  2 cups chicken or duck stock, heated

TURNIPS AND GREENS

  2 small bunches baby turnips with
    greens attached

  1 tablespoon butter

  Pinch of sugar

  Pinch of salt

  Freshly ground black pepper

  1 sweet orange, peeled and sectioned
    or sliced into rounds

TO PREPARE THE DUCK:

The night before serving, season the duck legs with salt and pepper and refrigerate.

The next day, make a glaze by combining the orange zest, juice, and sugar in a small saucepan and reducing until only a few table-spoons remain. Strain out the zest. If you're not using Seville oranges, return the juice to the heat and continue to cook until the sugar begins to caramelize. This will give the glaze a marmaladelike bitterness that is similar to the flavor of Seville oranges. If you are using Seville oranges, caramelization is unnecessary. Remove from the heat and set aside.

Preheat the oven to 375°. Sprinkle the bottom of a pan that will just hold the duck legs with a little thyme and the bay leaf. Arrange the legs in the pan, skin side up, and roast for 1 hour. Baste the legs with the glaze twice during the last 15 minutes of cooking. Pour off the rendered fat and reserve it. Pour enough hot stock over the legs just to reach the skin. Add orange zest strips and continue to cook for 30 minutes. The legs are ready when the meat is tender and the skin is crisp and golden.

TO PREPARE THE SAUCE:

Brown the shallot and innards in a little of the rendered duck fat. Add the thyme, a bit of crumbled bay leaf, peppercorns, and a strip of

(continued)

51

zest. Make sure no pith is attached. Add the stock and lower the heat to a simmer. Skim the scum frequently. Add more stock as the sauce reduces down. When no more stock remains, reduce the sauce to a spoon-coating consistency; this will take about 40 minutes. Add some reduced orange juice and adjust the seasoning. Strain through a fine strainer before serving.

TO PREPARE THE TURNIPS:

Trim and wash the greens thoroughly. Scrub the turnips and peel them if the skin seems tough. Quarter the turnips, unless tiny enough to sauté whole, and sauté them in a little rendered duck fat and butter. When the turnips begin to color, add the sugar and salt and a little water. Cook until the turnips are tender and there is no more liquid in the pan, about 5

minutes. Just before serving, add the greens to the pan and toss until wilted. Season with salt and pepper.

TO SERVE:

Serve the duck, orange sauce, orange pieces, turnips, and greens onto individual plates or a medium platter.

SERVES 4

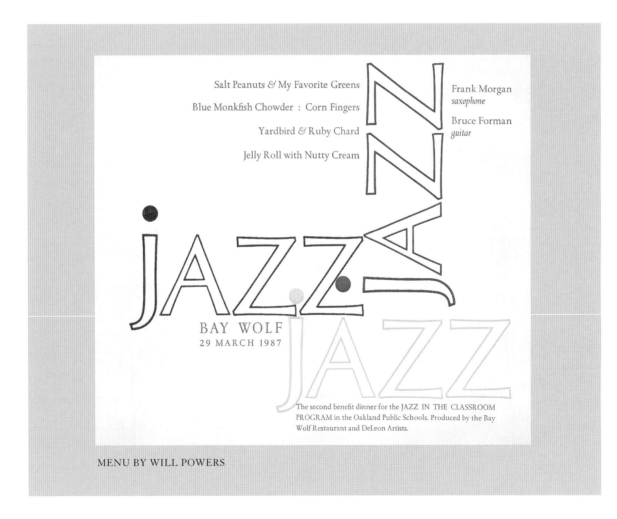

Salt Peanuts & My Favorite Greens

Blue Monkfish Chowder : Corn Fingers

Yardbird & Ruby Chard

Jelly Roll with Nutty Cream

Frank Morgan
saxophone

Bruce Forman
guitar

BAY WOLF
29 MARCH 1987

The second benefit dinner for the JAZZ IN THE CLASSROOM PROGRAM in the Oakland Public Schools. Produced by the Bay Wolf Restaurant and DeLeon Artists.

MENU BY WILL POWERS

MEYER LEMON MERINGUE TART

There is something ineffably immortal about the perfect layering of buttery sweet tart crust, lemon-scented filling, and the fluffy softness of slightly crisped meringue that seems to make individuals of a certain type (mine!) blissfully happy.

SWEET TART DOUGH
3/4 cup sugar

1 1/4 cups unsalted butter, at room temperature

1 whole egg

3 cups all-purpose flour

FILLING
1 cup Meyer lemon juice

Zest of 2 Meyer lemons, removed in strips

1 cup sugar

8 egg yolks

4 whole eggs

MERINGUE
4 egg whites

1 cup sugar

TO PREPARE THE TART SHELL:

Slowly beat the sugar with the butter in a mixer fitted with a paddle attachment until well combined. Add the egg and mix well, scraping the sides to incorporate the egg and butter thoroughly. Roll out into a 1/4-inch-thick round. Line a 9-inch tart pan with half the dough, reserving the other half for another purpose. Refrigerate until firm.

Preheat the oven to 350°. Line the shell with parchment and weight it with pie weights or dried beans or rice. Bake for 20 to 30 minutes, until the shell is light brown and dry. Remove the weights and parchment and let cool.

TO PREPARE THE FILLING:

Mix the juice, zest, sugar, egg yolks, and whole eggs in a stainless steel mixing bowl and place over a pot of boiling water. Cook, whisking constantly, for 20 to 30 minutes, or until thick. Strain out the zest through a fine strainer into a bowl. Let cool. Pour the filling into the cooled tart shell, spreading evenly. Refrigerate until cold. If the filling isn't cold, the meringue will weep and form a layer of moisture on top of the tart.

TO PREPARE THE MERINGUE:

Preheat the oven to 450°. Whisk the egg whites in the stainless steel bowl of an electric mixer until foamy. Add the sugar, place over a pot of boiling water, and heat, stirring constantly, until the sugar is melted. Whip until stiff with the electric mixer. With a spatula, pile the meringue onto the cooled tart. Completely cover the filling. Bake for 5 to 6 minutes, or until the meringue starts to brown. Cool completely on a rack. Cutting the tart with a wet knife will prevent it from sticking to the knife.

MAKES ONE 9-INCH TART

PROFITEROLES *with*
Strawberry Ice Cream and Chocolate Sauce

Profiteroles are little cream puffs filled with custard, whipped cream, or, in this incarnation, ice cream. At the BayWolf, we prepare them ahead to facilitate rapid service. At home, fill them just before serving, stack four on a plate, and drizzle with chocolate. You can substitute a commercial high-quality strawberry ice cream in this recipe, but freshly made ice cream is intense and wonderful.

PÂTE À CHOUX

1¼ cups water

¼ teaspoon salt

1 teaspoon sugar

3 tablespoons sweet, unsalted butter

1¼ cups all-purpose flour

4 whole eggs

STRAWBERRY ICE CREAM

2 cups hulled and chopped fresh strawberries

¾ cup sugar

¾ cup heavy whipping cream

¾ cup whole milk

Seeds scraped from ½ vanilla bean

8 egg yolks

¾ cup sugar

1 cup heavy whipping cream, whipped until stiff

CHOCOLATE SAUCE

8 ounces dark chocolate

½ cup heavy whipping cream

TO PREPARE THE PÂTE À CHOUX:

In a large saucepan, bring the water, salt, sugar, and butter to a boil. Add the flour all at once and beat over the heat until the mixture forms a sticky paste. Remove from the heat. Transfer to the bowl of an electric mixer fitted with the paddle attachment. Add 1 egg at a time, beating until incorporated. Preheat the oven to 400°. Line 2 baking sheets with parchment.

**TO SHAPE AND BAKE
THE PROFITEROLES:**

Using 2 large soup spoons dipped in water, scoop 2-inch rounds of dough onto the baking sheets, leaving at least ½ inch between puffs. Bake for 15 to 20 minutes, or until golden brown. Let cool.

TO PREPARE THE ICE CREAM:

Place the berries and sugar in a saucepan and cook over low heat for 10 to 15 minutes, or until thick. Remove from the heat. Let cool. Purée in a processor or blender. You should have 1 cup of purée. Set aside.

Heat the ¾ cup heavy cream with the milk and vanilla. Mix the egg yolks with the sugar in a stainless steel bowl. Add the cream, a few tablespoons at a time, to the yolk mixture, mixing well. Place atop an ice bath and stir until completely cooled. Strain through a fine strainer. Add the strawberry purée to the cream mixture and fold in the stiffly whipped cream. Freeze in an ice cream freezer according to the manufacturer's instructions.

TO PREPARE THE CHOCOLATE SAUCE:

Chop the chocolate into small pieces. Heat the cream in a small saucepan. Pour it over the chocolate. Mix until the chocolate is completely melted. Keep warm in a bain-marie or the top of a double boiler over hot water.

TO SERVE:

Slice the profiteroles in half horizontally and set the bottom halves on the serving plates or platter. Seat a generous scoop of strawberry ice cream on each profiterole bottom. Place the top halves of the profiteroles atop the ice cream. Drizzle with the chocolate sauce and serve right away.

MAKES ABOUT 36 PROFITEROLES

MIXED CITRUS NAPOLEONS

This napoleon is a crispy, crunchy, creamy dessert composed of layers of puff pastry, lemon cream, and refreshing winter citrus fruits. Puff paste is not difficult to make, but it is a little time-consuming. You can substitute commercial puff paste, cut into 4-inch squares, pricked with a fork, and baked at 400° for 15 to 20 minutes.

PUFF PASTE

2 cups all-purpose flour

Pinch of salt

Pinch of granulated sugar

1 pound sweet, unsalted butter, cut into small pieces

1/4 cup ice water, more if needed

LEMON FILLING

1 1/2 cups freshly squeezed lemon juice

1 1/2 cups granulated sugar

6 egg yolks

2 whole eggs

1/2 cup heavy whipping cream

2 cups mascarpone cheese

3 cups peeled and sliced mixed citrus fruits, such as grapefruits, oranges, tangerines, and blood oranges

Powdered sugar for dusting

TO PREPARE THE PUFF PASTE:

Combine the flour, salt, and sugar in a large mixing bowl. Cut the butter into the flour until the butter is the size of small peas. Add the ice water, a little at a time, and work the dough together. Roll into a rectangle 6 inches by 12 inches. Fold the dough in thirds, folding one third toward the center and then the other third overlapping the top of the first fold. This is the first turn. Rotate the dough one-quarter turn to the right or left and roll out again to a 6 by 12-inch rectangle. Fold again as before. Wrap in plastic wrap and refrigerate for 20 minutes. Roll and fold again. Refrigerate for 20 minutes. Roll out to 1/4-inch thickness. Refrigerate for 20 minutes.

Preheat the oven to 400°. Cut the puff paste into sixteen 4-inch squares. Prick the squares with a fork. Bake on a parchment-lined baking sheet for 15 to 20 minutes, or until the squares are a nice golden brown. Let cool.

TO PREPARE THE FILLING:

Mix together the lemon juice, sugar, egg yolks, and whole eggs in a nonaluminum pan and cook over low heat, stirring constantly, until thick. Remove from the heat. Strain through a fine strainer into a bowl. Cover with plastic wrap. Refrigerate until cold. Incorporate the cream, a little at a time, into the mascarpone. Place in a mixer and whip until stiff. Fold into the cold lemon filling.

TO SERVE:

Place 1 piece of puff paste on a serving plate, spread with some of the filling, and top with some fruit and a second piece of puff paste. Dust each napoleon with powdered sugar.

MAKES 8 NAPOLEONS

TANGERINE CHAMPAGNE TRIFLE

Trifle is a traditional English composition of cake and cream interlaced with fruit. It is both delicate and comforting. Although slightly old cake can be used, I like to make it with this somewhat coarse sponge cake: it holds plenty of moisture without becoming soggy.

SPONGE CAKE

6 whole eggs, separated

1 1/2 cups sugar

2 teaspoons vanilla extract

1/2 cup hot water

1 1/2 cups all-purpose flour

1 1/4 teaspoons baking powder

1/4 teaspoon salt

TANGERINE SAUCE

2 cups freshly squeezed tangerine juice

Zest of 1 tangerine, removed in strips and chopped

1 cup sugar

CHAMPAGNE SABAYON

6 egg yolks

1/3 cup sugar

3/4 cup dry champagne

1 cup whipped cream

TOPPING

1 cup heavy whipping cream

1/2 teaspoon vanilla extract

1/4 cup sugar

———

3 large tangerines

TO PREPARE THE CAKE:

Preheat the oven to 375°. Using an electric mixer, whip the egg yolks with 1 cup of the sugar and the vanilla until light and fluffy. Slowly add the hot water and whip until cold. Sift the flour with the baking powder and salt. Fold into the yolk mixture. Whip the whites with the remaining 1/2 cup sugar until stiff. Fold the whites, a little at a time, into the yolk mixture. Pour into a parchment-lined rimmed 12 by 16-inch baking sheet and spread evenly. Bake for 15 to 20 minutes. The cake should spring back when pressed with your hand. Let cool in the pan.

TO PREPARE THE SAUCE:

Place the juice, zest, and sugar in a saucepan over low heat and reduce by half. Let cool. Strain out the zest.

TO PREPARE THE SABAYON:

In a stainless steel or copper bowl set over a pot of boiling water, whip the egg yolks, sugar, and champagne until tripled in volume. Place over an ice bath and continue to beat until cold. It will decrease in volume slightly. Fold in the whipped cream.

TO ASSEMBLE THE TRIFLE:

Make the topping by whipping the cream with the vanilla and sugar. Peel the tangerines and cut along the membranes to remove the citrus sections. Put a dab of sabayon on the bottom of a 2-quart glass bowl or trifle dish, and cover with a layer of sponge cake, cut to fit. Soak the sponge cake with some of the tangerine sauce. Spread with more sabayon and a layer of tangerine sections. Continue layering the cake, sabayon, and tangerines until all have been used. Cover the top of the trifle with the sweetened whipped cream. Let sit for 1 hour before serving.

SERVES 8

Sidney Weinstein's abundant, exuberant garden supplies us and other restaurants with lettuces, herbs, berries, and Meyer lemons.

April In Paris

It is a truth universally acknowledged that Paris in April is everyone's homeland. People everywhere think of April in Paris, not April in Warsaw or April in Beijing. I love the sound of "April in Paris." It's incantatory; it resonates. It's where I was born, when I was born. It just fits, like bread and butter. I love to eat white asparagus and potage Crécy. I love the vital, sensual blitz of crocuses and daffodils and weird flowers brought in from the country, mushrooms, shellfish plucked from cold waters, cured pork with little lentils, cornichons, pickled onions, mustard. Fall is decadence and shoring up for the winter, but spring is the Parisian sky opening up after relentless months of lowering gray. By April, Europeans are starved for sun. In the Jardin du Luxembourg, you see citizens exposing themselves to the unfamiliar sun, taking off their clothes with unexceptional abandon.

I didn't see Paris from the time we emigrated to America when I was seven until I returned with my parents at fifteen. On that trip, every time we were together as a family, we were eating. We didn't play golf or go bowling or go for long walks or wander in museums. We ate. We went to pâtisseries and charcuteries, boulangeries, épiceries, bonboneries, and chocolatiers. The visuals were appealing, but what overwhelmed me were the smells. The butter-nut fairy smell of pastry shops, that blissful blend of marrons glacés and Jordan almonds encased in sugar. Waves of sugar and vanilla. The cool, meatily dense aroma of the charcuterie. It's wonderful to walk into a shop or restaurant and have it smell like food. In some restaurants today they've done everything possible to eliminate smell, to neutralize its impact. When you walk by BayWolf, you smell food. The kitchen smells are vented onto the sidewalk and into the street. It smells. It's wonderful.

My father and I knew how to enjoy each other best at mealtime. I loved to eat and he loved to watch me. I got whatever I wanted, when we could afford it. I rediscovered or connected with some sort of European aspect of my life that I hadn't been clear about in Los Angeles. Once I was in Europe I discovered there were things I knew how to do that made no sense in America. I'd been eating two-handed, European style, cutting with my right hand and spearing with my left, without knowing it was acceptably and essentially European.

I discovered I really liked pâté and had a taste for it. Wherever we went, I started every meal with some kind of country ham because I loved its infinite variety. It touched something inside me. I became completely conscious of my nose and its ability to ferret out treasures.

After that first reunion with France, I went back again and again, often in April. We'd go to Zeyer and La Coupole and eat oysters, just oysters. One very cold spring we huddled in a garret near Les Halles, sitting on packing crates and watching our host elegantly and skillfully open dozens and dozens of small double zero Belon oysters with a beautiful knife (not an oyster tool) held in a fine linen napkin. We ate off good dishes with silverplate. We grilled bread in the fireplace, grouted it with bliss-inducing foie gras, and accompanied it with many bottles of Côtes du Rhône.

I can detail dozens of meals in April in Paris—with friends, with my family, with my sons. In the earliest visits the French fries were fabulous, still cooked in suet. Every bistro's *pommes frites* were different. Strawberries were served in huge bowls, family style, with mounds of crème fraîche. I couldn't stop eating them. Years later, I watched my sons put away similar mountains of strawberries and familiar ladles of crème fraîche.

When I'm in France in the spring, I'm going to eat whatever is perfectly in season. I am going to fulfill my destiny by eating white asparagus and sauce mousseline, an enormous mound of it, made by someone who knows what a sauce mousseline is, loves to cook, loves to eat, and knows the best place to buy the asparagus and how to prepare and serve it—someone who has been eating this combination all his life, who knows that a mousseline is made with the wrist and elbow, and who can sense when it's light and frothy and right.

BABY LEEK VINAIGRETTE
with Shellfish Salad

When I'm in Paris, I cook leeks. Now that smaller leeks are more universally available, this is an even more perfect and manageable accomplishment. Steaming is the most delicate medium because the leeks don't absorb any undesirable water and it allows you greater control than simmering. Combined with mustard vinaigrette and a piquant shellfish salad, this is unbelievably beautiful—all pale pastels.

LEEK VINAIGRETTE

12 baby leeks

Salt

Finely chopped zest and juice of 3 Meyer lemons

1 shallot, finely minced

1 small garlic clove, smashed

Freshly ground black pepper

2 to 3 tablespoons Dijon mustard

1 to 1½ cups extra virgin olive oil

1 tarragon sprig, minced

SHELLFISH SALAD

½ cup dry white wine

1 thyme or tarragon sprig

8 ounces shrimp

8 ounces mussels, soaked and debearded

4 ounces cooked crabmeat

1 cup aioli without garlic (page 48)

1 celery stalk, minced

1 tablespoon thinly sliced chives

Ground cayenne pepper

Salt and freshly ground black pepper

Juice of 1 Meyer or Eureka lemon

1 head Belgian endive, julienned

1 small handful chervil leaves

TO PREPARE THE LEEK VINAIGRETTE:

Trim the root and the dark green part of the stem from the leeks, leaving just enough of the root end attached to hold the leeks together. Split the leeks lengthwise, leaving the root end attached. Soak the leeks in cold water to remove any soil left from the farm. Arrange the leeks in a steamer, season with salt, and cook until just tender and they're no longer squeaky if you bite into them. Baby leeks will take only a few minutes; larger leeks require longer steaming. Set aside in a shallow dish.

Macerate the lemon zest with the shallot and garlic in the lemon juice. Add salt and pepper and set aside for at least 15 minutes. Finish the vinaigrette by whisking in mustard, oil, and tarragon. Pour over the leeks. The leeks can be prepared up to this point several hours in advance. It's best to serve them at room temperature.

TO PREPARE THE SHELLFISH SALAD:

Heat the wine in a sauté pan over medium-high heat with the thyme or tarragon, and add the shrimp in their shells. Turn them individually just as they begin to turn orange. When the second side colors, transfer the shrimp from the pan to a large plate. To prevent them from overcooking, don't mound them on the plate as they come off the heat. While the shrimp are cooling, add the mussels to the same pan, cover, and steam until the shells open. Remove the shrimp and mussels from their shells, chop small but not fine, and mix with the crab, aioli, celery, and chives. Season to taste with cayenne, salt, black pepper, and lemon juice. Cover and refrigerate until ready to serve.

TO SERVE:

Toss the endive with some leek vinaigrette. Divide the leaves among 4 to 6 plates. Top with the seafood salad. Garnish with the chervil leaves.

SERVES 4 TO 6

SPRING CARROT SOUP
with Chioggia Beets

This fresh soup is the very essence of spring. It doesn't simmer long, but it does require a very flavorful chicken stock. Chioggia beets are not essential to this preparation, but they are richly colored, milder than red beets and, unlike red beets, won't bleed into your golden soup.

CRÈME FRAICHE

2 cups heavy whipping cream

3 tablespoons buttermilk

BEETS

5 small Chioggia beets

2 tablespoons white wine vinegar

1 tablespoon water

Pinch of salt

Pinch of sugar

CARROT SOUP

2 onions, diced

2 tablespoons butter

1 tablespoon olive oil

Salt

2 thyme sprigs

3 tarragon sprigs

1 bay leaf

3 pounds spring carrots, peeled and roughly chopped

12 cups light chicken stock

Ground white pepper

Ground nutmeg

Juice of 1 lemon

— —

1 tablespoon butter

TO PREPARE THE CRÈME FRAICHE:

Combine the cream and buttermilk in a glass jar. Loosely cover with plastic wrap and let sit in a warm place, between 65° and 70° for 2 to 3 days, or until thickened.

TO PREPARE THE BEETS:

Preheat the oven to 425°. Place the beets in a baking pan with a little water, cover, and roast. They are done when their skins peel away easily. This will take 45 minutes for small to medium-sized beets, $1^1/2$ hours for large beets. Cool, then peel and dice. While you make the soup, pickle the beets lightly in the vinegar mixed with the water, salt, and sugar.

TO PREPARE THE CARROT SOUP:

In a large soup pot, sweat the onions in the butter and olive oil, seasoning with salt. When just starting to color, tie the herb sprigs in a bundle and add to the onions with the bay leaf and carrots. Sweat until the carrots begin to soften, about 15 minutes. Add the stock. Simmer gently for 20 minutes or so. Adjust the seasoning with salt, pepper, nutmeg, and lemon juice. Be frugal with the white pepper and nutmeg; their flavors should remain just below the surface. Remove the herb sprigs and bay leaf and pass the soup through the finest holes of a food mill. If you prefer a smoother texture, purée it in a blender or food processor. Reheat over low heat.

TO SERVE:

Stir a pat of butter into the pot of soup. Ladle the soup into bowls. Garnish each bowl with some of the beets and a small dollop of crème fraîche.

SERVES 10

65

DUCK LIVER FLAN
with Green Peppercorns and Marsala

It is impossible to tire of this beloved flan. It has been on the BayWolf menu forever. Even those individuals who believe themselves immune to the pleasures of liver find themselves enamored of this savory preparation. At the restaurant we bake it in bread pans, but it can easily be adapted for individual ramekins. To extend the life of individual flans, fill them only three-quarters full, then cover them with 1/4 inch of rendered duck fat (see page 6) before cooking. They will keep, refrigerated, for several weeks. Serve the flan on grilled or toasted bread with cornichons and pickled onions.

1 cup dry marsala

3 tablespoons pickled green peppercorns, rinsed

1 pound duck livers

2 1/2 cups heavy whipping cream

4 eggs

1 teaspoon finely chopped fresh thyme

2 tablespoons salt

1/2 teaspoon ground white pepper

1 teaspoon sugar

Brush a glass bread pan or ceramic terrine with olive oil and line with a piece of parchment or waxed paper. The paper should extend at least 1/2 inch over the side of the pan. Place the pan in a larger pan at least 2 inches deep. If you want to bake the flans in smaller containers, reduce the cooking time by half, oil but do not line the containers, and watch them carefully to make sure they do not overcook. These smaller flans are meant to be served in their baking molds.

Preheat the oven to 325°. Combine the marsala with the green peppercorns and reduce by two-thirds. Drain the peppercorns and spread them on the bottom of the prepared pan. Set the marsala aside to cool. Place 2 strainers over a bowl. One of the strainers should be very fine. Place this one on the bottom. Purée the livers in a food processor until totally smooth, about 3 minutes. Pass the livers through the strainers. Add the cream and the eggs to the food processor bowl and process just long enough to clean the liver from the sides of the bowl. Pass the cream mixture and then the marsala through the strainers. Stir in the chopped thyme, salt, pepper, and sugar. Taste and adjust the seasoning. Pour the mixture into the prepared pan, and cover with foil. Add 1 inch of hot water to the larger outer pan and bake until just set, about 1 hour. Remove the flan from the pan of water and cool for 30 minutes at room temperature. Refrigerate the flan until completely chilled. To remove the flan from the pan, run a knife around the edges and then invert it onto a rectangular plate. Tug on the parchment paper until the flan releases.

SERVES 12

LINGUINE WITH POACHED SALMON
and Its Roe, Chives, and Crème Fraîche

At the restaurant, we like to celebrate all aspects of a single vegetable or animal in one dish. We might do this with a double or triple duck dinner or an appetizer of celery root and heart or an accompaniment of beets and their greens. It's our way of acknowledging the multifaceted usefulness of so many foods and of showcasing, often in surprising ways, their versatility. This pasta with salmon and its roe is simple, delicate, and pure.

2 cups water

2 cups white wine

1 thyme sprig

2 garlic cloves, lightly bruised

1 bay leaf

1/4 onion, roughly chopped

4 white peppercorns

Salt

3 medium leeks, washed and split lengthwise, with enough root attached to hold layers together

1 pound salmon fillet

1 to 2 tablespoons butter

1 medium-sized red onion, julienned

Ground white pepper

4 to 5 tablespoons crème fraîche (page 65)

1 1/4 pounds fresh linguine, cooked right before serving

3/4 cup salmon roe or caviar (from your local fishmonger)

2 tablespoons minced chives

Juice of 1 lemon

TO PREPARE THE SALMON:

Make the poaching liquid by bringing the water, wine, thyme, garlic, bay leaf, onion, and peppercorns to a boil. Simmer gently for 10 minutes, then add salt to taste. Add the leeks and simmer until tender, about 25 minutes. Remove the leeks, cool, and then cut into julienne. Add the salmon in one piece to the poaching liquid. Add more water if necessary to cover. Poach gently for 4 to 8 minutes, depending on desired doneness. Remove the salmon, cool briefly, then break into smaller pieces.

TO PREPARE THE PASTA:

Heat the butter in a large sauté pan. When bubbly, add the onion and cook over medium heat until translucent. We don't want any color here. Add the leeks and season with salt and white pepper. Add the poached salmon and crème fraîche and rewarm if necessary. Off the heat, add the pasta, roe, and chives. Toss well and adjust seasoning with salt, white pepper, and lemon juice. Serve immediately.

SERVES 4

SHORT RIBS BRAISED
in Red Wine with Spring Vegetable Ragout

The nicest way to prepare a braise is to brown it on the stovetop and then braise it very slowly in the oven, in a delicious stock of red wine and aromatic vegetables. The juxtaposition of the melting meat, with its voluptuous interior, and the crispy, browned, caramelized exterior is the very definition of braising in my personal canon. The trickiest part of a braise is knowing when and how to remove the fat. Our solution is to cook it a day ahead, let it sit overnight until the fat rises and congeals, skim the fat, and gently reheat.

BRAISED SHORT RIBS

2 pounds beef short ribs

Salt and freshly ground black pepper

Olive oil

1 carrot, peeled and diced

2 celery stalks, diced

2 onions, diced

Splash of water or wine for deglazing

6 garlic cloves

A few black peppercorns

1 bay leaf

2 juniper berries

6 thyme sprigs

6 savory sprigs

1 bottle dry red wine, heated

SAUCE

2 shallots, minced

1 tablespoon olive oil or rendered beef fat

About 1 1/2 cups beef fat, trimmed from the ribs or scraps from butcher

1 thyme sprig

8 cups beef stock, or 4 cups each stock and strained, degreased braising liquid, heated

1 tablespoon butter

VEGETABLE RAGOUT

3 tablespoons butter

1 bunch baby carrots, peeled

1 cup asparagus tips

1 cup shelled peas

Salt and freshly ground black pepper

Freshly squeezed lemon juice

TO PREPARE THE SHORT RIBS:

At least 2 days before serving, season the meat with salt and pepper and refrigerate.

The next day, preheat the oven to 325°. Brown the short ribs in the olive oil, and transfer them to an ovenproof pot that will just hold them comfortably. Brown the carrot, celery, and onions in the same pan, and transfer them to the pot with the ribs. Deglaze the pan with a little water or wine and add to the pot. Add the garlic, spices, herbs, and wine. Cover with parchment and then with foil or a tight-fitting lid. Braise slowly in the oven until the meat is meltingly tender. Check after 1 1/2 hours. Cool the short ribs in the liquid, then refrigerate overnight or until ready to serve. When ready to serve, remove the congealed fat and reheat, uncovered, in an oven no hotter than 350°. If the liquid is covering the meat, pour some of it off so that the meat is exposed. This will allow the meat to brown and crisp a bit on top. Bring to a boil on top of the stove. Place in a 400° oven for 10 minutes.

TO PREPARE THE SAUCE:

Brown the shallots in the oil or fat. Add the beef fat trimmings, thyme, and 2 cups of the hot stock. Reduce by half, then add 2 cups more stock. Skim the scum frequently. Continue in this manner until the stock is gone. Reduce to a spoon-coating consistency. Be careful if you are using braising liquid in addition to clear stock, as it tends to be salty. Strain the sauce through a fine strainer and finish with a pat of butter. Keep warm over low heat while you make the ragout.

TO PREPARE THE VEGETABLE RAGOUT:

Heat the butter in a sauté pan and add the carrots. Cook for a minute or so over medium-high heat, then add the remaining vegetables. Season with salt and pepper, and add a few tablespoons of water to the pan. Cook for 5 to 8 minutes, or until the liquid is almost gone and the vegetables are just cooked through.

TO SERVE:

Squeeze a little lemon juice over the vegetables and serve with the braised short ribs and sauce.

SERVES 4

SEAFOOD SAUSAGE *with Citrus-Braised Fennel and Blood Orange Beurre Blanc*

This sausage is very delicate—delicate in texture and delicate to handle. It is a total nightmare to make but is so wonderful that it is well worth it. Be sure to schedule two days off from work before embarking on this project, and God be with you. Serve with French lentils.

SEAFOOD SAUSAGE

1 pound halibut fillet or other boneless white fish

8 ounces scallops

8 ounces rock shrimp, peeled

2 to 3 cups heavy whipping cream

Salt and ground white pepper

1/2 cup minced fennel

1/2 cup minced leek

Olive oil

2 tarragon sprigs, minced

1 bunch chives, minced

5 feet hog casings, rinsed

CITRUS-BRAISED FENNEL

2 fennel bulbs

Salt and freshly ground black pepper

Finely chopped zest and juice of 2 oranges

Finely chopped zest and juice of 2 lemons

1 tablespoon sugar

2 thyme sprigs

1/2 cup dry white wine

A few black peppercorns

Olive oil

BLOOD ORANGE BEURRE BLANC

Minced zest and juice of 2 blood oranges

1 teaspoon sugar

2 tablespoon white wine vinegar

2 tablespoons white wine

1 tarragon sprig

1 shallot, minced

1/2 bay leaf, crumbled

1 tablespoon heavy whipping cream

1/2 cup butter, cut into small chunks

TO PREPARE THE SAUSAGES:

Remove any errant bones from the halibut and cut it into 1-inch chunks. Put into the bowl of a food processor with half of the scallops and half of the rock shrimp. Process for a couple of minutes until smooth. Add 2 cups of the cream and some salt and white pepper. Pulse just until the cream is incorporated. If you overmix the purée at this point, it may break. If this happens, add some more cream and pulse just enough to smooth it out. With a small rubber spatula, transfer the puréed fish to a large bowl. Finely chop the remaining scallops and shrimp and add to the bowl. Sauté the minced fennel and leeks very briefly in a little oil. Cool completely, then add to the bowl with the tarragon and chives. Mix all the components thoroughly, then make a little patty, fry it up, and taste to check the seasoning. If it seems flat, it probably just needs more salt. Go easy on the white pepper.

Chill the sausage mixture for a few hours (use the freezer if you are short on time, but do not freeze the unstuffed sausage) before attempting to stuff it into the casings. The colder the fish is, the less gooey and messy it will be when you assemble the sausages. Do not freeze it. To form links, pinch down 5 inches from one end of the sausage, avoiding air pockets, and twist it several times away from yourself. Next pinch down 5 inches farther and twist toward yourself. Continue in this fashion, alternating backward and forward twists the length of the sausage, and then hang them in the refrigerator until you're ready to use them.

TO PREPARE THE BRAISED FENNEL:

Preheat the oven to 375°. Trim the fennel and cut into 1/2-inch wedges. Arrange in a glass or ceramic ovenproof dish in a single layer. Season well with salt and pepper. Put the citrus zest and juice in a saucepan with the sugar, thyme, wine, and peppercorns. Bring to a boil and reduce by half. Remove the peppercorns and herbs. Pour the liquid over the fennel, drizzle with a little oil, and cover. Braise in the oven for about 20 minutes, or until tender. Uncover and pour any remaining liquid back into the saucepan. Reduce to a glaze, and then pour back over the fennel. Serve hot or at room temperature.

TO PREPARE THE BEURRE BLANC:

Put the blood orange juice, zest, and sugar in a small saucepan and bring to a boil. Immediately lower the heat and reduce to 2 tablespoons. Set aside. In another saucepan, bring the vinegar, wine, tarragon, shallot, and bay leaf to a boil. Reduce slightly and add the cream. The cream helps to stabilize the sauce. Reduce to 2 tablespoons and strain into the blood orange reduction. The sauce can be prepared ahead of time up to this point. Just before serving, vigorously whisk in the butter over medium-low heat. When all of the butter is incorporated, remove from the heat and adjust the seasoning.

TO SERVE:

Poach the sausages first and then grill very gently so that they do not explode. To poach the sausages, bring a pot of water to a boil, then lower the heat to a bare simmer. Add the sausages and simmer gently for 5 to 8 minutes. Divide the fennel among the serving plates. Place the sausages alongside. Spoon the beurre blanc over the sausages.

SERVES 6

FRENCH SWEET CREAM
with Fresh Berries

This innocent treat is the ideal triumvirate of the evocative essence of vanilla with the soft richness of cream and the complementary color and texture of the freshest and finest berries you can find.

SAUCE

4 cups mixed fresh berries

1 cup sugar

Splash of brandy

CREAM

2 tablespoons cold water

1 teaspoon powdered gelatin

3/4 cup sugar

3/4 cup sour cream

1 pound mascarpone cheese

1 cup plus 3 tablespoons heavy
    whipping cream

2 teaspoons vanilla extract

1 pint fresh berries

TO PREPARE THE SAUCE:

Combine the berries, sugar, and brandy in a saucepan and cook over medium heat until the berries start to break down and the sauce thickens. Strain the sauce through a fine strainer, discarding the pulp. Set aside to cool.

TO PREPARE THE CREAM:

Place the cold water in a small metal bowl and sprinkle the gelatin over the top. Allow the gelatin to be absorbed by the water, about 5 minutes. Mix the remaining ingredients together and place in a medium pan over low heat to warm the mixture. Do not let it get hot or it will curdle. Bring some water to a boil in a small pot and place the bowl of gelatin over the hot water to melt the gelatin. Pour the gelatin into the cream mixture and mix well. Pour into 8 custard cups. Refrigerate for about 1 hour, or until firm.

TO SERVE:

Run a butter knife around the edge of each custard and unmold onto individual plates. Mix some fresh berries into the berry sauce, then spoon the sauce and the remaining berries around the sweet cream. Enjoy.

MAKES 8 CUSTARDS

RUBY GRAPEFRUIT SORBET AND TANGERINE ICE *with Lime Cooler Cookies*

From the latter part of winter into early spring, citrus in California is colorful, abundant, and irresistible. The Ruby Red grapefruit is so full of sugar that it needs only a little additional sweetness to make a beautiful sorbet. I like serving a citrus-flavored ice, finely chopped, under the scoops of sorbet to fill out the plate and add a texture counterpoint to the smooth sorbet.

GRAPEFRUIT SORBET

4 cups freshly squeezed Ruby Red grapefruit juice, pulp and seeds discarded

3/4 cup granulated sugar

TANGERINE ICE

2 cups freshly squeezed tangerine juice

1/4 cup granulated sugar

LIME COOLER COOKIES

1/2 cup sweet, unsalted butter

1/4 cup powdered sugar, plus more for dusting

1 teaspoon freshly squeezed lime juice

1/2 teaspoon finely chopped lime zest

1 cup all-purpose flour

1/8 teaspoon salt

TO PREPARE THE SORBET:

Mix together the juice and sugar until the sugar is dissolved. Transfer to an ice cream freezer and freeze according to the manufacturer's instructions.

TO PREPARE THE ICE:

Mix together the juice and sugar until the sugar is dissolved. Transfer to a large pan and place in the freezer. When frozen, chop into fine chips, with a blunt pastry scraper. (Do not use a sharp knife.) This will take some muscle.

TO PREPARE THE COOKIES:

Preheat the oven to 325°. In a medium mixing bowl, beat the butter with the sugar until smooth. Add the lime juice and zest and mix well. Add the flour and salt, mixing well. With a small scoop or teaspoon, scoop the dough onto a parchment-lined baking sheet and bake for 8 to 10 minutes. The cookies will be light in color. Dust with powdered sugar while hot. Cool and dust again with powdered sugar.

TO SERVE:

Place some of the chipped ice in a chilled bowl and top with 2 scoops of sorbet. Arrange a cookie or two on the side.

MAKES 2 QUARTS SORBET, 2 CUPS ICE, AND 16 COOKIES

MEYER LEMON POTS DE CRÈME
with Vanilla Shortbread

Pot de crème is one of those lovely enchanted nursery sweets, those custards and creams, puddings, bavarians, brulées, and blancmanges that our patrons understandably never seem to tire of. A cookie or two is the perfect companion.

LEMON POTS DE CRÈME

2 Meyer lemons

2 cups heavy whipping cream

1 cup whole milk

1 teaspoon vanilla extract

7 egg yolks

1/2 cup granulated sugar

Pinch of salt

VANILLA SHORTBREAD

1/2 cup sweet, unsalted butter

1/4 cup powdered sugar

1 cup all-purpose flour

1 teaspoon vanilla extract

Whipped cream

TO PREPARE THE POTS DE CRÈME:

Remove the lemon zest with a zester that will cut off the zest in little threads or with a peeler that will peel off the dark yellow portion of the skin in strips. There is no need to chop the zest.

Preheat the oven to 300°. Combine the zest, cream, milk, and vanilla in a heavy-bottomed saucepan. By infusing the flavor of the zest in the pot de crème base, you avoid the possibility that the acid in the lemon juice will cause the cream to curdle. Heat to a boil and turn off the heat. Let the mixture steep for 15 minutes. Mix the yolks with the sugar and salt. Temper the yolk mixture by mixing in a small amount of the cream mixture at a time. This will warm the yolks slowly and avoid lumps. Pass through a fine strainer to remove the zest and any undissolved bits of egg. Pour into six 4-ounce custard cups. Using a small spoon, skim off any surface air bubbles on the surface.

Place the cups in a large pan at least as tall as the cups. Fill the pan with hot water, reaching three-fourths of the way up the sides of the cups. Cover with aluminum foil and place in the oven. Bake for 1 hour, checking halfway through by placing a clean finger in the top of the custard (it won't burn you). It should coat the finger lightly. If it is thickening too quickly, reduce the baking time. It is better to underbake custard than to overbake it. Overbaking will give them a curdled texture. Remove the cups from the water bath and refrigerate, uncovered, for at least 1 hour.

TO PREPARE THE SHORTBREAD:

Preheat the oven to 300°. Place the butter, sugar, and flour in an electric mixer fitted with the paddle attachment. Mix on low speed for 15 to 20 minutes, or until the dough comes together. Mix in the vanilla. On a floured board, roll out the dough to 1/4 inch thick and cut into desired shapes. I like 1 by 2-inch rectangles. Place on a parchment-lined baking sheet and chill before baking. Bake for 20 minutes, or until lightly browned.

TO SERVE:

Serve the pots de crème with a dollop of whipped cream and the cookies.

MAKES 6 POTS DE CRÈME AND 18 COOKIES

75

PARIS BREST

This dessert was originally created to commemorate a bicycle race from Paris to Brest, France. The traditional ring shape signifies the bicycle tires and is made of puff pastry covered in sliced almonds and filled with chocolate whipped cream. At the Bay-Wolf, we replace the single large ring with individual rings so that diners can each have their own chocolate-filled tire.

CAKE
> Pâte à choux (page 54)
> 1 cup sliced blanched almonds

CHOCOLATE CREAM FILLING
> 10 ounces dark bittersweet chocolate
> 2 cups heavy whipping cream

> Powdered sugar for dusting

TO PREPARE THE CAKE:

Line a baking sheet with parchment paper and draw six 2¹/2-inch rings in pencil. Set aside.

Fit a pastry bag with a large star pastry tip. Using the pencil markings as a guide, pipe the pâte à choux over the markings into nice circles. Cover each with sliced almonds, pressing the almonds into the surface. Bake for 30 to 40 minutes, or until fully puffed and medium golden brown. Let cool.

TO PREPARE THE FILLING:

Chop the chocolate into small pieces and place in a bowl. Bring the cream to a boil in a small saucepan. Pour the cream over the chocolate and stir until the chocolate is well melted. Place this bowl on top of a bowl filled with ice and a little water. Stir until the cream mixture is cold. Whip until stiff.

TO ASSEMBLE:

Cut each "tire" in half horizontally. Using a clean piping bag with another large star tip, pipe a ring of filling inside the bottom half of each circle. Place the other half on top. Dust with powdered sugar and serve.

MAKES 6 PASTRIES

When Northern Italy Took Hold

Much as I revere peanut butter, the after-school snack that still carries the most weight with me would have to be the refrigerator bin full of meatballs and tomato sauce in the home of my first American friend, Franklin Scarlata. We'd eat them straight from the bin, scooped out by the handful, with our fingers.

Franklin's Sicilian grandmother had taught his Polish mother how to make meatballs and the best tomato sauce, the sort of sauce I still make today and consider the gold standard: with basil, olive oil, garlic, and a big piece of pork shoulder slow-cooked for 24 hours. The meatballs were created separately. The drawer was always available to us and, incredibly, always full. Imagine this: after years of deprivation during the war, a whole drawer filled with meatballs! It's possible that my lifelong love of Italian food evolved from that bin.

I remember my first fettuccine Alfredo. It was in the 1960s, in New York City, before embarking on a pilgrimage to Europe. I had never seen it, much less seen it made with a quart of cream, a pound of butter, a mound of Parmesan, and a bouquet of garlic. It was fabulous.

Later, in the 1970s, when I was traveling a little more upscale, I spent a week with my friend Paola and her mother in an apartment in Torino. When we walked into the apartment, we were surrounded by the unbelievable odor of our dinner roasting in her pressure cooker: rolled veal, filled with prosciutto and fontina, tied, heavily browned, and slowly cooked with rosemary and wine. While it roasted, she dispatched us to the central Torino food market to shop for salad greens, fruit, cheese, and grissini. The meal was as good as that first "wow" smell. Her mother had come up from Allessandria for the week just to cook for us. She cooked every day, lunch and dinner, shopped, and cleaned up. I reveled in it: the largesse, the generosity, the perfect and extensive introduction to the local foods. I'd passed through northern Italy before, but this time it took.

Paola escorted us to a hunting lodge she knew would amuse me. They were serving twenty-three courses (I counted them) on communal tables, most of it family style. Some of it was extraordinary; all of it was interesting, pleasing, and good. Sort of like a rustic he-man–style dim sum. Next door, a famous, very old chocolate shop was oozing its sweet-fabricating scent. They roasted the beans and prepared the chocolate. It's formidable to watch hundreds of pounds of molten chocolate being poured onto marble slabs and worked by master craftsmen.

We ate the best Italian home cooking from that area. I got a feeling for the food, and I liked it. I knew I loved things like prosciutto and salami, but I liked them even more when I got to Italy and tasted them in the wild.

I remember the first time I was conscious of the taste, that there *was* a specific and spicy taste, to olive oil. I was twenty-one, sitting on a warm terrace west of Tuscany, in a little café up a mountain road, pleased with my incredible view, my bottle of water, my bottle of wine, salt, bread, and oil. It was delicious, aromatic, perfumed, a complete meal. I had never eaten just bread and oil.

You'd think the Italians invented coffee, so good is it, so strong and intense and hair-raising. They buy the best beans, and they know what to do with them. You can cross the border from France into Italy, stop at the first unassuming mountain outpost or gas station, and have the perfect cup of coffee, like nothing on earth—deep, rich, bitter, balanced.

I also learned to eat bitter greens in northern Italy: *cavolo nero* (black cabbage), dandelion greens, a dozen kinds of radicchio. I learned that you sweeten them by grilling and then combining them with salt, olive oil, and vinegar for the just right combination of bitter and sweet. Grilling or sautéing caramelizes the edges and brings out the latent sweetness. We'd eat them in cafés and in people's homes and found them healthful and cleansing.

There's nothing quite like eating vegetables in the spring if you've been deprived all winter and can suddenly eat tiny peas in a spring soup or be out touring and come across a little mill (at the side of a raging creek with a waterfall for a background) and spy a small shop selling fresh cherries. Big, black, burst-in-your-mouth, quintessential cherries. Or the wild asparagus that you see popping up and that is consumed on the spot. Everyone seems to be out hunting the birds, the *uccelletti,* that are migrating from North Africa onto your platter of polenta.

At BayWolf, we like to re-create these indelible taste memories with our own local produce, acquired at its peak and prepared with a similar lack of preciousness, a sustaining robustness, a lively delicacy, and a soupçon of rustic charm.

SMOKED MUSSELS

Smoked mussels are so delicious and easy to make, and so prohibitively expensive in a store, that it just makes sense from every perspective to make them at home.

2 cups dry white wine

2 thyme sprigs

2 garlic cloves, smashed

A few black peppercorns

As many mussels as you want

Salt

Freshly squeezed lemon juice

Chopped Italian parsley

Virgin olive oil

In a large pot with a properly fitting lid, bring the wine, thyme, garlic, and peppercorns to a boil. Simmer gently for 5 minutes. Meanwhile, soak the mussels in cold water for a few minutes, then remove their beards. The beard is a little hairy thing that protrudes from the mussel. Use a towel to grasp it and then yank it out. Add some salt and the mussels to the pot, cover, and simmer for about 5 minutes, or until the mussels have opened. Pour off the liquid and spread the mussels out on a baking sheet to cool. Discard any that refused to open. If you detect "funky mussel" odor, smell your way through each of them until you locate the culprit and discard him. Sprinkle the mussels with a little salt, and then smoke them very slowly in your smoker. See page 109 for smoking instructions. By slowly, I mean that the smoker should not be too hot. The idea is to get a good amount of smoke on the mussels without turning them into jerky. Dress the mussels with some lemon juice, parsley, and virgin olive oil and serve hot or at room temperature. The mussels will keep, refrigerated, for a couple of days. Bring to room temperature before serving.

SERVES AS MANY AS YOU WANT

Michael Wild and his partners have always treated me and, I feel sure, all of their vendors, as if we were part of the family. Whenever I'm in their restaurant, be it for business or pleasure, there is a kind word of inquiry about my family, enthusiastic praise for a product they have particularly liked, and invariably deliciously well-chosen treats from the kitchen.

I've always felt with Michael as if we're trying to reach common ground that is mutually beneficial. I've developed such a feeling of personal responsibility and great loyalty toward the BayWolf that makes it enjoyable for me to provide them with the freshest fish and best service possible.

—PAUL JOHNSON, *Monterey Fish*

FENNEL SALAD

This lightly pickled salad provides a fresh, crunchy contrast to an antipasto platter composed of smoked mussels, arancini, *and olive or fava bean toasts.*

3 fennel bulbs
Juice of 2 Eureka or Meyer lemons
Salt
Pinch of sugar
Mint leaves (optional)

Slice the fennel crosswise paper-thin with a mandoline or sharp knife. Put it in a bowl with the juice, salt, and sugar. Squeeze the fennel with your hand and let it sit for 20 minutes. Pour off any excess lemon juice and adjust the salt. If the fennel is too acidic due to particularly juicy lemons, give it a quick rinse in cold water. If you like, julienne a few mint leaves and toss them with the fennel just before serving.

SERVES 6 TO 8

HAND-PICKING PRODUCE WITH
GROWER EXTRAORDINAIRE
SIDNEY IN HER GARDEN.

FAVA BEAN TOASTS

Fava beans are fabulous. Some people avoid them because they think they require too large an investment of time and effort. I disagree. It's possible to learn to shell and relieve them of their skins quickly. Alternatively, relieve yourself of the notion that cooking is an activity that requires speed and enjoy the process.

2 to 3 pounds fava beans

1/4 cup olive oil

Salt

1 small garlic clove, minced

Freshly squeezed lemon juice

1/4 cup virgin olive oil

Rounds of levain or baguette, toasted

TO PREPARE THE BEANS:

Shell the beans slowly or quickly, whichever suits you. Drop them into a large pot of salted, boiling water. Do not add any oil to the water, or it will make the beans slippery and difficult to handle. Boil for a minute or so to loosen the skins, then drain the beans and plunge them into a large bowl or basin of ice water. If the water is not freezing cold, the beans will lose their vibrant green color. Remove the rubbery skin from the beans.

TO PREPARE THE PASTE:

Heat 1/4 cup olive oil in a pan and add the beans. Salt. Cook over medium heat for about 3 minutes for small beans, or until the beans are tender. Add the garlic and transfer the mixture to a bowl or mortar. Mash the beans with a wooden spoon or pestle. You can put them in a food processor, but the texture is far superior when they are mashed by hand. Mash until most of the beans are puréed but a few chunky bits remain. Adjust the salt. Add lemon juice to taste and the virgin olive oil. Push the salt and acid here. The paste will need them to keep its integrity on the toast. Serve on the toasts.

MAKES ABOUT 2 CUPS PASTE

SMOKED DUCK BREASTS
with Cherries, Nasturtiums, and Cracklings

It is hard to decide which aspect of a duck I love the most: the dark breast meat, the gamy legs, the buttery fat, or the crispy skin. While weighing the philosophical implications of my preferences, I dive into this.

1 whole duck breast, smoked (page 162)
2 tablespoons balsamic vinegar
Salt and freshly ground black pepper
16 Bing cherries, pitted and quartered
3 small handfuls tiny nasturtium leaves and flowers

Remove the skin and fat from the breast and cut them into small dice. Leave the breast meat itself whole for now. Heat a sauté pan that will just hold the dice for a couple of minutes over medium heat. Add the diced fat to the dry pan. The fat will begin to render out. It should not smoke or burn. Cook until the skin is crispy and the majority of fat is rendered out. Whisk the fat with half the vinegar and some salt and pepper. If the vinaigrette needs more acidity or sweetness, add the remaining vinegar. Remove the cracklings from the pan and drain on paper towels.

Right before serving, slice the duck breast meat thinly across the grain. (It should be warm or at least at room temperature.) Dress the slices in some of the vinaigrette and arrange on individual plates. Toss the cherries, cracklings, and leaves and flowers lightly and arrange next to the duck. Serve immediately.

SERVES 4

BRAISED ARTICHOKES
with Pancetta

Choose small artichokes if you are serving this as an appetizer, larger ones to serve as a light dinner or lunch. Serve with crusty bread to absorb the juice.

4 artichokes

Lemon wedge

3 ounces pancetta, diced

1/4 cup olive oil

1 onion, diced

1 carrot, peeled and diced

1 bay leaf

2 thyme sprigs

6 garlic cloves

4 cups chicken stock, heated

Salt and freshly ground black pepper

1 tablespoon butter

1 tablespoon chopped Italian parsley

Freshly squeezed lemon juice

Trim the artichokes so that only tender, edible leaves remain. Scoop out the choke, trim the stem, rub with the lemon wedge, and put into acidulated water until ready to use.

In a pot that will just hold the artichokes, sauté the pancetta in the oil until it is halfway cooked. Add the onion and carrot and cook until lightly browned. Add the bay, thyme, garlic, and stock. Season lightly with salt and pepper. Add the artichokes, stem ends down. Cover the pot with a tight-fitting lid and simmer gently for 25 to 35 minutes, or until the artichokes are just tender. Remove them from the pot and reduce the remaining liquid by half. It is because of this reducing that you must salt lightly earlier in the process. Just before serving, stir in the butter, parsley, and a squeeze of lemon juice.

Place the artichokes on individual plates or on a platter. Spoon the sauce into and over the artichokes, and serve.

SERVES 4

BRAISED LAMB SHOULDER

with Rosemary, Artichokes, and Olives

Lamb, artichokes, olives, and rosemary: these elements are flawlessly complementary. This braise, like all braises, benefits from several days of rest in the refrigerator. I suggest starting two days in advance. The dish will taste better, and the prep work on serving day it will be simplified. A bed of creamy polenta is a great partner for the lamb.

BRAISED LAMB

Salt and freshly ground black pepper

4 pounds boneless lamb shoulder, fat trimmed, meat cut into 2-inch pieces

2 carrots, peeled and diced

1 celery stalk, diced

1 onion, diced

4 tablespoons olive or peanut oil

4 cups lamb stock, heated

4 thyme sprigs

4 parsley stems

2 small rosemary sprigs

3 allspice berries

2 whole cloves

A few black peppercorns

2 bay leaves

2 juniper berries

6 black olives

6 garlic cloves

ARTICHOKES

3 artichokes

1 thyme sprig

3 tablespoons olive oil

3 lemon zest strips

Salt

SAUCE

2 shallots, minced

Reserved lamb trim without too much fat

2 tablespoons olive oil

1 thyme sprig

1/2 bay leaf

5 cups lamb stock, heated

3 black olives

Tiny rosemary sprig

— — —

1/4 cup pitted kalamata olives

TO PREPARE THE LAMB:

Two days before serving, season the lamb with salt and pepper and refrigerate. Save any meaty trim for the sauce.

The next day, preheat the oven to 350°. Sauté the carrots, celery, and onion in the oil and transfer to the bottom of an ovenproof pan that will just comfortably hold the lamb meat. Brown the meat in the oil. Do not add additional salt or pepper. The meat should be very brown, with no light gray parts. Deglaze the pan with a little of the lamb stock. If there are any burned parts in your pan, forget deglazing. Put the meat on top of the vegetables. Tie up the herbs and add them to the pan with the spices, olives, and garlic. Pour the remaining stock into the pan. It should reach at least half the height of the lamb chunks. Cover with parchment and then foil. Braise in the oven. Check for doneness after 1 1/2 hours. The meat will be meltingly tender when done. It may take up to 2 1/2 hours to finish. When done, uncover one corner of the pan, and let cool. Refrigerate overnight.

TO PREPARE THE ARTICHOKES:

Trim away the artichokes' leaves, pare to heart and stem, and halve lengthwise. Place the artichokes in a sauté pan with the thyme, oil, and zest. Add water almost to cover. Salt and simmer gently until the artichokes are tender. Remove the artichokes and reduce the liquid until it is mostly oil. Pour over the artichokes and set aside until ready to serve.

TO PREPARE THE SAUCE:

Brown the shallots and lamb trim in the olive oil in a 4-quart saucepan. Add the thyme, bay leaf, and 2 cups of the lamb stock. Simmer gently and skim the scum frequently. When reduced by half, add 2 more cups of stock. Reduce further, then add the last cup of stock and the olives. Reduce to a light glaze. Add the rosemary. Let sit for a few minutes before straining through a chinois or fine strainer.

TO SERVE:

Half an hour before serving, bring the sauce just to a boil on top of stove. Uncover the lamb and return it to the top rack of the oven to reheat at 375° and brown the top part of the lamb for about 10 minutes. The goal is to have a little crispiness on the outside to contrast with the tenderness on the inside. Serve the lamb with the artichokes, olives, and sauce.

SERVES 4

B*ayWolf was a place of change for me: serious conversations about life and love took place over white tablecloths with wine and food and the promise that all would be well in the world. As a cure for existential blues, a good meal at BayWolf seemed the ideal nonprescription mood enhancer.*

These years later I bring radio show guests to this haven, to introduce them to fine Bay Area cuisine. I come to BayWolf for solace and conversation and to eavesdrop on the next table, to see the art, to feel good about life.

— SEDGE THOMSON, *Impresario,* West Coast Live

ROAST SALMON
with Beet Vinaigrette

This dish is beautiful on the plate—the brilliant red beets, the pinkish orange salmon, the spritz of green parsley. A perfect accompaniment would be horseradish mashed potatoes, prepared by soaking grated horseradish in a little lemon juice and then stirring it into finished potatoes just before serving.

4 portions salmon fillet, 5 ounces each
Salt and freshly ground black pepper
1 tablespoon finely minced Italian parsley
3 medium beets
1 shallot, minced
Finely chopped zest and juice of 2 lemons
1 thyme sprig
3/4 cup virgin olive oil

Season the salmon with salt and pepper and sprinkle with the parsley. Arrange in a baking pan, and set aside until a few minutes before serving.

Preheat the oven to 425°. Place the beets in a baking pan with a little water, cover, and roast. They are done when their skins peel away easily. This will take 45 minutes for medium-sized beets, 1 1/2 hours for large beets. Cool, then peel and cut into a tiny dice.

Place the shallot in a small bowl with the finely chopped zest, juice, and thyme. Let macerate for 20 minutes, then whisk in the olive oil. Add the beets and season with salt and pepper. Let marry for 30 minutes. Preheat the oven to 450° and roast the salmon for 8 minutes for medium-rare, a few minutes longer for medium. Serve immediately with beet vinaigrette.

SERVES 4

GOAT CHEESE RAVIOLI
with Asparagus, Pancetta, and Toasted Breadcrumbs

Little ethereal pillows are the model for ravioli. The dough needs to be soft, with a certain degree of elasticity and tooth, but neither chewy nor rubbery, and the ravioli must puff up. Goat cheese crottins are one of the first flavors I remember from childhood. I like their purity and their own way of demonstrating richness. Fresh goat cheeses have a tart freshness that is appealing in ravioli, sharp and light and a nice alternative to the heaviness of using all cream or butter without any loss in flavor.

PASTA DOUGH

1 cup unbleached all-purpose flour

2 whole eggs plus 1 egg yolk

Pinch of salt

1 teaspoon extra virgin olive oil

GOAT CHEESE FILLING

8 ounces fresh goat cheese

1/4 cup heavy whipping cream

Rice flour or semolina for dusting

SAUCE

1 red onion, diced

2 tablespoons olive oil

1 bunch pencil-thin asparagus, sliced on the diagonal

Salt and freshly ground black pepper

1 garlic clove, chopped

6 ounces pancetta, diced and cooked until soft

Finely chopped zest of 4 Meyer lemons

1/2 cup duck or chicken stock

1 tablespoon butter

1 small handful Italian parsley, chopped

Extra virgin olive oil

Freshly grated Parmesan cheese

1/2 cup dried levain breadcrumbs, toasted, seasoned, and tossed in olive oil

TO PREPARE THE PASTA DOUGH:

Mound the flour on a work surface. Make a well in the center and add to it 1 of the whole eggs, the yolk, salt, and oil. Whisk the contents of the well with a fork, gradually incorporating flour. Have a little water on hand in the event you need more liquid. Pasta for ravioli should be a bit wetter than pasta for noodles. Bring the dough together and knead for a few minutes. Put the dough in a plastic bag and let rest for 30 minutes.

TO PREPARE THE FILLING:

Season the goat cheese with salt. Beat the cream into it to make it smoother.

TO ASSEMBLE THE RAVIOLI:

Roll the pasta out into very thin sheets. Beat the remaining egg with a little salt and brush it over half of the pasta sheets. Spoon little blobs of goat cheese over the egg-washed pasta. Leave 1 inch between the blobs. Make 24 blobs for 6 people. Arrange the dry pasta sheet over the first sheet. Press gently around the cheese to get rid of any air bubbles. Cut the ravioli into squares and store on a baking sheet lined with a napkin and a thin layer of rice flour to prevent sticking. Do not substitute all-purpose flour: the pasta will absorb this flour and then stick.

TO PREPARE THE SAUCE:

Sauté the onion in the olive oil. Just as it begins to color, add the asparagus and season to taste. Cook a minute more, then add the garlic, pancetta, chopped zest, and stock. Reduce the stock to a few tablespoons, and then add the butter. Add the parsley and a squirt of extra virgin olive oil.

TO SERVE:

Cook the ravioli in a large amount of salted simmering water. They will take 30 to 60 seconds to cook. Boil them gently, not rapidly; if boiled too vigorously, they may burst open in the water. Add the cooked ravioli to the sauce. Adjust the seasoning and arrange on plates. Garnish with grated Parmesan and toasted breadcrumbs.

SERVES 6

LEMON RISOTTO

with Peas, Parsley, Prosciutto, and Parmesan

Some of the BayWolf's most delicious dishes have been developed out of my communicable affection for the use of alliteration in the written menus. This felicitous combination sounds so edible and appealing even before you indulge in the first taste.

1 tablespoon olive oil

2 tablespoons butter

1/2 medium onion, diced

1 generous cup Arborio rice

1 cup dry white wine

4 cups chicken stock, heated

Salt and freshly ground black pepper

Finely chopped zest of 2 lemons

1 cup shelled peas, blanched

1/2 cup freshly grated Parmesan cheese

1 handful Italian parsley, roughly chopped

Freshly squeezed lemon juice

4 prosciutto slices, julienned

Heat the fats in a large saucepan until hot and bubbly, then add the onion. Cook over medium heat until translucent. Don't let the onion brown. Add the rice and fry for a minute, stirring constantly. Add the wine and reduce for a few minutes. Over medium-low heat, add 1 cup of the stock, and season lightly with salt, pepper, and lemon zest. Stir occasionally while the rice absorbs the stock. Add another cup of stock and proceed in the same fashion until all of the stock has been added and the rice is just done. This will take 25 to 30 minutes. Stir in the peas, Parmesan, and parsley. Adjust the seasoning with salt, pepper, and lemon juice. Keep in mind that the prosciutto will provide some of the salt. Right before serving, stir in the prosciutto. It should not cook. Serve immediately.

SERVES 4

ALMOND CAKE
with Rhubarb Sauce and Strawberries

Fresh, full-flavored almonds are a versatile and useful nut in pastry production. They can be used raw, toasted, candied, blanched, or flavored with spices or herbs. Each preparation has a different aspect and imparts a different flavor or texture to the finished tidbit, soup, salad, entrée, or dessert. I love warm almond cake. The fragrance of the warmed almonds and the sweet scent of butter is enough to make me feel light-headed. Paired with the first fresh fruits of spring, strawberries and the more exotic rhubarb, it is refreshing, light, and delightful.

ALMOND CAKE
   1/2 cup blanched almonds
   1/2 cup sugar
   1/2 cup almond paste
   1/2 cup sweet, unsalted butter
   1/2 cup all-purpose flour

1/2 teaspoon baking powder
3 eggs
1/4 teaspoon vanilla extract
1/4 teaspoon almond extract

RHUBARB SAUCE
1/4 cup water
1 cup sugar
4 cups chopped rhubarb

1 pint fresh strawberries, hulled and
   quartered

TO PREPARE THE CAKE:

Line a 9-inch cake pan with parchment. Preheat the oven to 350°. In a food processor or blender, grind the almonds into a fine meal, using a few tablespoons of sugar to aid in the grinding. In the bowl of an electric mixer fitted with the paddle attachment, beat the almond paste with the remaining sugar until it forms a fine meal. Add the ground almonds and mix well. Beat in the butter, scraping the bottom of the bowl. Sift the flour with the baking powder. Mix the eggs with the vanilla and almond extracts. Beat the egg mixture into the butter mixture, a little at a time, scraping the bowl and mixing thoroughly. Add the flour mixture and mix well. Pour into the cake pan and bake for 45 minutes, or until a toothpick inserted into the center of the cake comes out clean. Let cool on a rack. Remove from the pan and slice into 12 wedges.

TO PREPARE THE SAUCE:

Bring the water and sugar to a boil in a medium saucepan. Add the rhubarb and cook for 10 to 15 minutes, or until soft. Do not overcook or the sauce will be an unattractive color. Purée in a blender or food processor and let cool.

TO SERVE:

Place a piece of cake on a plate, pour some of the sauce over it, and accompany it with a generous serving of strawberries.

MAKES ONE 9-INCH CAKE

93

HAZELNUT-RAISIN BISCOTTI

I eat more of these than of any other sweet in the restaurant. I cannot walk by one and not eat it. As a professor in San Francisco, I conducted my office hours at Caffè Trieste in North Beach over cups of cappuccino and ultimately hundreds of biscotti. They're fun to eat, have great flavor and texture, and are the perfect dunking device. I never visit my mother without taking her a large container of these.

1/2 cup hot water

1/2 cup golden raisins

1/2 cup plus 2 tablespoons all-purpose flour

1/2 cup plus 2 tablespoons sugar

1/4 teaspoon baking powder

1/2 cup hazelnuts, toasted and skinned

2 teaspoons ground aniseed

2 teaspoons minced orange zest

2 teaspoons vanilla extract

2 teaspoons anisette

1 egg yolk

Pour the hot water over the golden raisins to plump them. Place the flour, sugar, baking powder, hazelnuts, anise, and orange zest in a mixer fitted with the paddle attachment. Drain the raisins, reserving the liquid. Add the raisins to the dry ingredients. Mix all together on low speed. Mix the vanilla, anisette, and egg yolk together and add to the flour mixture while mixing on low speed. When well mixed, add 1 or 2 tablespoons of the raisin water to make the dough come together. The dough should be firm, not sticky. You may not need to add any of the water.

Preheat the oven to 350°. Line a baking sheet with parchment. On a floured work surface, roll the dough into a log the length of the baking sheet. Bake for 30 minutes. Press the log. If it presses back, it is done. Remove from the baking sheet and let cool on a cooling rack. Reduce the oven to 300°.

Cut the log into 1/2-inch-thick slices, using a sharp knife. Cut each one at a slight angle. Lay the slices cut side down on a parchment-lined baking sheet with another baking sheet underneath. This double lining will allow the biscotti to dry out without browning and will ensure that they're light and crisp. Bake for another 30 minutes. Remove from the baking sheet and let cool on racks. If you do not remove the biscotti from the baking sheet, moisture will collect under them and they will be soft and not crisp.

MAKES 2 DOZEN BISCOTTI

BUDINI

These individual Italian puddings consist of cake or breadcrumbs bound with butter and eggs and flavored with chocolate. Deceptively simple, unnaturally good. The cakes can be prepared several days in advance and then reheated in preparation for their final destination beneath the custardy chocolate sauce and cream.

¹/₂ cup sweet, unsalted butter, at room temperature

¹/₂ cup sugar

2 tablespoons unsweetened dark cocoa powder (increase to 4 tablespoons if you are not using chocolate cake crumbs)

2 tablespoons all-purpose flour

¹/₂ cup plus 2 tablespoons dry cake crumbs (chocolate if you have them) or breadcrumbs

4 egg yolks

1 teaspoon brandy

1 teaspoon vanilla extract

¹/₂ cup heavy whipping cream

SAUCE

9 egg yolks

¹/₄ cup sugar

2 cups whole milk

1 teaspoon vanilla extract

4 ounces bittersweet chocolate, finely chopped

Sweetened whipped cream for topping

TO PREPARE THE BUDINI:

Butter six 4-ounce ramekins. They will cook in a steam bath. A large pot with a good lid and a rack on the bottom is best, although a vegetable steamer will also work fine. Have the steamer in place and hot before starting to make the budini.

Beat the butter with the sugar. Sift the cocoa powder with the flour and mix into the crumbs. Mix the egg yolks with the brandy, vanilla, and cream. Beat the egg yolks and flour alternately into the butter mixture, scraping the sides and bottom of the bowl, until well incorporated. Scoop the batter into the buttered ramekins and steam for 30 to 40 minutes, or until a toothpick inserted into the center comes out dry.

TO PREPARE THE SAUCE:

Place ice in a large bowl with a few tablespoons of water and set aside. Mix the yolks with sugar and set aside. Heat the milk and vanilla to a boil. Add the hot milk, a little at a time, to the egg mixture until well mixed. Pour back into the cooking pan and cook over low heat for 15 to 20 minutes, or until the sauce has thickened and will coat the back of a spoon. Remove from the heat and add the chocolate, mixing until it has melted. Strain through a fine strainer into a metal bowl and place on top of the ice bath to cool. Refrigerate.

TO SERVE:

Unmold the budini and serve warm with chocolate sauce and dollops of whipped cream.

CHERRY-CHEESE TART

In early spring, Earl develops his pastry chef version of spring fever: a longing for the fresh fruits that will bury him by mid-May and pour into his grateful hands and the restaurant's coffers all summer long. The earliest takes on this tart will be prepared with the last of the cherries brandied the previous year. Later in May, we'll move on to the sweet varieties, the Bing, Brooks, Burlat, and Queen Anne that are so suitable for this vivid tart. Sour cherries won't do.

SWEET TART DOUGH

3/4 cup sugar

1¼ cups sweet, unsalted butter

1 whole egg

3 cups all-purpose flour

FILLING

8 ounces cream cheese or mascarpone cheese

1/4 cup sugar

4 egg yolks

1 teaspoon vanilla extract

3 cups pitted, halved cherries, fresh or brandied (page 20)

TO MAKE THE TART SHELL:

Slowly beat the sugar with the butter in an mixer fitted with the paddle attachment until well combined. Add the egg and mix well, scraping the sides to thoroughly incorporate the egg and butter. Roll out into a 1/4-inch-thick round. Line a 9-inch tart pan with the dough. Refrigerate until firm.

Preheat the oven to 350°. Line the shell with parchment and weight it with pie weights or dried beans or rice. Bake for 20 to 30 minutes, or until the shell is light brown and dry. Remove the weights and parchment and let cool.

Leave the oven at 350°. Beat the cream cheese with the sugar until smooth. Add the egg yolks and vanilla and mix well. Lay the cherries in the tart shell and pour the filling over the top. Bake for 15 to 20 minutes, or until the filling is just set.

MAKES ONE 9-INCH TART

June

Wine Matters

Wine is a beautiful thing. One of the qualities that attracted me to wine makers as I began to know more of them better is that a good wine maker is like a good cook. There are ineffable aspects to the processes of cooking and making wine—ineffable in the sense that they aren't quantifiable. You can't religiously follow recipes. The magic is in the mouth or hand or soul. The joy of cooking is in the improvisation, but improvisation evolves from love and knowledge in equal measure.

I wasn't born understanding what makes wine or food move into the galaxies beyond palatable. I taught myself about wine out of necessity. I cultivated the friendship of wine makers like Jim Clendenen, Bob Lindquist, and Tony Cartlidge and wine merchants like Kermit Lynch, who had incredible palates and taste memories and were eager to share their wines and their insights.

In 1977 I arranged to meet Kermit and Joe Swan in Burgundy, and we spent a week tasting wine, all day every day, starting at nine in the morning. Being in the cellars filled with old Burgundies, pulling corks, showing off, and trying to guess what wine, what vineyard, what vintage. It was an unbelievable education about the wines I most like to drink: Burgundies, Pinot Noirs, and Pinot Chardonnays. I've never had an experience that was so focused and disciplined, and I've never been drunk for so many days.

You can't know for sure what heights or glories a wine might attain, but you can tell which wines have the potential to develop into something good. Some wines seem completely shy but then come around. Although some of it can be learned, what makes a wine maker a master is the innate gift possessed by someone like Jim Clendenen. He understands so clearly what's good about someone else's wine and how to translate it into his own. He gets all the technical stuff, but he also knows how to play with it. Wine makers are just working with grapes, but it isn't what they have. Instead, it's what they understand, what they know, what they do with it. Jim's winery and the home of our BayWolf Noir are aptly named Au Bon Climat. It is indeed the right spot.

Jim remembers just about every bottle of wine he's ever had. The vintage, what it tasted like, what he ate with it, what the circumstances were, who was there. His ability to describe wines is incomparable. It isn't hyperbolic buzzwords; it's perfect, precise, and descriptive.

A wine can be cleansing, can whet your whistle or wash away the road dust, or it can knock your socks off. It isn't wise to drink more than one complex wine per meal. Instead follow the French ideal of structuring the meal by starting with the most complex dishes and the simpler wines and then progressing into less baroque and more straightforward dishes partnered with more complex, richer wines. Point, counterpoint.

Once I found my calling, France was irresistible to me. It's such an affirmation of what I do for a living; so much energy is brought to bear on eating and restaurants. I couldn't get enough of it. When you're a chef in France hanging out with wine makers and restaurateurs, all kinds of wonderful people gravitate to you and you to them. You cross paths, especially in Burgundy, with people who have enormous income as well as those of very little means, all of whom have discovered the beauties of food and wine and the joys of being at the table together. Enthusiasts from any country and any social class are ideal companions.

GRILLED APRICOTS
with Wilted Escarole, Pancetta, and Hazelnut Vinaigrette

What a fine combination: the sweet apricots, the bitter greens, the sweet saltiness of the pancetta, the rich little crunch of the hazelnuts. Grilled apricots are a wonderful thing. Caramelizing them on the exterior deepens their flavor, softens them, and concentrates their essence. Select apricots that are just ripe: an all-over deep orange color, yielding to pressure but not too soft. If they are too ripe, they will fall apart on the grill. My love for hazelnuts goes back forever. It was my first nut. In the Europe of my youth, chocolate was inevitably paired with hazelnuts. The first ice cream that ever stopped me in my tracks was an Italian hazelnut gelato. Similarly, hazelnuts add an irresistible charm to this perfect mix.

1 shallot, minced

2 to 3 tablespoons sherry vinegar

1 thyme sprig

1/2 cup hazelnut oil

1/4 cup hazelnuts, toasted and chopped

Salt and freshly ground black pepper

8 thin pancetta slices

8 apricots

1 tablespoon olive oil

1 head escarole, cut into 2-inch pieces

Soak the shallot in the vinegar with the thyme for 20 minutes, and then whisk in the hazelnut oil. Stir in the hazelnuts and season with salt and pepper.

Preheat the oven to 350°. Arrange the pancetta on a baking sheet and bake until just done. Cool and break into smaller pieces. If there is any delicious, rendered fat, add it to the escarole. Cut the apricots in half, season with salt and pepper, and grill over a hot fire.

Right before serving, heat some of the vinaigrette in a large stainless steel bowl directly over the burner. Add the escarole and pancetta and toss until the escarole is lightly wilted. Arrange the greens on plates, then briefly toss the apricots in the vinaigrette. Arrange on the greens and serve immediately.

SERVES 4

GOAT CHEESE WRAPPED IN FIG LEAVES

Fig leaves lend a distinctive flavor to foods. If the leaves are very thin and delicate, they may be eaten, but the appeal is primarily in the aroma and the flavor, not the texture, of the leaf.

3 ounces goat cheese per person

Olive oil

1 fig leaf per person, washed and stems trimmed

1 small thyme sprig per person

Levain or baguette, sliced and brushed with olive oil

Light a fire in the grill. Form or cut the goat cheese into little patties. Bring a large pot of water to a boil. Add some oil to the water. Blanch the fig leaves in the water for 3 minutes, or until pliable. The water will turn a beautiful gold color and smell vegetal. I love this smell. Lift out the leaves and transfer them to a bowl of ice water to chill. Drain well and pat dry.

Line up the leaves on a work surface with the outer part of the leaf, the smooth side, down. Place a goat cheese round in the center of each leaf and mark with a little sprig of thyme. Fold the leaves around the cheese, turn the bundles over, and line them up on a plate. Brush the outsides with a little olive oil, then place them on the grill, folded side down. Grill them hard for about 5 minutes; they should have significant grill marks and start burning a bit at the edges. Transfer the bundles to the individual plates, folded side up, and open the leaf a bit so people have an idea of what's inside and how they might eat it. Grill the bread, cut it into triangles, and serve with the goat cheese.

CAESAR SALAD

We make a creamy Caesar dressing at the restaurant that is addictive for many of our regulars. Some notes on this dressing: It should be on the acidic side to cut through the richness of the cheese and pick up the anchovy and garlic flavors. Use day-old levain for the croutons; there is no compromise in quality and fresh levain is a nightmare to cube. Finally, make the dressing no more than a few hours before you intend to serve it. Sometimes the garlic, especially if it is winter garlic, develops a metallic taste after a few hours.

3 garlic cloves

1^{1}/$_{2}$ cups olive oil

^{1}/$_{4}$ loaf levain or sourdough baguette, crusts removed and cubed

Salt and freshly ground black pepper

4 salt-packed anchovies, filleted, rinsed, and chopped

3 to 4 tablespoons sherry vinegar

^{1}/$_{4}$ cup freshly squeezed lemon juice

1 egg yolk

2 tablespoons water

Leaves from 4 hearts of romaine

Freshly grated Parmesan cheese

Smash one of the cloves of garlic, heat ^{1}/$_{4}$ cup of the olive oil in a sauté pan, and add the smashed clove. When the garlic just begins to sizzle, remove from the heat and let sit 10 minutes. Remove the garlic, and then fry the bread in the oil until golden and crispy. You may need to add a little more olive oil. Season well with salt and pepper and drain.

Chop the remaining 2 cloves garlic and macerate with the anchovies in the vinegar and lemon juice for 15 minutes. Put the yolk in a blender with the water. Turn the blender on and add the remaining 1^{1}/$_{4}$ cups olive oil in a thin and steady stream. If the dressing becomes too thick, add a little more water. Add the anchovy mixture and season well with salt and a lot of freshly ground pepper. Adjust garlic, anchovy, acid, and oil as necessary.

Toss the romaine leaves and croutons with some of the dressing and grated Parmesan. Serve immediately.

SERVES 6

COQ AU VIN

I must have crispy skin. In this version of wine-braised chicken, the meat is partially immersed in wine, but the skin is left exposed. The problem with most coq au vin and other chicken sautés and braises is that after browning, the chicken is immersed in stock, and loses its crispy skin. Exposed skin is the way to go with all bird braises.

6 chicken legs and thighs, separated

Salt and freshly ground black pepper

3 pancetta slices

1¼ pounds small fresh domestic mushrooms

3 tablespoons butter

5 tablespoons olive oil

1¼ pounds pearl onions

1 carrot, peeled and finely diced

1 celery stalk, finely diced

Shot of brandy

5 thyme sprigs

2 small bay leaves

2 dried porcini mushrooms

12 new potatoes, cut in half

3 cups dry red wine, heated

1 cup chicken stock, heated

1 tablespoon butter

Several hours ahead or the day before serving, season the chicken pieces well with salt and pepper. Refrigerate until ready to use.

When you're ready to cook, cut the pancetta into lardons and cook in a dry sauté pan until just done. It should be soft, not crispy. If you have small mushrooms, keep them whole. Otherwise, cut them in half. Brown the mush-

W*ho would think that it could be harder to be a wine supplier to a forward-thinking, cosmopolitan restaurant in Oakland than to cross the silk ropes at Studio 54 in Manhattan during its heyday? Once your name is on the list at the BayWolf, you're practically on for life, but getting the first wine in is not an evident proposition.*

Michael Wild knows wine. He knows what he likes and emphatically knows what he doesn't like. But the wine program at the BayWolf is not just a matter of Michael's personal taste, although it almost is. Michael's taste in wine and my personal taste in wine are not identical, but they overlap a lot. At the table, dining in the restaurant, we both know what works, and the succession of chefs over the last twenty-five years have presented balanced, textural, savory food that welcomes delicious wines.

The ease with which the wine program works is deceptive. Few restaurants have the maturity to have enough wines, enough price diversity, enough geographic diversity, enough mature wines,

rooms in 1 tablespoon each of butter and olive oil in the same pan in which you cooked the pancetta. The mushrooms will release a lot of liquid. Do *not* pour this off; it will reduce down and the mushrooms will reabsorb it. Cook for a long time, very slowly, until the mushrooms are brown all over and caramelized. It may take 45 minutes. If the mushrooms shrink to the point that there is a lot of extra space in the pan, and the pan is very dry, transfer them to a smaller pan and add a little more fat.

Trim the stem and a bit of the root from the pearl onions, keeping enough of the root attached so they hold together. Blanch the onions and then refresh them in ice water. Drain. Peel away the outer skin. Brown in 1 tablespoon each butter and olive oil, mix with the mushrooms, and set aside.

Sauté the carrot and celery in 1 tablespoon each of olive oil and butter. Deglaze with the brandy and then transfer to the bottom of an ovenproof pan that will hold the chicken comfortably in a single layer. Add the thyme, bay leaves, pancetta, fresh and dried mushrooms, and onions.

Preheat the oven to 350°. Brown the skin side of the chicken pieces in 2 tablespoons of olive oil, and then arrange the chicken, skin side up, over the vegetables. If the pan in which you browned the chicken has no burned parts, deglaze it with a little wine, then add it to the braise. Salt and tuck in the potato pieces. Pour in the wine. It should just reach the skin. The idea here is to keep the meat moist and the skin crisp. Braise, uncovered, on the top rack of the oven until the meat is tender and wanting to fall off the bone. Check for doneness after an hour. Rotate the potatoes periodically so that they don't dry out.

Before serving, pour off most of the braising liquid through a strainer into a saucepan. Degrease the liquid, add the stock, and reduce by half. The liquid may have picked up a lot of salt, so don't over-reduce it. Finish with the butter, pour the sauce back over the chicken and vegetables from the cooking vessel, and serve.

SERVES 6

and their own specially labeled wines that are distinctive. Few restaurants have the familiarity with their suppliers to allow absolute confidence in recommending all the wines on the list.

I don't know how to get a bottle placed on the BayWolf list. It's not genius or artistry, patience or belligerence, renown or anonymity, experience, familiarity, social connection, or random encounter. But as a BayWolf supplier, when you are a part of the BayWolf wine program, you are a part of a special family. It gives an immense amount of pleasure and you can't pinpoint why. It is obvious at an anniversary dinner or a special wine function. It involves an intuitive relationship with Michael that extends to the whole restaurant family. And the result is the accessibility of a perfect amount of carefully selected bottles for the enjoyment of the BayWolf's customers. Without a big fuss, just as it should be.

—JIM CLENDENEN, *Wine Maker*

DUCK *with Red Wine Flan and Chanterelles*

This is one of the simplest and most delicious duck dishes we prepare. The flan can be made several hours ahead and then reheated gently in a 350° oven. The only part of this recipe that is best prepared at the last minute is the mushroom sauté.

DUCK

4 duck legs

Salt and freshly ground black pepper

1 teaspoon dried thyme

2 dried porcini mushrooms

1 bay leaf

2 cups duck or chicken stock, heated

SAUCE

2 shallots, minced

Duck gizzards or hearts (optional)

1 thyme sprig

Piece of bay leaf

1 dried porcini mushroom

A few black peppercorns

6 cups duck stock

4 cups dry red wine, reduced to $^1/_2$ cup

RED WINE FLAN

2 onions, minced

1 tablespoon butter

1 tablespoon olive oil

Pinch of chopped fresh thyme

Salt and ground white pepper

$^1/_4$ cup red wine reduction, reserved from sauce (above)

3 eggs

2 cups heavy whipping cream

- - - -

1 pound chanterelles, sliced or quartered

TO PREPARE THE DUCK:

The day before serving, season the duck legs with salt, pepper, and thyme and refrigerate.

The next day, preheat the oven to 375°. Arrange the legs in an ovenproof pan that will just hold them comfortably, skin side up. Roast for 1 hour. Pour off and reserve the rendered fat, leaving the duck in the pan. Add the mushrooms, bay leaf, thyme, and hot stock to the pan. Cook for 30 minutes more, uncovered, until the meat is tender and the skin is golden and crispy.

TO PREPARE THE SAUCE:

Brown the shallots and gizzards in a little of the rendered duck fat. Add the thyme, bay leaf, mushroom, peppercorns, and 2 cups of the stock. Reduce by half and add 1 to 2 cups more stock. Skim the scum frequently to produce a clear and clean-tasting sauce. Add the remaining stock, 1 to 2 cups at a time, reducing after each addition. Reduce until the sauce is a spoon-coating consistency. Add $^1/_4$ cup of the red wine reduction, reserving the rest for the flan. It is important to reduce the red wine to just a few tablespoons; otherwise the acid in the wine may curdle the cream when you prepare the flan. Strain the sauce through a fine strainer and keep warm until ready to serve.

TO PREPARE THE FLAN:

Caramelize the onions in the butter and oil with the thyme over medium to low heat, frequently scraping in the caramelized bits from the bottom of the pan. This will take about 45 minutes if you do it properly. Caramelized onions are not the same as browned onions. The flavors will not develop in the same way if you try to rush the process. If the onions begin to stick to the pan, add a little more butter. When the onions are caramelized, season well with salt, season lightly with white pepper, and add the remaining $^1/_4$ cup wine reduction. Reduce until there is no liquid left.

Cool the onions, and then divide between among 4 custard ramekins that you have arranged in a larger pan with sides at least 2 inches high. Preheat the oven to 325° to 350°. Beat the eggs well, then whisk in the cream. Season with salt and white pepper. Strain through a fine strainer. Pour into the ramekins. Pour water to a depth of $1/2$ inch into the larger pan. Cover the pan loosely with foil and bake for about 30 minutes, or until set.

TO PREPARE THE MUSHROOMS:

In the remaining rendered duck fat, sauté the chanterelles over high heat. The pan should not be too crowded or the mushrooms will steam rather than brown. Chanterelles release a lot of liquid. Do not pour this off. Let it reduce and be reabsorbed by the mushrooms. Season with salt and pepper.

TO SERVE:

Remove the flans from the ramekins by running a knife around the inside of the ramekin. Invert the flan into your hand, then place right side up on an individual plate. Divide the duck and sautéed chanterelles among the plates and serve with the sauce.

SERVES 4

The Spring Double Duck Dinner

BAY WOLF RESTAURANT · JUNE 3, 1985 ·

Turnovers of giblet confit with rhubarb sauce

Minced duck & fried rice noodles in lettuce cups

Blond duck livers with pickled baby garlics & tarragon

Roast spring duckling glazed with ginger & basil

Duck egg zabaglione with sour cherries in armagnac

'83 Duckhorn Sauvignon Blanc

'81 Duxoup Napa Gamay (magnum)

'81 Duxoup Zinfandel (magnum)

DUXOUP WINE WORKS · BAY WOLF RESTAURANT · REICHARDT DUCK FARM

MENU BY ROBIN CHERIN

LASAGNA
with Smoked Duck, Morels, and Peas

There is hearty lasagne and there is delicate lasagne. This is a delicate lasagne constructed from thin pasta lightly layered with wine-braised smoked duck, a flavorful duck stock, herbs, peas, and morels. It's perfect with a pinot noir.

BRAISED DUCK

4 duck legs

Salt and freshly ground black pepper

1 teaspoon dried thyme

1/2 bottle red wine

MORELS

1 medium-sized red onion, julienned

1 tablespoon rendered duck fat (page 6) or olive oil

2 tablespoons butter

1 pound fresh morels, quartered lengthwise

2 garlic cloves, minced

2 tablespoons chopped Italian parsley

Sherry vinegar

SAUCE

8 cups duck or poultry stock

1 tablespoon rendered duck fat (page 6) or olive oil

1 shallot, minced

1 thyme sprig

3 dried morels

─────

1 pound pasta dough (page 31)

1 cup shelled peas, blanched

2 large handfuls arugula

TO PREPARE THE BRAISED DUCK:

The day before you smoke the duck, season the duck legs with salt, pepper, and dried thyme and refrigerate overnight.

The next day, soak applewood chips for 30 minutes and prepare a fire in a smoker or grill. When the coals are gray, add some drained wood chips. Put the duck legs on the top rack and cover. Smoke as slowly as possible for 2 to 3 hours. Continue feeding the coals wood chips over this period.

Preheat the oven to 375°. Transfer the legs to a 2-inch-deep pan that will just hold them. Heat the wine and pour it over the legs, immersing the meat but leaving the skin on top exposed. Cover the pan and braise in the oven for 30 to 40 minutes, or until the meat is just falling from the bone. Cool in the wine, and then remove the skin from the legs and reserve for snacking or some other purpose. Remove the meat from the bone, then break it into smaller pieces by hand. Do not chop it with a knife or you will compromise the texture. Set the meat aside. Add the bones to the duck stock for making the sauce.

TO PREPARE THE MORELS:

Sear the onion in the duck fat and set aside. Heat the butter in a large sauté pan over high heat. Add the fresh morels and cook until tender. Add the garlic and cook for a minute more. Remove from the heat and add the parsley and a shot of sherry vinegar. Set aside.

(continued)

109

TO PREPARE THE SAUCE:

Heat the duck stock and bones and simmer gently while you prepare the reduction. Heat the duck fat in a small saucepan. Add the shallot and brown lightly. Add the thyme, dried morels, and 2 cups of the stock. Reduce the sauce over medium heat, skimming any scum that rises to the top. When the sauce has reduced by half, add another 2 cups stock. Continue in this fashion until no more stock remains and the sauce is almost a spoon-coating consistency. It should be thinner than a reduction sauce would normally be. Strain through a chinois or fine strainer. Warm before serving.

TO ASSEMBLE THE LASAGNE:

Roll the pasta dough paper-thin, then cut into 3-inch squares. Cook in a large pot of generously oiled, salted, boiling water. It is very important that the pasta water be well oiled; otherwise the sheets will stick together once they're chilled. Drain the pasta squares and transfer to an ice bath to stop the cooking.

Preheat the oven to 375°. Arrange 6 squares in a single layer in an oiled 9 by 13-inch pan. Leave 2 inches between the squares. Put a light layer of duck, morels, red onions, and peas and a poof of arugula on each square. Cover with another square of pasta and continue to layer until the ingredients are all used. Set aside some morels for the sauce. Make at least 4 thin layers. Finish with a square of pasta on top. Bake for 20 minutes, or until heated through.

TO SERVE:

Place the lasagne on warm plates. Drop the reserved morels into the sauce. Ladle some of the sauce and morels over each lasagne. Serve immediately.

The lasagne can be prepared up to 8 hours ahead, the top oiled, covered with plastic wrap, and refrigerated.

SERVES 6

JIM CLENDENEN AND MICHAEL WITH THE BAYWOLF'S FIRST PINOT NOIR VINE.

PHOTO BY JEANNE O'CONNOR

APRICOT ICE CREAM
with Almond Crisps

When we prepare ice cream at the restaurant, it is always full-cream ice cream. It's the type of ice cream Earl grew up making and the type we most enjoy eating. The crisps are deceptively simple treats of baked sweetened almonds that provide a delicious contrast.

APRICOT ICE CREAM

2 cups apricots, preferably fresh, but high-quality dried apricots can be substituted

1/2 cup water (3/4 cup if using dried apricots)

1/2 cup sugar

1/4 teaspoon almond extract

8 egg yolks

1/2 cup sugar

1/2 vanilla bean, split

3 cups heavy whipping cream

1 cup whipped cream

ALMOND CRISPS

1 cup slivered blanched almonds

1 tablespoon water

1/2 cup sugar

1 tablespoon sugar for sprinkling

TO PREPARE THE ICE CREAM:

Wash the apricots and cut into small pieces. Combine the apricots, water, sugar, and extract in a heavy saucepan. Cook over a low flame until the apricots are soft and can be puréed. Purée them in a food processor or blender and then push the purée through a fine strainer. Set aside and let cool.

Combine the yolks with the sugar. In a heavy saucepan, scrape the seeds from the vanilla bean into the cream, drop in the bean, and heat to a boil. Add the hot cream, a little at a time, to the egg mixture. Mix thoroughly. Remove the vanilla bean. Place the cream mixture over an ice bath consisting of a bowl of ice drizzled with water. When the cream mixture is cold, strain it through a fine strainer and fold in the whipped cream. Pour into an ice cream freezer and freeze according to the manufacturer's instructions. Fold in the apricot sauce to make ribbons throughout the ice cream. Freeze for at least 2 hours before serving.

TO PREPARE THE CRISPS:

Line a baking sheet with parchment paper. Preheat the oven to 350°. Mix the almonds with the water. Add the sugar and mix well. Pile sugar-coated almonds in little mounds on the baking sheet. They will not spread, so don't worry about spacing them closely. Sprinkle with more sugar and bake for 10 to 12 minutes, or just until they stick together and are golden in color.

TO SERVE:

Scoop ice cream into bowls and serve with crisps on the side.

MAKES 2 QUARTS ICE CREAM AND 12 CRISPS

RHUBARB AND ALMOND GALETTE

Galette is another fancy name for a rustic tart. Many galettes derive from specific cities in Europe and are created with regionally specific pastry doughs. This is not one of them. This came from Earl's head and his love of rhubarb and almonds.

ALMOND DOUGH

1/2 cup plus 2 tablespoons blanched almonds

3/4 cup sweet, unsalted butter

1/2 cup powdered sugar

1/2 cup plus 2 tablespoons all-purpose flour

Egg wash of 1 egg, pinch of salt, and a few drops heavy whipping cream, beaten together

FILLING

5 cups chopped rhubarb

1/2 cup granulated sugar

1/4 cup blanched sliced almonds

Granulated sugar for dusting

Fresh strawberries, hulled, sliced, and tossed with sugar

TO PREPARE THE DOUGH:

Preheat the oven to 350°. Toast the almonds on a cookie sheet in the oven for 6 to 10 minutes, or until lightly browned. In a food processor or blender, grind the almonds into a fine meal. Using an electric mixer, beat the butter with the powdered sugar. Add the flour and the ground almonds and mix until it forms a soft dough. Divide the dough into 4 equal pieces. Press the dough pieces into flat rounds and wrap in plastic wrap. Refrigerate until firm. Roll out the dough on a floured surface into rounds about 4 inches in diameter and about 1/4 inch thick. Transfer to a parchment-lined baking sheet. Brush the entire top surface of the dough rounds with the egg wash. Refrigerate until firm.

TO ASSEMBLE AND BAKE:

Preheat the oven to 400°. Mix the rhubarb with the sugar. Place the rhubarb in the center of the dough rounds, leaving a 1-inch edge all around. Fold the edge over to form a rim to hold in the filling. You may have to pinch it to get it to lie flat. Brush the edge with the egg was, gently press 1 tablespoon of almond slices along the outside of each tart shell, and dust with sugar. Bake for 20 to 30 minutes, or until the dough is light golden brown and the rhubarb is soft. Serve the tarts with the sweetened berries.

MAKES FOUR 3-INCH TARTS

NECTARINE AND CHERRY CROSTATA

Crostata is a fancy (Italian) name for a rustic open-faced tart. Easy to make and, with its mosaic of multicolored fruits and sparkling sugar, this crostata is lovely to look at.

DOUGH

2¼ cups sweet, unsalted butter

¾ cup powdered sugar

1 egg

1¾ cups plus 2 tablespoons all-purpose flour

Egg wash of 1 egg, pinch of salt, and a few drops of cream, beaten well

FRUIT FILLING

½ cup granulated sugar

2 tablespoons all-purpose flour

2 or 3 large nectarines, unpeeled

1 pound pitted sweet cherries, such as Burlat, Bing, or Queen Anne

Granulated sugar for sprinkling

Whipped cream or vanilla ice cream

TO PREPARE THE DOUGH:

In the bowl of an electric mixer fitted with the paddle attachment, beat the butter with the powdered sugar. Add the egg and mix until well combined. Add the flour and mix until the dough comes together. Press the dough into a round. Roll out on a floured surface into a round almost about 15 inches in diameter and ½ inch thick. Fold in half and transfer to a parchment-lined baking sheet. Unfold and brush the entire top surface of the dough with the egg wash. Refrigerate while you prepare the fruit filling.

TO PREPARE THE FILLING:

Mix the sugar and flour together and set aside. Cut the nectarines into thick slices. Combine the nectarines and cherries with the sugar and flour.

TO ASSEMBLE AND BAKE:

Unfold the dough and mound the fruit in the center, spreading it out evenly to within 1 inch from the edge. Fold the edge over to form a rim to hold in the filling, and crimp it to the fruit. Brush the crimped edge with egg wash and sprinkle it with sugar. Refrigerate for 45 minutes to 1 hour, or until firm.

Preheat the oven to 400°. Bake for 20 to 30 minutes, or until slightly browned. The filling should be soft but not mushy.

TO SERVE:

When cool, cut into slices, and serve with whipped cream.

MAKES ONE 12-INCH TART

MIXED SUMMER BERRY PUDDING
with Crème Fraîche

This is not a pudding at all in the true sense of the word. It is neither boiled nor baked, it is not a firm childhood custard, nor does it have a cereal base. It is more closely related to trifle and yet is more firmly compressed and almost cakelike in its density. Sponge cake is layered into a mold or casserole dish, soaked with a sauce of the most beautiful berries you can acquire, layered with more smashed fresh berries and bits of cake, and then left to sit for several hours or overnight. It is then unmolded and served with whipped crème fraîche. The ingredients marry into softness and tenderness and yet retain a comely shape and form.

MIXED BERRY SAUCE

3 pints mixed fresh berries, such as strawberries, raspberries, blueberries, and blackberries

1 cup sugar

¹/₂ cup water

- - - -

1 pint extra mixed fresh berries

Sponge Cake (page 57)

Crème fraîche (page 65), chilled

Sugar

TO PREPARE THE BERRY SAUCE:

Combine the berries, sugar, and water in a large, heavy-bottomed saucepan and bring to a boil over medium heat. Remove from the heat. Let cool slightly. Purée in a food processor or blender. Strain through a fine strainer.

TO ASSEMBLE THE PUDDING:

Up to a day before serving, line a 2-quart dish with plastic wrap (this will help you unmold the pudding later). Cut the sponge cake into rounds that will fit into the dish. Save the scraps. Take one-fourth of the sauce, the 1 pint berries, and the sponge scraps and mix together, crushing the berries. Place a layer of the berry sauce in the bottom of the dish. Place a layer of sponge cake on top of this. Spread with more sauce, the scrap and berry mixture, and another layer of cake. Continue layering until the dish is filled to the top. Coat the top with some of the sauce. Cover with plastic wrap and weight with a heavy object. Refrigerate for at least 1 hour or as long as overnight.

TO SERVE:

Whip the crème fraîche until silken and smooth, sweetening to taste with sugar. Umold the pudding onto a large plate. Cut into wedges and serve with dollops of the crème fraîche.

SERVES 8

Throughout the twenty years I've worked at BayWolf, it's been a workplace, a home, a dining room, a living room. Michael and Larry have been my friends and teachers. From the beginning I've watched them go to great lengths to ensure the well-being of the staff, the sort of personal attention and attention to the human details that makes us feel like family. The reality and sincerity of this effort may be why several generations of families have worked here.

The highly personal, hands-on management style at the BayWolf encourages forming bonds of friendship with many of the diverse and talented people who make their home in the Bay Area and find their way to the Wolf. Our customers always clean their plates and

almost invariably seem well pleased. This is gratifying to me as the middle man between the great food emanating from the kitchen and the people who are and have been our customers. My job is to see to the extras and socialize with people I would not otherwise have been likely to meet and befriend. The staffs I've worked with over the years have been equally talented and diverse and up to the task. BayWolf was created almost by accident, reinforced by good luck and great management. It is so much more than a workplace. It's been a large part of my life and my personal history.

—Danny Ray Robinson, twenty-year wait yet

Larry and the Love of Oranges

July

started cooking when I was ten. It was summertime in Los Angeles, both of my parents worked, and eating wasn't an event you squandered on sandwiches. My mother believed that a sandwich was something you ate if you were unfortunate enough to be stuck in a train station, nothing you'd have at home. In the 1940s, for a European, eating at home meant eating a meal. In the beginning, I learned how to heat up portions of the mega-meals that were designed to last several days. Then I started playing with them, making things up, trying my own untutored variations, amendments, additions. I developed a sort of ease. If you love to eat, that's what you do. My mother loved to relate the story of my invention of an open-faced sandwich consisting of a slice of bread, a slice of bologna, a slice of tomato, and some Parmesan shaken from the can, run under the broiler to warm the bread, melt the cheese, and brown the bologna. Not a classic and maybe not a keeper, but the beginning of a long career of improvisation.

I hung out at Griffith Park. It was a huge park from another era, with four full-sized baseball fields, two of them with bleachers, all sandlots with grass outfields surrounded by oleanders and sandstone walls. There were trails through the oleanders for walking and biking, tennis courts and football fields, and the biggest swimming pool in the city of Los Angeles.

In the 1950s, the happening sport in America was baseball. Ball players of every age and range of skills, with their cleats and fungo bats, would make a pilgrimage to Griffith Park. Indulging in my ballpark food concession preferences one day, I found myself drawn to another teenager, a lefty, all skinny and gawky, opening a big paper bag filled with oranges. I watched him as he began methodically to peel and eat them. Here was a world-class orange peeler, someone who knew innately how to start them and how to accomplish the peeling quickly and efficiently. He offered me one. The idea of someone bringing a bag of oranges to a ballpark was congruous with my life. I wanted to eat all the junk food in the park, but then I met this kid who was unembarrassed to bring a bag of oranges and he made perfect sense to me.

Larry and I became friends and committed co-eaters after high school, when I moved to San Francisco and was able to lure him out to the dozens of Italian delis and cafés and ethnic restaurants that make this place the City That Knows How to Eat. Larry and I lived in the Haight across the street from Michael McClure. We'd go to Molinari's in North Beach and buy sliced meats and cheeses and loaves of French bread that we'd take to Washington Square Park and turn into huge sandwiches. To this day, I think of a Molinari's sandwich as a thing of beauty.

We had a taste for the minestrone at Mike's Pool Hall. We tried the Russian, the Indonesian, the Chinese shops and restaurants. We had friends all over the city, and we'd drop in at dinnertime and all eat together, or Larry, always studying, would make a big pot of chili and I'd stop by and do my part to make it disappear. People would come out from New York or Minneapolis or Chicago and we'd cook and eat, often sitting on the floor.

Our idea of a hamburger would be a Little Joe's burger loaded with onions and piled on a French roll. Why have buns if you could have a freshly baked, crunchy, crispy big hunk of French bread?

I moved to Berkeley, but we remained friends; we shopped and cooked and ate and raised our kids together. One of the beautiful things about my relationship with Larry, then

MICHAEL WILD AND LARRY GOLDMAN

and now, is that my mom has known Larry since he was a kid, his mom has known me since I was a kid, and the fact that we're partners has made both of our mothers happy. From the beginning, from that first bag of honest oranges, I have always known Larry to be totally rigorous and honorable, uncompromisingly fair, and always on the up and up, with a clear and quick sense of what's good and what isn't, in food as in life.

TRIO OF SUMMER SALADS

This is another irresistible combination. It isn't unique to BayWolf, but we give it our own twist by including our house-made tuna confit and fresh instead of dried shell beans. The chopped salad is a chiffonade of different lettuces mixed with carrots, and celery—some things with crunch and texture to play off the softness of the shell beans and the richness of the tuna. Although this recipe is perfect as outlined, it is also a delightful canvas upon which to improvise.

Tuna Confit Salad

Tuna confit is delicious in a niçoise salad with green beans, boiled potatoes, eggs, and mayonnaise, or you can make spaghetti with Tuna Confit, Tomatoes, and Capers (page 128). Everything that you love made with tuna is better with confit: tuna melts, tuna sandwiches, tuna casserole. This tuna is far from its familiar home in plebeian tins. Avoid purchasing perfect yellowfin steaks for confit, as this would be an expensive misuse of a premium product. Tuna belly meat is perfectly suited to confit.

TUNA CONFIT
- 1 pound tuna belly meat
- Salt
- 3 thyme sprigs
- 3 garlic cloves, bruised
- 1 teaspoon fennel seed, toasted
- 5 black peppercorns
- 4 lemon zest strips
- 4 cups pure olive oil

SALAD
- 1/2 pound Tuna Confit or yellowfin tuna
- 1/2 red bell pepper, diced
- 1/2 red onion, diced
- 1 celery stalk, diced
- 1/2 cup aioli (page 48)
- 1 tablespoon chopped Italian parsley
- 1 tablespoon capers, rinsed
- Finely chopped zest and juice of 1 lemon

TO PREPARE THE CONFIT:

The day before making the confit, season the tuna generously with salt and place it in a 2-inch-deep, nonreactive pan. Add the thyme, garlic, fennel, peppercorns, zest, and 2 tablespoons of the olive oil. Cover and refrigerate overnight. The next day, preheat the oven to 200°. Cover the tuna with the remaining olive oil and bake, uncovered, until just done, 1 to 1¹/₂ hours. When the tuna is done, remove it from the oven and cool it in the olive oil. Store the tuna, totally immersed in olive oil, in glass jars. It will keep for 2 weeks stored in the refrigerator.

TO PREPARE THE SALAD:

If not using the confit, light a fire in the grill. Brush the yellowfin tuna with 1 tablespoon olive oil and season with salt and pepper. Rub 1 tablespoon fennel seed, toasted and ground, over the fish and grill over a hot fire for a couple of minutes. The flesh should be rare. Remove from the heat and let cool. Dice the confit or yellowfin and mix.with the remaining ingredients. Serve at room temperature.

SERVES 4

Shell Bean Salad

Every year I look forward to the moment when the shell beans are ripe and ready for me to reintroduce this salad.

   2 cups fresh shell beans, such as lima beans, cranberry beans, or black-eyed peas
   1 onion, quartered but left attached at the root end
   1 bay leaf
   Salt and freshly ground black pepper
   Juice of 2 lemons
   2 garlic cloves, finely minced
   ³/₄ cup virgin olive oil
   14 cherry tomatoes, cut in half
   10 black olives, pitted and roughly chopped
   1 tablespoon chopped oregano
   1 teaspoon chopped Italian parsley

Cook the shell beans over medium heat in water to cover with the onion and bay leaf until tender. If you are using more than one bean variety cook them separately. Drain and remove the onion and bay leaf. While the beans are still warm, season with salt and pepper. Add some of the lemon juice, the garlic, and the olive oil. When the beans cool to room temperature, toss in the tomatoes, olives, and herbs. Adjust seasoning and serve.

SERVES 4

Chopped Salad

This salad is the Wild family daily salad. I can eat it every day of the year, incorporating greens and vegetables as they come and go through the seasons.

   1 heart of romaine, chopped small
   2 tablespoons chopped mint
   2 tablespoons chopped cilantro
   1 cup diced cucumber
   1 tomato, peeled, seeded, and diced
   Freshly squeezed lemon juice to taste
   Virgin olive oil
   ¹/₂ cup crumbled feta cheese
   Salt and freshly ground black pepper

Mix together all of the ingredients except the seasonings. Season well with salt and a lot of pepper. Serve immediately.

SERVES 4

ARUGULA AND NECTARINE SALAD
with Almonds and Purple Basil

Use perfectly ripe, perfumed nectarines for this salad. Look for arugula that is neither the super baby, toothless stuff nor the tough, burning hot variety. We want leaves with tooth and a hint of spiciness. If you cannot find such arugula, substitute baby spinach.

VINAIGRETTE

1 ripe nectarine, chopped

2 tablespoons honey

1 thyme sprig

Finely chopped zest and juice of 1 lemon

1/2 cup virgin olive oil

Salt and freshly ground black pepper

GOAT CHEESE TOASTS

2 small (8 ounces total) logs fresh goat cheese

10 black peppercorns

5 lemon zest strips, minced

6 thyme sprigs

1 bay leaf, crumbled

1 garlic clove, minced

2 cups virgin olive oil

Rounds of baguette, toasted

SALAD

4 ripe nectarines, unpeeled, thinly sliced

1/2 cup almonds, toasted and coarsely chopped

4 handfuls arugula

1 head Belgian endive, julienned

Basil or hyssop leaves, torn

Salt and freshly ground black pepper

TO PREPARE THE VINAIGRETTE:

Place the nectarine in a small saucepan with the honey, thyme, zest, and a few tablespoons of water. Simmer until the liquid has reduced to a sweet syrup. Remove the thyme. Transfer the nectarine syrup to a blender and purée. Transfer to a bowl and cool. Squeeze the lemon juice into the bowl. Finish with oil, salt, and pepper.

TO PREPARE THE CHEESE TOASTS:

Cut the cheese into little rounds and place in a bowl. Sprinkle with the peppercorns, lemon zest, thyme, crumbled bay leaf, and garlic. Cover with oil. Let sit for a minimum of 2 hours. Spread the cheese generously on the toasts, allowing 3 toasts per serving. Serve with the salad. If you don't have the time or inclination to marinate your goat cheese, worry not. Simply proceed without marinating.

TO ASSEMBLE THE SALAD:

Wait to slice the nectarines until just before serving. If they are truly ripe, they will be a little fragile. Place the nectarines, almonds, arugula, endive, and basil in a bowl and season with salt and pepper. Add some vinaigrette and toss gently and thoroughly.

SERVES 6

123

PROVENÇAL VEGETABLE SOUP
with Shell Beans, Tomato, and Pistou

It is important when making this soup to "layer" it. That is, instead of adding all of the vegetables to the pot at the same time, add them gradually. Cook one vegetable for a few minutes, and then add the next. In this way, you prepare a more complex soup, one that is multidimensional and more delicious for being so. The anchovies will not make the soup fishy. Their function here is to salt and to give the soup a greater depth of flavor.

SOUP

Olive oil

1 onion, diced

2 ounces pancetta, in one piece

1 carrot, peeled and diced

1 celery stalk, diced

1/2 fennel bulb, diced

1 leek, white part only, diced

2 cups peeled, diced butternut squash

1 bay leaf

3 thyme sprigs

2 summer savory sprigs

Salt and freshly ground black pepper

3 garlic cloves, minced

2 salt-packed anchovies, filleted, rinsed, and minced

8 cups chicken stock, heated

4 tomatoes

1 cup fresh shell beans, cooked until tender and salted while warm

Freshly squeezed lemon juice

PISTOU

1 to 1 1/2 cups virgin olive oil

Leaves from 1 bunch basil

1 large garlic clove

1/4 cup toasted walnuts or pine nuts

1/4 cup freshly grated Parmesan cheese

Freshly squeezed lemon juice

GARNISH

1/2 cup small pasta, such as riso or macaroni, cooked and refreshed

1 handful green beans, blanched, iced, and cut into 1/2-inch lengths

1 summer squash, such as crookneck or pattypan, grilled and diced

TO PREPARE THE SOUP:

Heat a little oil in a large, heavy-bottomed pot. Add the onion and pancetta. Cook over medium-high heat until just starting to color. Add the carrot and celery and cook for a few minutes more, scraping the bottom of the pan for any caramelized bits. Add the fennel and leek and cook for 8 to 10 minutes. Add a little more olive oil if necessary, then add the squash and bay leaf. Tie the herbs together and add to the pot. Season the vegetables well with salt and pepper. Increase the heat to high and stir in the garlic and anchovies, then immediately add the hot stock. Lower the heat and simmer gently for 40 minutes. Meanwhile, oil and then blacken the tomatoes in a dry cast-iron pan or directly over a gas flame. Place a food mill over the soup pot and strain the tomatoes directly into the soup. Alternatively, purée the tomatoes in a blender and then strain them through a sieve into the soup. Add the beans during the last 15 minutes of cooking. Season the soup well with salt, pepper, and lemon juice.

TO PREPARE THE PISTOU:

Purée 1 cup of the oil with the basil in a blender or food processor until finely ground and bright green. Do not run the blender any longer than necessary or the basil leaves may blacken. Add the garlic and nuts and process again. Add the remaining olive oil if the pistou is extremely thick and not blending. Remove the pistou from the blender. Stir in the cheese and lemon juice to taste. If the cheese is processed, it may make the pistou grainy. Add salt if the cheese does not provide enough.

TO SERVE:

Stir the garnishes and a couple tablespoons of the pistou into each soup serving and serve immediately.

SERVES 6 TO 8

DAVID WILD HELPING MICHAEL SHELL PEAS.

GRILLED SWORDFISH WRAPPED IN FIG LEAVES *with Black Olive Tapenade*

In the backyard of the BayWolf, we have a huge fig tree, variety unknown. Sometimes the fruit is spectacular, sometimes it's unremarkable. We use the leaves to wrap and flavor fish or cheese. I take home any prunings to stoke the grill. We use some of the fruit and the birds take the rest. We climb this tree, smoke under it at the end of the night, and cry under it when the activity and stress of the kitchen sends one of us over the edge. The following recipe is entirely inspired by that tree.

About 4 tablespoons olive oil

4 large fig leaves, washed and stems trimmed

4 swordfish or yellowfin or tombo tuna steaks, skin removed

Salt and freshly ground black pepper

8 ripe figs

1 cup Black Olive Tapenade (page 24)

4 handfuls arugula

Juice of 1 lemon

2 tablespoons virgin olive oil

Bring a large pot of water to a boil. Add 1 tablespoon of oil to the water. Blanch the fig leaves in the water for 3 minutes, or until pliable. Lift the leaves out and transfer them to a bowl of ice water to chill. Drain and pat dry.

Arrange the fig leaves on the counter with the underside of the leaf face up. Oil the fish steaks with the remaining olive oil and season with salt and pepper. Place a steak on each leaf and wrap in a neat little package. Put on a plate, folded side down, until ready to grill.

Light a fire in the grill. Right before grilling, brush the fig leaves with olive oil so that they don't stick to the grill. Grill swordfish over a blazing hot fire for 4 to 5 minutes per side. For tuna, grill just a couple of minutes per side, or longer if you prefer your fish cooked through. Oil, season, and grill the figs at the same time.

When the fish is ready, put it on a plate and unfold the leaf. Unless the leaf is very young and tender, it is meant only as a flavoring, not to be eaten. Put a couple of spoonfuls of tapenade on top of each steak. Serve with the grilled figs, halved, and the arugula, tossed in lemon juice and oil.

SERVES 4

127

SPAGHETTI
with Tuna Confit, Tomatoes, and Capers

This dish is best prepared with good-quality dried pasta. It provides better tooth than fresh pasta.

3 tablespoons olive oil

1 medium-sized red onion, julienned

2 garlic cloves, slivered

3 medium-sized tomatoes, peeled, seeded, and diced

1 pound Tuna Confit (page 120), drained and broken into bite-sized chunks

1¹/₂ tablespoons capers, rinsed

2 tablespoons chopped Italian parsley

¹/₂ pound dried spaghetti

Juice of 1 lemon

Virgin olive oil

Salt and freshly cracked black pepper

Heat the olive oil in a large sauté pan over a hot flame. When the oil is on the verge of smoking, add the onion and brown lightly. Add the garlic and cook several minutes longer, until the garlic has a little color and toastiness. Do not let it darken and become bitter. Immediately add the tomatoes and cook until the liquid has reduced slightly. Add the confit, capers, and parsley.

Cook and drain the pasta and add it to the pan. Squeeze in some lemon juice and add a little virgin olive oil. Season well with salt and a lot of cracked pepper. Toss well and serve immediately.

SERVES 4

ARTWORK BY KINDE NEBEKER

BAKED NECTARINES, BLUEBERRIES, AND RASPBERRIES

Topped with Cake and Sweet Cream

This simple dessert is very popular at the height of summer. I have great affection for French sweet creams, for panna cotta, zuppa inglese, *and everything else on the ladder that leads to crème anglaise and custard. There was a time in my life (before the invention of cholesterol) when the ultimate treat was a beer glass filled with crème anglaise sipped like a milk shake.*

FRUIT

2 or 3 nectarines (depending on size), unpeeled, sliced

1 pint fresh blueberries

1 pint fresh raspberries

1/2 cup granulated sugar

STREUSEL TOPPING

13/4 cups all-purpose flour

1/4 cup cornstarch

1/4 teaspoon salt

1/2 cup firmly packed brown sugar

1/2 cup granulated sugar

1/2 cup sweet, unsalted butter, cut into small pieces

CAKE

2 eggs

1 teaspoon vanilla extract

1 cup sour cream

13/4 cups cake flour

1 cup granulated sugar

2 teaspoons baking powder

1/2 teaspoon baking soda

1/4 teaspoon salt

SWEET CREAM

1 cup heavy whipping cream

2 tablespoons granulated sugar

1/2 vanilla bean, split

TO PREPARE THE FRUIT:

Mix together the nectarines, blueberries, raspberries, and sugar and place in the bottom of a buttered 9 by 13-inch baking pan.

TO PREPARE THE TOPPING:

Preheat the oven to 350°. Sift together the flour, cornstarch, and salt. In the bowl of an electric mixer, combine the flour, sugars, and butter on low speed until they form a coarse meal. Set aside.

TO PREPARE THE CAKE:

Preheat the oven to 350°. Beat together the eggs, vanilla, and sour cream. Sift together the dry ingredients. Mix into the egg mixture. Pour the batter over the fruit in the pan and top evenly with the streusel. Bake for 25 to 30 minutes, or until the cake springs back when touched.

TO PREPARE THE SWEET CREAM:

Combine the cream and sugar with the sticky scrapings from the inside of the vanilla bean. Mix; do not whip.

TO SERVE:

Cut the cake into squares and serve warm with sweet cream.

SERVES 9 TO 12

129

APRICOT AND CHERRY UPSIDE-DOWN CAKE

Apricots and cherries are such a fine combination. The colors are beautiful visually, and the flavors of each are simultaneously sweet and acidic. All upside-down things have the crunch of caramelization to recommend them. Top this cake with extra caramel sauce.

CARAMEL SAUCE

   3 cups sugar

   $1/2$ cup water

   1 cup heavy whipping cream

CAKE

   4 to 6 apricots, halved

   1 cup cherries, pitted and halved

   $1/2$ cup sweet, unsalted butter

   $1^{1}/_{3}$ cups sugar

   $1^{3}/_{4}$ cups cake flour

   2 teaspoons baking powder

   $1/4$ teaspoon salt

   2 teaspoons ground cardamom

   $3/4$ cup whole milk

   2 teaspoons vanilla extract

   4 egg whites

TO PREPARE THE CARAMEL SAUCE:

Place the sugar and water in a heavy-bottomed pan and bring to a boil. Continue boiling until the mixture is the color of dark brown sugar. Remove from the heat and add the cream a little at a time, mixing it in with a whisk and being careful not to burn yourself in the steam.

TO PREPARE THE CAKE:

Cover the bottom of a parchment-lined 9-inch round, 2-inch-deep cake pan with some of the caramel sauce. A good layer of caramel will give the apricots great flavor. Arrange the apricots, cut sides up, on the caramel. Lay the cherries between the apricots. Make sure the bottom of the pan is fully covered with fruit.

Preheat the oven to 350°. Beat the butter with 1 cup of the sugar. Sift the flour with the baking powder, salt, and cardamom. Beat the flour mixture into the butter mixture, alternating with the combined milk and vanilla. Scrape the bottom of the bowl to ensure that the batter is well mixed. In a clean bowl, whip the egg whites until stiff, and then beat in the remaining $1/3$ cup sugar. Fold the egg whites into the butter mixture and pour the batter over the fruit in the cake pan. Bake for 45 minutes, or until a toothpick inserted into the center comes out clean. Let cool for 20 minutes and then run a knife around the edge. Unmold onto a serving plate while still warm. Peel off the parchment and cover the top with the rest of the caramel sauce, warmed.

MAKES ONE 9-INCH CAKE

CHERRY-SAFFRON CAKE

Saffron is one of the world's most magical spices. Here in the United States we tend to think of it as a savory spice, suitable for coloring Middle Eastern pilafs, essential in paella and risotto, and for Indian biryani. In England and most Mediterranean countries, it is just as often used to color and add its spicy pungency to sweets. This is one of my favorite summer desserts for after dinner or as an afternoon snack with tea or coffee.

CAKE

1/4 teaspoon saffron threads, finely chopped

1 cup heavy whipping cream

1 tablespoon white vinegar

2 cups all-purpose flour

1 cup sugar

2 teaspoons baking powder

1/2 teaspoon baking soda

1/4 teaspoon salt

2 eggs

1 teaspoon vanilla extract

1 teaspoon finely chopped lemon zest

2 cups pitted Bing or Burlat cherries, halved

Sugar for dusting

CHERRY COMPOTE

1 cup water

1 cup sugar

3 cups pitted cherries, halved

1/4 teaspoon almond extract

1 tablespoon kirsch

1 tablespoon cornstarch

TO PREPARE THE CAKE:

Preheat the oven to 350°. Toast the saffron in a sauté pan. Remove from the heat and add a few drops of water to the pan to hydrate the saffron. Mix the cream and vinegar into the saffron and let sit. Sift the dry ingredients into a large bowl. Mix the eggs, vanilla, and lemon zest into the saffron mixture and then mix it into the dry ingredients. Add the cherries and mix well. Pour into a 9-inch cake pan lined with parchment. Dust the top with sugar and bake for 45 minutes, or until a toothpick inserted into the center comes out clean.

TO PREPARE THE COMPOTE:

Mix the water and sugar in a medium saucepan and bring to a boil. Add the cherries, almond extract, and kirsch. Add a little cold water to the cornstarch to make a slurry, then add this to the cherry mixture and cook for 1 or 2 minutes, or until thick. Remove from the heat immediately.

TO SERVE:

Slice the cake into wedges and serve with the warm compote.

MAKES ONE 9-INCH CAKE

HAZELNUT, PLUM, AND BLACKBERRY TART

Hazelnuts seem to have an affinity for any sweet thing: pastries, confections, cookies, and many of the world's most beautiful and labor-intensive chocolates. This fragrant nut enhances the flavor of almost any fruit but seems especially alluring in this painterly tart.

Tart Dough (page 39)

1 pound plums

1 cup fresh blackberries

6 tablespoons sugar

3 eggs, separated

1/2 teaspoon vanilla extract

1 tablespoon sweet unsalted butter, melted

3/4 cup hazelnuts, ground into a fine meal

Whipped crème fraîche (page 65) or whipped cream

Preheat the oven to 350°. Line a 9-inch tart pan with half the dough, reserving the other half for another purpose. Thinly slice the plums. Lay them in the tart shell and place the blackberries over them. Set aside. Beat 3 tablespoons of the sugar with the yolks and vanilla until light and fluffy. Mix the butter into the hazelnuts and fold into the yolk mixture. Whip the egg whites until stiff, then add the remaining 3 tablespoons sugar. Beat until well blended. Fold the whites into the nut mixture a third at a time. Pour over the fruit and bake for 45 minutes, or until the surface springs back when pressed. Let cool. Serve with whipped crème fraîche.

MAKES ONE 9-INCH TART

Peak Experience

August

There's no great cooking without generosity of spirit, and no human being more perfectly embodies this spirit than Alice Waters. Alice has found a middle path that inspires creativity yet remains faithful to the traditional organizing principles of the French canon. Without excess or irrelevant reverence for the icons of haute cuisine, she has taken the best and improved on the rest.

In 1976, before she was anybody and when I was less than anybody, Alice spontaneously pressed on me her copy of an Elizabeth David book that I subsequently devoured. That book has meant more to me than any single other food book, and I owe my introduction to it to that typical and emblematic Alice gesture. The gods reward generosity when it has such innocence and warmth and heart. Alice's generosity extended to suggesting suppliers for us, advising us on practical matters, and loaning us equipment—even bringing it over herself.

A friend of mine took his wife to a big benefit at the Mondavi Winery. There were chefs and wine mavens from everywhere. The food and wine were intended to impress, and they were having themselves a fine old time, so my friend walked up to Alice and said it was a pleasure to meet her, that he hated to bother her but his wife was a huge fan and would she mind autographing her copy of the Chez Panisse (Paul Bertolli) book. Alice graciously complied. Emboldened, his wife appeared and was introduced to Alice, who spontaneously hugged her. The wife cried. It's so wonderful that Alice can still be so friendly, so genuine, to a total stranger, to bring this woman to tears, to embrace her. I loved that. I'm a big fan of Alice.

Alice has the most extraordinary visual sense. I remember a perfectly constructed plate that she just threw together: a crown of figs, a corolla of different colors of berries, purple flower blossoms on a bluish platter with golden edges. It was effortless, gorgeous, and painterly—both edible and visually stimulating.

Cooking from the marketplace isn't a foodie fad; it's the soundest of principles. In August everything is at its most desirable. The garden is wildly profuse and diverse. This is prime time here and in Italy and France and Spain. Waltzing into a garden is a feast for the eyes, but the hand and mouth soon follow. How can you not pick wild berries or grapes that are cascading toward you or pluck a peach or nectarine that's hanging in front of you? At this point, in a place like California, we can get the food that is near perfect.

Start with the best and freshest and most homegrown ingredients you can find, the ones least abused by chemicals and long storage. It will make the process of shopping and cooking more pleasurable and the end result more satisfying. At home as well as in the restaurant, it makes the most sense to work with what's available locally.

I'm not interested in fruits from South America or New Zealand. If I could, I'd use only things grown within fifty miles of the restaurant. We live in the midst of a cornucopia. It's a luxury I never tire of or underrate. Alice Waters introduced the awareness of this bounty into our lives and our restaurants; she encouraged and subsidized their increased variety and availability and made possible their quantum leap in quality.

In France you still can't find tender baby spinach. There might be a hundred varieties of sausage in France, but here we now have an unsurpassed palette of lettuces and greens. Alice made it possible for us, not single-handedly, but she was the first.

At home you can guiltlessly indulge in the perfect simplicity of the ideal tomato, sliced and served unadorned or eaten out of hand. In a restaurant, the expectation is for a different level of peak experience. It takes a great deal of confidence to serve a solitary sliced tomato, however masterfully vine-ripened it may be or however scholarly its origins.

I learned the meaning of abundance when we came to America in 1947, when I was seven, after spending the war years hiding in France, where my mother traded her sewing skills for meager amounts of food that, like all good home cooks, she managed to transform into something palatable. When we first arrived, we were in a coffee shop in the Hotel Edison on Lexington Avenue in New York. We were eating a breakfast that was far beyond the kid in the candy store model for me: I saw platters of bacon, stacks of this, sides of that, an unimaginable show of abundance. The people at the table next to us had left an egg, some bacon, and some toast—a meal for four in our recent existence in France—and the busboy came along and swept it into the garbage. My mother turned to me and said, "This is the place to which we've come." In the gutter outside we saw a loaf of bread. I don't remember what people were wearing or what they were driving or what the weather might have been, the food, with its apparent abundance, was such a focus for me.

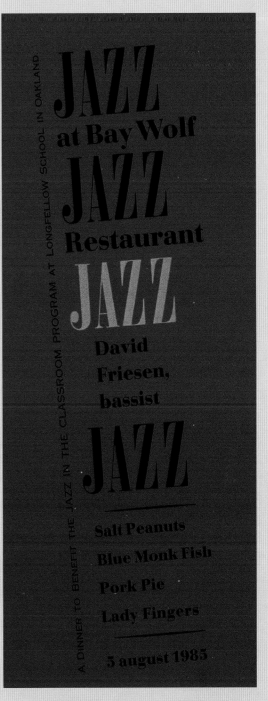

MENU BY WILL POWERS, CHERYL MILLER, AND ROBIN CHERIN

135

TAPAS PLATE
with Tomato and Celery Salad, Salt Cod Crostini, Fresh Anchovy Toasts, and Rock Shrimp Fritters

This is a perfect palette of appetizers for a party buffet. It is equally attractive served as individual composed plates. Follow it with a less labor-intensive second course that is very simple and direct: grilled meat, roasted potatoes. Follow the French approach of serving an elaborate first course with simple wines followed by simpler foods and more complicated wines.

Tomato and Celery Salad

This very simple and quickly prepared salad is a delicious component in tapas plates and antipasto platters. The freshness and crunch provide relief from richer accompaniments.

1 basket cherry tomatoes, halved

4 tender celery stalks, cut in very thin julienne, blanched, iced, and drained

1 handful Italian parsley leaves

Salt and freshly ground black pepper

Juice of 1 lemon

Virgin olive oil to taste

Right before serving, toss the tomatoes, celery, and parsley leaves in a bowl. Season with salt and pepper, then add the lemon juice and olive oil. Toss well and serve immediately.

SERVES 4

Salt Cod Crostini

Make sure that you finely and completely shred the salt cod before adding any potato. The idea is to work the mixture as little as possible once the potato is added. Otherwise, the final spread may be gummy.

SALT COD

2 pounds Atlantic cod, in one piece

2 cups kosher salt

1/2 bottle dry white wine

1 fennel bulb, thinly sliced

1 tablespoon fennel seed, toasted

5 garlic cloves

1 teaspoon white peppercorns

Zest of 1 lemon, removed in strips

5 thyme sprigs

3 tablespoons olive oil

— — —

2 pounds Yukon Gold potatoes

Extra virgin olive oil

Freshly squeezed lemon juice

Thin rounds of baguette

1 red bell pepper, roasted, seeded, and finely chopped

Chopped Italian parsley

TO PREPARE THE SALT COD:

Several days before serving, heavily salt the cod, with the skin on, pouring all 2 cups of salt over it. Let sit, refrigerated, for 2 to 3 days.

When you're ready to poach the cod, make a poaching liquid with the white wine, sliced fennel, fennel seed, garlic, peppercorns, lemon zest, thyme, olive oil, and water to cover. Boil this liquid for a few minutes and remove from heat. Rinse the cod. If it is very thin, and therefore very salty, you may need to soak it in cold water for a while. Put the fish in the poaching liquid on the lowest heat possible. When the cod is just cooked through, gently remove it from the pan and let it cool. Reserve the garlic cloves from the poaching liquid. Finely shred the fish into a bowl.

TO PREPARE THE CROSTINI:

Boil the potatoes and pass them through the finest holes of a food mill. Take the garlic cloves from the poaching liquid—they should be soft—and purée them. Add some of the potato, some extra virgin olive oil, lemon juice, and a bit of the garlic purée to the cod. Incorporate these ingredients with your hands. Brush the baguette rounds lightly with olive oil and toast on a baking sheet in the oven. Taste the mixture on a toasted baguette slice. In my experience, it tends to taste too salty on its own but just right on unsalted toast. Smear the toasts with the salt cod mixture and garnish with a little chopped red pepper and parsley.

MAKES ABOUT 32 CROSTINI

(continued)

Fresh Anchovy Toasts

Fresh silver anchovies are beautiful to look at and delicious to eat. You cannot purchase them sans guts, but do not let that prevent you from preparing these intensely tasty toasts.

1 pound fresh anchovies

Salt and freshly ground black pepper

2 tablespoons olive oil

1 red onion, minced

4 garlic cloves, minced

1 tomato, peeled, seeded, and diced

Pinch of dried red chile flakes

$^1/_3$ cup white wine vinegar

$^1/_4$ cup dry white wine

1 thyme sprig

1 bay leaf

Virgin olive oil

Chopped Italian parsley

Thin baguette slices, cut on the diagonal and toasted

TO PREPARE THE ANCHOVIES:

Gently tug the head toward the tail, using the tip of your finger to split the belly as you go. Lift out the bones and innards and discard. Rinse the anchovies, and then arrange them, opened flat and skin side down, in a single layer in a glass or ceramic pan. Season generously with salt, frugally with pepper. Refrigerate for several hours.

TO PREPARE THE TOASTS:

Heat the olive oil in a sauté pan until it is almost smoking. Add the onion and sear briefly. Add the garlic, tomato, pepper flakes, vinegar, wine, thyme, and bay leaf. Boil vigorously until reduced by a third. Pour this hot liquid over the anchovies and let cool to room temperature. Drizzle with a little olive oil. Taste an anchovy and adjust the salt and acid. Remove and discard the bay leaf. Sprinkle with the parsley and serve on toasts.

MAKES ABOUT 12 TOASTS

Rock Shrimp Fritters

Make the fritter base the day before you plan to serve it so it has plenty of time to chill and harden. Rock shrimp contain a lot of natural salt, so season prudently.

FRITTERS

$1/2$ cup unsalted butter

$3/4$ cup all-purpose flour

1 cup whole milk, heated

$1/2$ cup dry white wine

$1/2$ cup fish or chicken stock

1 pound rock shrimp, peeled

Salt

Ground cayenne pepper

1 bunch green onions, white parts and some green, minced

Minced Italian parsley

— — —

$1/2$ cup all-purpose flour

2 eggs, beaten

2 cups fresh breadcrumbs

Peanut oil for frying

Lemon wedges

Aioli (page 48)

TO PREPARE THE FRITTER BATTER:

Up to a day before serving, heat the butter in a heavy-bottomed saucepan over medium heat. When the butter has melted, add the flour and stir with a wooden spoon. Lower the heat and cook for 4 minutes. Gradually whisk in the milk, wine, and stock. The mixture should be totally smooth. Season with salt and cayenne. Simmer for 20 minutes, stirring occasionally. Meanwhile, purée half of the shrimp in a food processor. Chop the remaining shrimp. Add the puréed and chopped shrimp to the fritter batter the last 5 minutes of cooking. Remove from the heat and adjust the seasoning. Transfer to a bowl and cool. Add the onions and parsley. Cover and refrigerate for several hours or overnight.

TO COOK THE FRITTERS:

Just before serving, form the fritter batter into small balls and roll them first in the flour, then in the egg, then in the breadcrumbs. Fry in 2 inches of peanut oil until golden. Serve with lemon wedges and aioli.

MAKES ABOUT 30 SMALL FRITTERS

SHELL BEAN AND CORN SALAD
with Bacon and Grilled Green Onions

This salad is especially beautiful if prepared with a mixture of fresh shell beans such as lima and cranberry. Make the salad a few hours ahead of time if possible, but be sure to warm it before serving to avoid serving congealed bacon fat. You can save the corncobs, simmer them in water, and use the water for cooking polenta.

BEANS

   2 thyme sprigs

   1 bay leaf

   4 cups fresh shell beans, such as lima beans or cranberry beans

   Salt

VINAIGRETTE

   8 ounces bacon, cut into $^1/_2$-inch lengths

   1 shallot, minced

   $^1/_4$ cup white wine vinegar

   Virgin olive oil

   Salt and freshly ground black pepper

CORN

   Kernels cut from 5 corn ears

   Butter

   Chopped Italian parsley

   Green onions, lightly oiled, seasoned with salt and freshly ground black pepper, and grilled

TO PREPARE THE BEANS:

If you are using more than one variety of shell bean, cook them separately. Bring a pot of water to a boil with the thyme and bay leaf. Add the beans and simmer gently until tender. When the beans are done, remove from the heat and salt generously. It is very important to season them while they are still hot so that the salt penetrates the beans. Let the beans sit for about 30 minutes, then drain. Remove and discard the thyme and bay leaf. Check the seasoning again.

TO PREPARE THE VINAIGRETTE:

Cook the bacon until it just starts to crisp. Do not let it get so hot that the fat smokes. We need the fat. Remove the bacon from the pan and set aside. Pour the bacon fat into a bowl and set aside. Soak the shallot in the vinegar for 20 minutes, then whisk in the bacon fat and enough olive oil to balance the acidity. Season with salt and pepper.

TO PREPARE THE CORN:

Heat a little butter in a sauté pan and cook the corn gently until it is just cooked. Do not let it brown.

TO SERVE:

Add the corn and bacon to the beans and dress with the vinaigrette. Add some chopped parsley to the beans and serve on a platter with the green onions scattered over the top.

SERVES 6 TO 8

WHITE GAZPACHO
with Melon, Grapes, and Almonds

This unbelievably wonderful chilled soup is most perfectly composed of ripe, sweet, perfumed melons. You will want to make it when the weather warms and the melons are in season. Everything in this soup is a variation of paleness: white bread, melon, grapes for texture, white almonds. This paleness is strangely appealing on very hot days. If you are ever offered unformed almonds, float them in this soup. They are limpid, gossamer almond embryos with an intense almond essence.

3/4 cup almonds, blanched and peeled

1/4 to 1/2 cup freshly squeezed lemon juice

1 cup white bread, crusts removed

2 small honeydew or Sharlyn melons, peeled, seeded, and cut into large pieces (6 to 7 cups melon chunks)

Salt

Ground white pepper

1/4 cup almonds, toasted and julienned

1 cup seedless red grapes, halved

Crème fraîche (page 65)

Put the blanched almonds in a blender with 1/4 cup of the lemon juice. Purée until totally smooth, then add the bread and melon and purée again. If the melon needs more liquid to purée properly, add a little water. You will most likely need to purée the melon in batches. After puréeing one batch, pour out all but 1 cup of the liquid and then add the next batch. Season well with salt and white pepper. If the soup needs more acid, add the remaining lemon juice. If the soup is too thick, you can add a little water, but if the melons are really ripe, this shouldn't be a problem. Serve slightly chilled. Garnish with toasted almonds, grapes, and a swirl of crème fraîche.

SERVES 6 TO 8

ROMESCO SAUCE

Romesco sauce is delicious with grilled fish and all varieties of shellfish. It requires long, slow cooking and is best if it can sit for a few hours before serving at room temperature. We often serve it at the restaurant with grilled monkfish, boiled new potatoes fried in olive oil, and blanched green and yellow beans. It would also be good for dressing smoked mussels.

1/3 cup olive oil

2 onions, roughly chopped

4 red bell peppers

1 ancho chile

Salt

6 large garlic cloves

4 to 6 large, ripe tomatoes

1 to 2 tablespoons Spanish paprika

1 cup almonds, toasted and ground

Virgin olive oil

Sherry vinegar

Heat the olive oil in a heavy, wide-bottomed pan. Add the onions and cook over high heat for a few minutes. Stir to scrape up any caramelized bits that form on the bottom. Brown the onions well, then lower the heat and cook for about 20 minutes, or until very soft. Continue to scrape the pan as necessary. Don't let the onions burn.

Meanwhile, roast the peppers whole, either on a grill, directly over a gas burner, or in the oven at 500°. Blacken the peppers all over, then put them in a bag or covered bowl and let cool. When cool enough to handle, peel and seed the peppers. Do not run water over the peppers no matter what anyone tells you. Do, however, keep a small bowl of water nearby to rinse black bits from your hands as necessary.

Toast the ancho chile in the oven at 375° just until you begin to smell it, about 5 minutes. Place it in a saucepan with boiling water to cover. Let it stand for about 15 minutes, or until it has softened. Remove the chile from the water, then remove the stem and seeds. Cut the bell peppers into random strips and add to the onions. Add a little more olive oil, raise the heat to high, and fry the peppers for a few minutes, stirring frequently. Season with salt, then add the whole garlic cloves and whole chile and cook for a few minutes more.

Blacken 4 of the tomatoes over a flame, in a cast-iron pan, or in a very hot oven. Add the tomatoes, (seeds, charred parts, and all), to the onion-pepper mixture once the onions are completely softened. The onions will not soften further after you add the tomatoes because of the acid in the tomatoes. Lower the heat to a simmer. The tomatoes will give off their juice and make the sauce soupy. If the tomatoes are not very juicy, you may need to add a couple more. Add the paprika. Simmer the sauce for 30 minutes, stirring every 5 minutes. Check the salt again and pass the sauce through the largest holes of a food mill. If you don't have a food mill, you can use a food processor or blender, but the texture and color will be different. If you are hard-core and have some extra time on your hands, use a mortar and pestle. The sauce can be made up to this point 5 days in advance of serving and stored in the refrigerator.

Right before serving, add the almonds, a few shots of fruity virgin olive oil, and enough sherry vinegar to pick everything up. Always serve at room temperature or warmer. Always add the almonds right before serving so you detect a little crunch.

MAKES ABOUT 5 CUPS

143

BRAISED GAME HENS
with Red Wine, Chickpeas, and Chocolate

This seamless, tasty combination is akin to Spanish and Oaxacan moles, those lovely poultices of spices and herbs that thicken and flavor classic sauces. A small amount of chocolate adds flavor and deepens the color, and the nuts both thicken the mix and heighten its complexity. In Mexico cooks might substitute pumpkin seeds, in Spain hazelnuts or almonds. Feel free to experiment. I like the little game hens for this dish, but chicken or duck legs or any small birds would be equally suitable.

4 game hens, backbones removed, halved

MARINADE

Salt and freshly ground black pepper

2 small oranges

3 garlic cloves, sliced

Pinch of saffron threads

1 tablespoon paprika

2 bay leaves, crumbled

4 thyme sprigs, roughly chopped

A few black peppercorns

4 tablespoons olive oil

CHICKPEAS

2 cups chickpeas

1/2 carrot, peeled

1 celery stalk

1 onion

1 bay leaf

2 thyme sprigs

Zest of 1 orange, removed in strips

Pinch of salt

Pinch of saffron threads

Sherry vinegar

Virgin olive oil

BRAISING LIQUID AND SAUCE

3 ounces pancetta, diced

1 carrot, diced

1 onion, diced

1 celery stalk, diced

3 garlic cloves, minced

2 bay leaves, crumbled

3 thyme sprigs

Pinch of dried red chile flakes

1 bottle dry red wine

2 ounces Ibarra chocolate, chopped

2 cups chicken stock

2 tablespoons chopped Italian parsley

1/2 cup hazelnuts, toasted, skinned, and chopped

TO MARINATE THE HENS:

The day before serving, season the birds well with salt and pepper and arrange them in a glass pan. Remove the zest of the oranges with a peeler. Juice the oranges and add the zest and juice to the birds. Add the garlic, saffron, paprika, bay, thyme, and a few peppercorns to the marinade, pressing the ingredients into the skin. Coat the birds with a layer of olive oil, then cover and refrigerate for 24 hours. Turn once or twice during this period.

TO PREPARE THE CHICKPEAS:

The day before serving, soak the chickpeas in water to cover overnight.

The next day, drain the chickpeas and put in a pot with cold water to cover. Bring to a boil and skim any scum that rises to the top. Reduce the heat to a simmer. Cut the carrot, celery, and onion into large chunks and add to the chickpeas. Add the bay leaf, thyme, and orange zest. Simmer gently until the chickpeas are thoroughly tender, but not burst open, about 1 hour and 15 minutes. Season with salt, saffron, a few drops of sherry vinegar, and a little oil. Let sit for 30 minutes. Remove the bay leaves, zest, and thyme. Adjust the seasoning again, then reheat before serving.

TO BRAISE THE HENS:

Preheat the oven to 350°. In a large, heavy-bottomed, ovenproof saucepan, cook the pancetta with the carrot, onion, and celery until lightly browned. Add the garlic, bay leaves, thyme, chile flakes, and red wine. Bring to a boil, then turn off the heat. Arrange the halved birds, skin side up, on top of the vegetables. The meat should be immersed in wine, but the skin should remain exposed. Braise in the oven for 45 minutes to 1 hour, or until the meat is tender and the skin is crispy. Add the chocolate to the braise during the last 15 minutes of cooking. When the birds are ready, ladle off the braising liquid into a bowl. Let the liquid settle, then ladle off the top layer of fat. In a small saucepan, reduce the chicken stock to $1/2$ cup. Add the degreased braising liquid to the stock. Add the chopped parsley and hazelnuts and serve over the birds, with the chickpeas on the side.

SERVES 4 TO 6

DOUBLE DUCK DINNER

BAY WOLF RESTAURANT   AUGUST 6, 1984

Duck consommé with duck giblet confit,
duck egg royales, & herb flowers

Baby spinach salad with duck cracklings and
gamay verjuice vinaigrette

Fresh lemon-mint fettuccine with sautéed duck livers

Breast of duck grilled rare, served with blackberry-ginger
beurre rouge and succotash

Duck leg sausage wrapped in grape leaves with a zinfandel sauce

Sorbet of Babcock peaches and Duxoup Gamay

'82 DUXOUP GAMAY   '81 DUXOUP ZINFANDEL (magnums)
'81 DUXOUP GAMAY

Duxoup Wine Works · Reichardt Duck Farm · Bay Wolf Restaurant

MENU BY WILL POWERS, CHERYL MILLER, AND ROBIN CHERIN

SEAFOOD RISOTTO
with Shrimp, Mussels, Chorizo, and Saffron

This is a dish we might serve during a series of menus featuring the flavors and ingredients of Spain, so many of which seem appropriate to our corner of California. Here we can easily indulge in our own locally produced tomatoes and sausages, olives, numerous varieties of peppers, and abundant seafood. You can transform this dish into a paella simply by cooking it in a paella pan or large sauté pan and stirring less frequently. An authentic paella would have a crusty bottom.

1 tablespoon olive oil

1 tablespoon butter

1 onion, cut into small dice

1/2 fennel bulb, cut into small dice

1 small leek, diced

2 1/2 cups Arborio rice

2 cups dry white wine

8 cups chicken or fish stock, or a combination

Generous pinch of saffron threads, minced

1/2 red bell pepper, diced

Salt and freshly ground black pepper

4 ounces mussels, beards removed, or clams, or a combination of both

1 1/4 pounds shrimp, peeled and deveined

4 ounces scallops

4 ounces halibut or rock cod fillet, cut into 1/2-inch pieces

10 ounces chorizo sausage, poached, browned, and sliced into rounds

4 green onions, white and light green parts, finely chopped

1 tablespoon chopped Italian parsley

Freshly squeezed lemon juice to taste

1/2 to 1 cup aioli (page 48)

In a large, heavy-bottomed pot, heat the oil with the butter. Add the onion, fennel, and leek and sweat over medium heat until tender. Do not brown. When the vegetables are tender, about 10 minutes, raise the heat and add the rice. Stir to coat the rice completely with the fat. Add the wine. Simmer for a few minutes until the rice has absorbed the wine. Bring the stock to a boil, then reduce the heat to low. Add the saffron, red pepper, and 2 cups of the stock to the rice. Season the rice well with salt and pepper. Stirring frequently, add 2 cups of stock at a time as it is absorbed by the rice. Keep the rice higher than a simmer.

When the rice is almost cooked, 20 to 25 minutes, and you have added the last 2 cups of stock, stir the mussels into the rice and cover the pot. When they are just beginning to open, add the shrimp, scallops, halibut, and chorizo and replace the lid. When the fish is just cooked, about 5 minutes, add the green onions and parsley. Adjust the seasoning with salt and lemon. Stir in aioli to taste and serve.

SERVES 6

147

BASQUE CAKE

A version of this cake was ubiquitous in the '60s and '70s in student restaurants throughout France. It had a huge proportion of dough and a disappointingly tiny dab of custard. We've tried to redress the balance by increasing the custard and decreasing the dough, fragrantly flavoring it with orange flower water, rum, and brandy and accompanying it with sweet summer berries. Our version is richer and far more rewarding.

AROMATIC LIQUID

$1/3$ cup anisette

$1/3$ cup dark rum

$1/3$ cup brandy

2 tablespoons orange flower water

DOUGH

1 pound sweet, unsalted butter

1 cup sugar

3 wholee eggs

1 egg yolk

$2^1/4$ cups all-purpose flour

$1^1/2$ cups cake flour

$1^1/2$ teaspoons baking powder

PASTRY CREAM

2 tablespooons cornstarch

$1/2$ cup sugar

1 whole egg

1 egg yolk

2 cups whole milk

$1/2$ vanilla bean, split and scraped, or
   1 tablespoon vanilla extract

Egg wash consisting of whole 1 egg, pinch
   of salt, and 1 tablespoon heavy whipping
   cream or whole milk

Sugar for sprinkling

Fresh berries

TO PREPARE THE AROMATIC LIQUID:

Mix together the ingredients and set aside.

TO PREPARE THE DOUGH:

Beat together the butter and sugar. In a separate bowl, whisk the eggs and yolk with 2 tablespoons of the aromatic liquid. Beat into the butter mixture. Sift the flours with the baking powder and beat into the butter mixture. This dough will be very sticky. Wrap in plastic wrap and refrigerate for 4 hours or overnight.

TO PREPARE THE PASTRY CREAM:

Sift the cornstarch with the sugar. Mix into the egg and egg yolk. Bring the milk and the vanilla bean to a boil. Scrap out the vanilla bean once more, then discard the pod. Add a few tablespoons of the hot milk to the egg mixture to temper it. Add the egg mixture to the remaining milk and cook over low heat until thick. Stir in the remaining aromatic liquid and the vanilla extract, if using instead of bean scrapings. Strain through a fine strainer into a bowl. Cover with plastic wrap and chill.

TO ASSEMBLE AND BAKE THE CAKE:

Preheat the oven to 375°. Cut the dough into 2 pieces, one a little larger than the other. Roll out into 2 rounds 1/4 inch thick. Line the sides and bottom of a buttered 9-inch springform pan with the larger round of dough. Pour the cooled pastry cream into the dough-lined pan. Cut the second round the diameter of the pan and lay it on top of the pastry cream, fitting it inside the dough on the sides. Brush the top of the round with the egg wash and fold down the dough lining the sides of the pan. Take a fork and press the edges of the dough together. Brush the edge with the egg wash. Prick air holes in the top of the cake. Sprinkle with sugar and bake for 20 to 35 minutes, or until golden brown. Let cool.

TO SERVE:

Remove the rim of the pan, cut the cake into 12 slices, and serve with fresh berries.

MAKES ONE 9-INCH CAKE

LAVENDER HONEY AND FIG TART
with Lemon Ice Cream

I love everything about figs. The simple shape, the contrast of colors from outside to in, their delicate nature, and their ethereal flavor. They can range from sweet and soft to firm and nutty. Figs have been cultivated for thousands of years in numerous countries. At one time, fig production was in decline in the United States, as more popular fruits became widely available. Now it is rebounding, thanks in part to the increased use of figs in restaurant cooking. Figs can be eaten fresh, dried, preserved, grilled, baked into tarts, or stuffed inside meats and braised into stews. Their fragrance is beautifully complemented by the scent of lavender. If you cannot acquire lavender honey, substitute orange blossom honey. It has far more fragrance and a cleaner flavor than field-run or wildflower honeys.

Tart dough (page 39)

Egg wash of 1 egg, a pinch of salt, and 1 tablespoon cream

2 pints figs, quartered

1 cup lavender honey or light-flavored honey, heated with 2 tablespoons dried lavender, cooled, and strained

Sugar for sprinkling

LEMON ICE CREAM

3/4 cup heavy whipping cream

3/4 cup whole milk

1 vanilla bean, split and scraped

Zest of 2 lemons, removed in strips

3/4 cup sugar

8 egg yolks

1 cup heavy whipping cream, whipped until stiff

TO PREPARE THE TART:

Roll the tart dough out into a 14- to 16-inch round. Brush the entire top of the dough with the egg wash. Fold in half, transfer to a parchment-lined baking sheet, and unfold. Refrigerate until cold. Coat the figs with honey and place them on the tart dough, keeping them at least 1 inch from the edge. Fold the edge toward the center to form a rim and crimp if needed. Brush the edge with egg wash and sprinkle with sugar. Place back in the refrigerator and chill. Preheat the oven to 400°. Bake the tart for 20 to 30 minutes, or until the edges are a light golden brown.

TO PREPARE THE ICE CREAM:

Heat the cream and milk with the vanilla bean and lemon zest in a small saucepan. Mix the sugar with the egg yolks. Remove the vanilla bean and zest. Add a small quantity of the milk mixture to the yolks to temper them. Add the remaining milk mixture. Strain through a fine strainer and place over an ice bath to chill. When cold, fold in the whipped cream. Freeze in an ice cream freezer according to the manufacturer's instructions.

MAKES ONE 14-INCH TART AND 2 QUARTS ICE CREAM

151

PLUM AND HAZELNUT UPSIDE-DOWN CAKE

Brown butter has a very definite essence, just verging on caramel, that adds an extra dimension to this dessert. The hazelnuts provide a warm, toasty flavor. The plums are braised in a little sugar and brandy to create a thick sauce that is transformed into a delicious topping when the cake is unmolded.

PLUM SAUCE

Plums, 3 for sauce, 8 for topping

$1/2$ cup sugar

2 tablespoons brandy

CAKE

$3/4$ cup plus 1 tablespoon sweet, unsalted butter

1 vanilla bean, split and scaped

2 cups sugar

2 tablespoons brandy

6 eggs, separated

$1^1/4$ cups all-purpose flour, sifted

$1^1/2$ cups finely ground hazelnuts

Whipped cream or vanilla ice cream

TO PREPARE THE PLUM SAUCE:

Slice 3 of the plums into small pieces. Mix them in a saucepan with the sugar and brandy and cook over low heat until the plums are soft. Push them through a fine strainer. Let cool and pour into a parchment-lined 9-inch cake pan. Slice the remaining plums into thick slices and lay them in a nice pattern in the pan.

TO PREPARE THE CAKE:

In a thick-bottomed saucepan, heat the butter with the vanilla and cook until dark brown. Strain through a fine strainer. Let cool. Preheat the oven to 350°. Add $1^1/2$ cups of the sugar to the butter. Mix well. Add the brandy and egg yolks. Set aside. Mix the flour and hazelnuts. Add to the butter mixture. Whip the egg whites until stiff, then add the remaining $1/2$ cup sugar and whip until the sugar is well combined. Fold in the egg whites and pour into the plum-prepared cake pan. Bake

for 1 hour, or until a toothpick inserted into the center comes out clean. Let the cake cool. While still a little warm, run a knife around the edge and unmold onto a large plate.

TO SERVE:

Slice and serve warm with whipped cream.

MAKES ONE 9-INCH CAKE

WATERMELON ICE
with Mint Sorbet

Summer and watermelon are synonymous. This refreshing summer dessert is as low in calories as it is high in color and sweet in natural flavor.

MINT SORBET

2 cups sugar

2 cups water

3 large bunches mint

WATERMELON ICE

3 pounds watermelon, peeled, seeds removed, and diced

1/2 cup sugar

1 tablespoon dry marsala

TO PREPARE THE MINT SORBET:

Place the sugar and water in a saucepan and bring to a boil. Add the mint and let steep for 20 minutes. Remove and discard the mint. Place in the refrigerator to cool completely. Freeze in an ice cream freezer according to the manufacturer's instructions.

TO PREPARE THE WATERMELON ICE:

Place the watermelon in a blender and purée. Strain through a fine strainer. Add the sugar and marsala. Pour into a pan and freeze. When frozen, chop into fine chips with a blunt pastry scraper. (Do not use a sharp knife.) This takes some muscle.

TO SERVE:

Place some of the chipped ice in each bowl and top with 2 scoops of sorbet.

MAKES 1 1/2 QUARTS SORBET AND 2 CUPS ICE

I first came to BayWolf about two or three years after it opened. BayWolf's reputation for exotic feasts, which I never attended , still figured in my early forays into the East Bay from my San Francisco redoubt. A place willing to take risks must also be comfortable with the rest of its menu and confident in its skills. So I found that the Berkeley restaurant I was most drawn to was in fact in Oakland.

—SEDGE THOMSON, *Impresario,* West Coast Live

153

Double Duck

Like young people everywhere, Larry and I learned how to ferret out good cheap eats by scouring the ethnic neighborhoods. I liked to window-shop the food markets in San Francisco's Chinatown in the '60s. It was an exhilarating and practical form of entertainment. What could be more appealing than those glistening, warm brown ducks hanging whole in the windows of poultry shops? Their meat was dark, it was lean, it was provocatively spicy. Add a little rice and it was a complete meal. In my youth, I'd eaten a few of those throat-laminating, stomach-congealing hyper-fat Long Island ducklings, but these were very different.

We started serving ducks at the restaurant early in our history. There was a poultry shop nearby that I disliked; it didn't seem quite hygienic enough for my taste. To get the ducks I liked, I started going to Chinatown twice a week and loading up my car with boxes of oozing, bloody ducks. In the beginning I didn't realize that Reichardt Duck Farms in Petaluma raised all the ducks you'd find in Chinatown; I just knew they were the best.

I was cooking a dinner in Los Angeles and needed to procure ducks from their Chinatown. They weren't nearly as good as we'd been getting—they were poorly cleaned, and mangled—and that's when I began to appreciate what we had in the Reichardt ducks. Their skin was flawlessly unblemished; they were perfectly clean and glamorously alabaster.

At about the same time that we were getting serious at BayWolf, Jim Reichardt was seriously trying to extend the family business into local restaurants, and he started to deliver the ducks directly to us. We'd talk about creating the perfect ducks, about raising different ducks for different needs, about processing them with care and paying closer attention to how they lived and when they were killed. To Jim, it began to make sense to move from a medium-sized business to a smaller business, where he could focus on the details.

Fourteen years after joining the family business, Jim left to start his own. Chefs wanted leaner, meatier, fuller-breasted, more flavorful ducks, and he was anxious to try his hand at providing them. He established Sonoma County Poultry on twenty acres on the outskirts of Petaluma, six miles down the road from his family's farm—a nearly perfect climate for raising ducks.

Most commercial duck farmers specialize in one of three breeds: the most common being the Pekin, along with the lean and somewhat gamier Muscovy and Moulard. A Moulard is the offspring of a female Pekin and a male Muscovy, wonderful for foie gras but equally prized for its meaty breasts. Jim chose two particularly meaty and lean strains of Pekin developed in Denmark: the Legarth hybrid and the Berlill, which he raises to five and six pounds, respectively. Chefs who serve breast and leg want the five-pounder; those who serve just breast want the six-pounder.

This was at the beginning of the popularity of "free-range" poultry. When ducks have room to maneuver and fresh air, they're more resistant to diseases and less likely to need antibiotics. Jim's Pekins are not fatty: they're raised on a high-protein mixture of corn and other grains. He processes some fifteen hundred ducks a week; by comparison, a corporation like Foster Farms may process three hundred thousand chickens a day. We were his first customers, and he's committed to giving us all the ducks we want. BayWolf orders hundreds of pounds of whole ducks, parts, carcasses, livers, giblets, and eggs each week.

From the beginning, our Double Duck dinners were never precisely "double" duck; I just liked the alliteration. In the early years, it was more likely to be quadruple or quintuple duck. Maybe a first course of duck consommé with duck giblet confit or duck rillettes, a duck liver mousse, and then a spinach salad with duck cracklings accompanied with the duck crackling biscuits that we christened Quackers. Perhaps then a fettuccine with sautéed duck livers, followed by a rare grilled duck breast, and then a duck leg sausage, or we might smoke the breast and serve it with crispy pears and persimmons. Jim's ducks are the real right thing, exactly what I dreamed of procuring, serving, and eating when it first occurred to me that we should distinguish ourselves with the utility, versatility, and delectability of duck.

TOMATO AND AVOCADO SALAD
with Cilantro Vinaigrette and Grilled Onions

This is a delicious combination and a huge relief to diners and cooks who are weary of the ubiquitous tomato and basil combinations. We have a tomato salad on the menu from July through September, or for as long as we're able to acquire the tomatoes we most prize: ones of any size or color possessing deep flavor, tender skin, and innate sweetness.

1 shallot, minced

Finely chopped zest and juice of 1 lemon

1 to 2 teaspoons cumin seed, toasted and ground

Salt and freshly ground black pepper

$1/4$ to $1/2$ cup virgin olive oil

$1/2$ bunch cilantro, chopped

$1/4$ loaf levain or sourdough baguette, crust removed, cut into tiny dice

2 avocados

2 large tomatoes

1 bunch green onion, very light oiled, seasoned with salt and freshly ground black pepper, and grilled

Macerate the shallot and lemon zest in the lemon juice for 20 minutes, then add the cumin and some salt and pepper. Finish with olive oil and cilantro.

Toss the bread cubes with a little olive oil and then season them and toast in a 375° oven until golden.

To serve, peel and slice the avocados, then arrange on plates. Sprinkle with a little salt. Slice the tomatoes, season them well, and dress in the vinaigrette with the croutons and the grilled green onions. Arrange over the avocado and serve.

SERVES 4

156

CORN AND CLAM CHOWDER

Corn chowder is basic and essential for all corn lovers. Clam chowders have a venerable history in the New England states and maritime Canada. Mariner chowders of the eighteenth century more closely resembled puddings than our modern chowders, which are more stew than soup. If you are serving this soup as an appetizer, use a light hand with the cream.

2 onions, diced

2 tablespoons butter

6 corn ears

2 russet potatoes, peeled and diced

1 garlic clove, minced

10 thyme sprigs, tied together

Salt and ground white pepper

Ground cayenne pepper

10 cups chicken stock

2 pounds clams, steamed open in 1 cup dry white wine, meats removed and roughly chopped and liquor strained

1 cup heavy whipping cream

Croutons for garnish

In a heavy-bottomed pot, cook the onions in the butter over medium heat for about 10 minutes, or until translucent. Do not brown. Husk the corn and cut off the kernels with a knife. Do this into a large bowl to contain shooting kernels. Reserve the cobs. Add the corn to the onions. Cook for about 20 minutes, until the corn is soft, then add the potatoes, garlic, and thyme. Season well with salt, white pepper, and a little cayenne. Cook briefly.

In a large pot, simmer the corncobs with the stock, then remove the cobs from the stock and add the stock to the pot containing the corn. Simmer for 40 minutes. Remove the thyme bundle. Ladle about half of the soup into a blender and purée. Return the puréed soup to the pot. Stir in the clam meats and the liquor. Add the cream. Stir well and adjust the seasoning. Serve with croutons.

SERVES 6

STUFFED SQUID
with Shrimp and Saffron Beurre Blanc

This is one of our signature dishes. At one of my favorite Paris restaurants (Le Regalade), I was once served a dish of squid stuffed with tomato and tomato stuffed with squid. This evolved from that sensation. Our first attempt was for one of the special wine dinners. I knew Alice Waters would be in attendance, and so I was trying to create small, tasty dishes to please her. Squid is a natural casing for the rough-textured sausage. We often accompany it with the deep-fried tentacles for garnish. The faint acidity of saffron beurre blanc brings the complementary colors and flavors into perfect harmony.

SQUID

10 to 12 whole squid, cleaned, beaks removed from tentacles

1 tablespoon olive oil

$1/2$ red onion, minced

$1/2$ fennel bulb, minced

1 leek, minced

Salt and ground white pepper

1 garlic clove, minced

1 pound shrimp, peeled

1 tablespoon minced chives

$1/4$ cup heavy whipping cream

SAFFRON BEURRE BLANC

1 shallot, minced

1 thyme sprig

$1/4$ cup dry white wine

$1/4$ cup white wine vinegar

1 tablespoon heavy whipping cream (optional)

Pinch of saffron threads, chopped and mixed with 1 tablespoon hot water

$1/2$ pound unsalted butter, slightly softened

Salt and ground white pepper

Peanut oil 4 inches deep for frying

Seasoned flour for dusting

1 teaspoon minced chives

1 tomato, peeled, seeded, and finely diced

TO PREPARE THE SQUID:

Clean the squid and pat them dry with paper towels. Heat the olive oil in a sauté pan. Add the onion, fennel, and leek. Cook over medium heat until tender. Season with salt and white pepper, add the garlic, remove from the heat, and let cool. Purée half of the shrimp in a food processor. Finely chop the remaining shrimp and mix in a bowl with the cooled vegetables, chives, and cream. Season again, and then fry a small patty, taste, and adjust the seasoning if necessary. Stuff the shrimp mixture into the squid bodies. Block the open end with a toothpick. Make a small incision at the narrow end to allow steam to escape when cooking. Chill until ready to fry.

TO PREPARE THE BEURRE BLANC:

Place the shallot in a small saucepot with the thyme, wine, and vinegar. Reduce to a few tablespoons and strain. Add the cream and saffron to the reduced liquid and reduce 1 minute more. Over medium heat, whisk in the butter, a couple of tablespoons at a time. Season with salt and white pepper. Hold in a warm place. If the sauce gets too hot, it will break.

TO FRY THE SQUID:

Right before serving, heat the peanut oil in a deep pot. When the temperature reaches 375°, dust the squid bodies and tentacles in seasoned flour and deep-fry until golden and crispy. Drain on paper towels and season immediately with salt.

TO SERVE:

Ladle a couple of tablespoons of saffron beurre blanc onto individual warmed plates. Place 2 squid with tentacles over the sauce. Sprinkle with chives and tomato and serve immediately.

SERVES 6

BAYWOLF

Clam chowder with corn & garlic croutons

Spiced scallop salad with cucumbers, preserved lemon and tchermoula

Smoked trout salad with fennel, various beets, arugula and dill crème fraîche

Warm duck liver salad with spinach, radicchio and sherry dressing

Cabbage bundles with turkey and black eyed peas in spicy Creole broth

Grilled swordfish with eggplant, olives, tomatoes and red pepper

Cannelloni filled with crab, ricotta cheese and spinach with lemon sauce

Indonesian-style chicken and prawn curry with coconut and mint

Grilled duck with Gravenstein apple sauce and potato pancakes

Grilled Wolf Ranch quail, cheese polenta and various mushrooms

Caribbean Steel Drum Music

SWIMMERS & FLYERS

27 SEPTEMBER 1992

CELEBRATION MENU 17

MENU BY CLAY DOYLE

DUCK CONFIT

Whenever you prepare duck confit, keep in mind that it is very rich and should not be served with other very rich ingredients. Keep the combinations small and balanced. Make sure there is enough freshness, crunch, and acidity in the composition to offset the deep richness of the duck.

12 duck legs with thighs attached
1¹/4 cups kosher salt
2 teaspoons dried thyme
3 bay leaves, crumbled
3 quarts rendered duck fat (page 6)
12 garlic cloves
1 teaspoons black peppercorns
Parsley stems, tied

TOP LEFT, CLOCKWISE: DUCK LIVER FLAN ON TOAST (PAGE 66), DUCK LIVER WITH PANCETTA (PAGE 162), RILLETTES (AT RIGHT), GIZZARDS AND GRAPES (PAGE 180), AND SLICED SMOKED DUCK BREAST

Arrange the duck in a shallow dish. Season both sides with half of the salt and sprinkle with thyme and bay. Cover and refrigerate for 2 days. Two days later, heat the fat in a large pan that will hold the legs comfortably in 2 layers. Rinse the legs thoroughly under cold water, then pat dry with a towel. Add legs, garlic, peppercorns, and parsley stems to the fat. Cook in a 200° oven for about 2 hours, or until the meat is tender. Check by gently lifting out a leg. Press the meat near the bone with your finger. It should be tender to the point that the meat is thinking about falling from the bone. If it actually does fall from the bone, it has gone too far, but proceed anyway. Remove the pan from the oven and cool to room temperature. Carefully transfer the legs to a wire rack to drain. Strain the fat into a clean pot and bring to a boil. Simmer until all the duck juices have evaporated. Skim the scum as necessary. Do not let the fat begin to smoke. Cool the fat and reserve. Put the duck legs in a large glass jar or crock, or 3 small jars, with the remaining half of the salt on the bottom and pour over the cooled fat. Make sure the fat covers the legs by at least 2 inches. Store refrigerated for at least 2 weeks before using. It is best, however, to let the legs sit for 2 months. The legs will keep for several months if properly stored

What to Do with Duck Confit

Confit is an intense concentration of duck and its very essence. Cooked in its own flavored fat, it is great on a cold day accompanied with a cool Beaujolais and potatoes sautéed in and infused with duck fat. It is equally satisfying in hotter times and climes when paired with other crispy and focused flavors.

Rillettes

Whenever I go to Paris, my first night will invariably be spent at the Tabac Henri Quatre, enjoying a bottle of Vouvray and their admirable version of rillettes spread on toasted wedges of crusty Poilâne bread. You can go to France to have the same, or you can do what I do most of the time and make your own.

2 legs duck confit (page 160)

Duck fat from duck confit (page 160)

Salt

2 tablespoons chopped flat-leaf parsley

Shot of distilled white vinegar

1 baguette, thinly sliced on the diagonal and toasted

Let the jar of confit sit in a warm place for a while to gently melt the fat. Carefully pull out one leg at a time. Remove the skin from the legs and finely shred the meat by hand into a bowl. Add a little duck fat from the jar, salt if needed, add some chopped parsley and a shot of vinegar. Knead throughout with your hands. Spread on toasts and serve.

SERVES 4 TO 6

(continued)

Duck Liver with Pancetta

Serve this warm paste on warm toast. If you are hardcore in your love for duck products, serve on sliced levain fried in duck fat. Make sure you remove any traces of green bile from the livers, or your paste will taste bitter.

1/4 cup rendered duck fat (page 6)

2 shallots, minced

Salt and freshly ground black pepper

2 to 3 garlic cloves, minced

2 thyme sprigs , leaves picked and chopped

3 tablespoons dry sherry

4 ounces pancetta, diced small

1 tablespoon chopped Italian parsley

8 duck livers, veins and bile sack removed

2 tablespoons capers, rinsed well
and chopped

1 tablespoon sherry vinegar

Heat 2 tablespoons of the duck fat in a heavy-bottomed sauté pan. Sauté the shallots until golden, season with salt and pepper, then add the garlic, thyme, and sherry. Cook for a minute, then transfer to a bowl.

Cook the pancetta in the same pan until it is just cooked. Don't let it get too crispy. Add the pancetta and its fat, the parsley, and capers to the bowl. Heat the remaining fat in the pan. Pat the livers dry with a towel, then season with salt and pepper. Cook over medium heat, turning once until the livers are just cooked, about 1 1/2 minutes per side. Test one liver before cooking them all. You want them to remain pink in the center, and they will continue to cook a bit after you remove them from the pan. Transfer the livers to a plate to cool. When cool enough to handle, dice the livers and mix with the remaining ingredients. Adjust the seasoning with salt, pepper, and sherry vinegar. Serve warm or at room temperature.

SERVES 8

Smoked Duck Breasts

Smoking duck breasts is easy if you don't let the fire get the best of you. One might think that building a fire is easy. I think it is, but it has intimidated most cooks I've seen come through the restaurant. I've seen staff standing around the smoker, blowing on the fire and fanning it, discussing the best way to get it going, as the initial flames die down and the coals grow cold.

Using lighter fluid to start or fuel the fire is not an option. It makes the food taste like, well, lighter fluid. To build a respectable fire, twist up several sheets of newspaper and put them in the bottom of your smoker or grill. Find some small dry sticks out in the yard, or break up some wood from a packing crate. Arrange the sticks or wood pieces on top of the newspaper. Put some small coals on top of the sticks or wood. Light the newspaper confidently and walk away. Don't stand there looking at it.

When the coals are gray, scatter some soaked apple wood chips over them. Put the duck breasts on the grill, skin side down. If the fire is too hot the fat will drip into the it, causing the fire to flame up and blacken the breasts. It's smart to put a metal bowl or something below the breasts to prevent flare-ups.

Smoke the breasts for about 40 minutes, or until they are just cooked through, scattering additional wood chips over the coals as necessary. The cooking time will depend on the intensity of your fire. Check the breasts after they have been smoking for 20 minutes, and then again 20 minutes later. Ideally, they will smoke slowly and evenly in 40 minutes. If they cook more quickly, they won't have much smoke flavor.

PORK CHOPS with Apples and Escarole

We are surrounded by multitudes of multitalented apples. It's fun to experiment with different varieties for this dish, as long as they're crisp and tart enough to play off the sweetness of the pork. I love to brown meats, but pork chops are one cut I no longer brown: the meat seizes and toughens. At the restaurant we take the whole loin and french it (trim off everything around the bones, leaving the loin intact). This gives us all the benefits of cooking the loin as a roast while still serving it as individual, neatly packaged chops. This recipe is a successful and delicious alternative for packaging similar succulence at home.

4 pork chops, 1$^{1}/_{2}$ inches thick

Salt and freshly ground black pepper

2 tablespoons olive oil

1 shallot, minced

1 thyme sprig

Shot of apple brandy, if available

8 cups veal or dark poultry stock, heated

$^{1}/_{2}$ cup unsweetened apple juice

4 tablespoons butter

3 green apples, unpeeled, cut into thick wedges

$^{1}/_{4}$ cup sugar

1 small red onion, diced

2 small heads escarole, cut into 2-inch pieces

Apple cider vinegar or lemon freshly squeezed juice to taste

If possible, season the chops with salt and pepper the night before serving and refrigerate.

Heat 1 tablespoon of the oil in a small saucepan, then add the shallot and brown lightly. Add the thyme, a splash of brandy, and 2 cups of the stock. Reduce by half, then add another 2 cups stock. Skim the scum frequently. Add the apple juice and continue to reduce. Continue in this fashion until all of the stock has been added. Reduce to a spoon-coating consistency and strain through a fine strainer. Keep warm.

Heat 3 tablespoons of the butter in a sauté pan, then add the apples and sugar. Cook over medium-high heat for about 10 minutes, or until the apples are thoroughly caramelized. Set aside. Heat the remaining 1 tablespoon each of butter and of olive oil in a sauté pan. Add the onion and cook until lightly browned. Add the escarole and cook until thoroughly wilted, about 5 minutes. Season with salt and pepper and adjust the acid with the apple cider vinegar.

Half an hour before serving, preheat the oven to 325°. Arrange the pork chops in a baking pan or a baking dish. Bake until just done, about 20 minutes. Let the chops rest for 10 minutes in a warm place, and then serve with the apples, escarole, and sauce.

SERVES 4

163

NORTHERN HALIBUT
with French Lentils, Caperberries, and Warm Saffron-Tomato Vinaigrette

Halibut is a great fish. We count ourselves blessed to be supplied by Paul Johnson at Monterey Fish Market. Paul brings us the greatest of the halibut: Northern halibut from Alaska, alabaster in color, peerless in quality. It's a big fish from very deep, cold water, a firm-fleshed beauty that cooks up gloriously. It is both delicate and flavorful, never bland or insipid and unlikely to become repetitious. It marries well, it's never fishy in an unbecoming way, and it's flaky without being dry. I find it perfect. You can substitute sea bass, a local halibut, or even petrale in this dish. The rule of thumb is to buy the best and freshest fish available. The best coating for pan searing (quick frying in a small amount of oil) is unequivocally semolina. It's the secret ingredient that every lover of things crispy needs in the arsenal.

4 portions Northern halibut, 5 ounces each
Salt and freshly ground black pepper

LENTILS
2 tablespoons olive oil
1/2 onion, diced
1 carrot, peeled and diced
1 celery stalk, diced
2 garlic cloves, minced
2 cups French lentils
2 thyme sprigs
1 bay leaf
4 cups chicken stock or water
Salt and freshly ground black pepper
2 tablespoons chopped Italian parsley

SAFFRON-TOMATO VINAIGRETTE
1 shallot, minced
1/4 to 1/2 cup white wine vinegar
1 thyme sprig
Pinch of saffron threads, minced
1 cup virgin olive oil
1 garlic clove, minced
2 tomatoes, peeled, seeded, and diced
Salt and freshly ground pepper

—––

4 handfuls pea sprouts
3/4 cup caperberries, soaked in water
    for 20 minutes and drained

TO PREPARE THE FISH:

Season the fish with salt and pepper and refrigerate until ready to cook.

TO PREPARE THE LENTILS:

In a large saucepan, heat the olive oil and sauté the onion, carrot, and celery until just starting to color. Add the garlic, lentils, thyme, bay leaf, and chicken stock. Bring to a boil, then lower the heat and cook for about 20 minutes, or until the lentils are just tender. Season with salt and pepper, add the parsley, and keep warm until ready to serve.

TO PREPARE THE VINAIGRETTE:

Soak the shallot in the vinegar for 20 minutes with the thyme and saffron. Heat the olive oil in a large sauté pan. When the oil is hot, add the garlic and cook for a minute. Before the garlic takes on any color, remove from the heat and add the tomatoes to stop the cooking. Add the vinegar and shallot mixture. Season with salt and pepper.

TO BAKE THE FISH AND SERVE:

Preheat the oven to 425°. Place the fish in a small baking pan and bake for 6 to 10 minutes, depending on the thickness of the fish, or until just cooked. Dress the pea sprouts in a little warm vinaigrette. Serve the fish on a small mound of lentils with the pea sprouts. Dress the fish with the vinaigrette. Garnish with the caperberries.

SERVES 4

BAY WOLF 22ND ANNIVERSARY DINNER
September 21, 1997

Baby Spinach and Butter Pear Salad
walnuts and blue cheese

Corn Soup
pickled shrimp and "confetti"

Tomato and Basil Tart
parsley and parmesan salad

———

Grilled Swordfish
*eggplant, gypsy pepper tian
and olive vinaigrette*

Liberty Ranch Duck
*red wine onion flan, grapes
and abc pinot noir sauce*

Roast Suckling Pig Stuffed with Herbs
*shell beans, mushrooms
and pancetta*

———

Last Chance Peach Tart
vanilla ice cream

Apple Galette
brandied crème anglaise

Chocolate Mousse Cake
raspberries

CHEF: Lauren Lyle
DESSERTS: Karen Nielsen

MENU BY CHRISTINE TAYLOR

BRAISED DUCK LEGS
with Pinot Noir and Summer Succotash

Duck is not just our gastronomic signature, it's our emotional preference. I prepared this splendid dish several times for the International Pinot Noir Celebration held in Oregon. To take full advantage of the fabulous duck legs, we'd dry-cure them with salt and pepper, juniper, thyme, and local herbs. The attending wine makers would provide me with gallons of Pinot Noir that I'd reduce in gigantic cauldrons. The succotash is an end-of-summer mélange of whatever vegetables are most perfect. Ideally it includes white and yellow corn, little bits of green beans, and shell beans cooked until they're little bundles of bean butter, everything as close as possible to the same size. The finished dish is a most attractive composition of burnished duck, dark wine sauce, and very fresh, brightly colored seasonal succotash.

BRAISED DUCK

4 duck legs

Salt and freshly ground black pepper

1 teaspoon herbes de Provence

3 cups Pinot Noir, heated

SAUCE

1 tablespoon olive oil or rendered duck fat (page 6)

1 shallot, minced

1 thyme sprig

1 bay leaf

8 cups duck or chicken stock, heated

SUCCOTASH

2 cups fresh shell beans, such as lima or cranberry beans

1/2 onion

1 bay leaf

2 thyme sprigs

Salt and freshly ground black pepper

Virgin olive oil

2 tablespoons butter

1 small red onion, diced

Kernels cut from 2 corn ears

2 large handfuls green beans and yellow wax beans, blanched and cut into 1/2-inch lengths

1 garlic clove, minced

Juice of 1 lemon

▃▃▃

2 handfuls arugula

TO PREPARE THE DUCK:

Preheat the oven to 375°. Season the duck legs with salt and pepper and the herbes de Provence. Put the legs in a pan that will just hold them comfortably. Roast for 1 hour, then pour off and reserve any rendered fat. Pour the wine over the legs. It should be just deep enough so that the meat is immersed but the skin is exposed. Cook the legs for 30 more minutes, or until the skin is golden red.

TO PREPARE THE SAUCE:

In a small saucepan, heat the olive oil and cook the shallot until lightly colored. Add the thyme, bay leaf, and 2 cups of the duck stock. Reduce by half, then add 2 more cups of stock. Skim the scum frequently. Continue until all of the stock has been added. Add 1 cup of the braising liquid and reduce to a spoon-coating

(continued)

consistency. Strain through a fine strainer. Keep the sauce warm.

TO PREPARE THE SUCCOTASH:

Cook the shell beans in water to cover with the onion, bay leaf, and thyme for about 25 minutes (or 1 hour if using dried beans), or until tender. Drain and season with salt, pepper, and virgin olive oil while still warm. Heat the butter in a sauté pan. Add the red onion and brown lightly. Add the corn and cook over medium heat until just tender. Add the green and yellow beans and the shell beans. Add the garlic, then season with salt and pepper. Add lemon juice to taste.

TO SERVE:

Dress the arugula in a little of the reserved duck fat. Serve the braised legs with some of the sauce spooned over and the succotash and arugula on the side.

SERVES 4

20TH
anniversary

Smoked duck ravioli in a rich duck broth

Sonoma County foie gras
with Silver Queen corn fritter, pancetta, and port

Stuffed calamari with shrimp,
shiitake mushrooms, and tomato vinaigrette

•

Sautéed Northern halibut with
crisp potato wrap and truffled vegetable ragout

Liberty Ranch duck with French Butter pears
and celery root galette

Grilled lamb loin with wild mushroom
"tambourine" and Provençal tomatoes

•

Last-chance peach "Pavlova"
with toasted almond ice cream

Mostly plum soup with ginger crème brûlée

Triple chocolate profiteroles
with mocha sauce and berries

September 1995

BAY WOLF MENU

CHEF: JOE NOUHAN

MENU BY CHRISTINE TAYLOR

BLACKBERRY AND FIG TART

In the fall, blackberries are full of sugar and as fat as your thumb. Abundant sun and early rain produce berries that are juicy and fragrant. These luscious berries and sweet, creamy fall figs form a simple and tasty tart. My ideal honey for this tart would be orange flower.

1 recipe Tart dough (page 39)

Egg wash of 1 egg, pinch of salt, and a little heavy whipping cream

1 pint full-flavored fresh blackberries

1 quart figs, quartered

1/4 teaspoon finely chopped lemon zest

1/4 cup light-flavored honey, such as orange flower honey

Sugar for dusting

Whipped cream

Roll half of the tart dough into a 12-inch round. Reserve the other half of the dough for another use. Place the tart dough on a parchment-lined baking sheet. Brush with egg wash out to the edge. Mix the berries, figs, zest, and honey. Place in the center of the tart dough, keeping at least a 2-inch edge all the way around the tart. Fold this edge toward the center to form a rim, crimping if needed. Brush this edge with egg wash and then dust the entire tart with sugar. Refrigerate until the dough is firm. Preheat the oven to 400°. Bake the tart for 20 to 30 minutes, or until the edge is light brown and the fruit has released some of its liquid. Serve warm with whipped cream.

MAKES ONE 10-INCH TART

EARL AT WORK.

169

BROWN BUTTER AND WALNUT CAKE with Poached Pears and Blue Cheese

We live in a most hospitable place for walnuts, almonds, and hazelnuts and consider ourselves fortunate to have access to this bounty. A walnut grove is a lovely thing: quiet, with a unique filtered light and an evocative fragrance. This dessert showcases the flavor and texture of these nuts. Poaching pears is not difficult, but it does take some time. The slower the pears are poached, the creamier their texture. The wine used in the poaching will affect the taste. For this recipe I like a slightly dry wine to provide a pleasing contrast to the creaminess of the pears and blue cheese.

POACHED PEARS

4 medium Bosc, Anjou, Bartlett, or French butter pears (or a combination of these varieties), firm and slightly green

2 bottles dry white wine

3 or 4 white peppercorns

3 cups granulated sugar

Zest of 1 lemon, removed in strips

BROWN BUTTER AND WALNUT CAKE

3/4 cup sweet, unsalted butter, at room temperature

1 vanilla bean, split

1 cup granulated sugar

6 tablespoons all-purpose flour

3 eggs, separated

1 cup chopped walnuts

BLUE CHEESE TOPPING

4 ounces good-quality blue cheese

1/2 cup sweet, unsalted butter, at room temperature

2 cups powdered sugar (measured and then sifted)

1 teaspoon freshly squeezed lemon juice

TO POACH THE PEARS:

Peel and core the pears. Combine the wine, peppercorns, sugar, and zest in a large pot. Bring to a boil and reduce the flame to very low. Add the pears. Cover the pears with a cloth or cheesecloth and place a plate or bowl on top to weight them down. You want to keep the pears submerged in the poaching liquid. Cook for about 2 hours over low heat, or until the pears are soft when pierced with a knife. Remove the pears from the poaching liquid, and place them in a container that will hold the pears and enough of the poaching liquid to cover. Place in the refrigerator and let cool. Cut the pears in half, slice thinly, and fan.

TO PREPARE THE CAKE:

Butter an 8-inch square baking pan and line with parchment. Preheat the oven to 350°. Place the butter and vanilla bean in a saucepan and brown the butter. It will smoke and look burnt, but it is just browning. Burnt butter takes on a wonderful aroma and a nutty, luscious taste. Strain it into a bowl and let cool, but do not let it become cold and harden. When cool, add 3/4 cup of the sugar and mix in the flour, yolks, and walnuts. In a clean bowl, whip the egg whites until stiff and add the remaining 1/4 cup sugar. Continue to whip until all of the sugar is absorbed into the whites. Fold into the butter mixture and pour into the prepared pan. Bake for 45 to 50 minutes, or until the cake springs back when pressed. Cool in the pan on a cake rack.

TO PREPARE THE TOPPING:

Place the cheese and butter in the bowl of an electric mixer fitted with the paddle attachment and beat together until smooth. Add the sugar and beat until well mixed. Add the lemon juice and mix well.

TO SERVE:

Cut the cake into squares and top each with a large scoop of topping and a pear fan.

MAKES ONE 8-INCH SQUARE CAKE

ARTWORK BY RUPERT GARCIA

CHOCOLATE PUDDLE CAKE
with Crème Anglaise

These individual bittersweet chocolate cakes ooze out a molten chocolate center when cut open at the table. The preparation is not difficult but is a little involved. It thoroughly repays the effort. For a dinner party, prepare the cakes in advance, chill them, and then bake them while you're clearing the table and preparing your coffee and brandies.

GANACHE

    4 ounces bittersweet chocolate

    1/4 cup heavy whipping cream

CRÈME ANGLAISE

    2 cups whole milk

    1/2 vanilla bean, split

    8 egg yolks

    1/4 cup sugar

CAKES

    4 ounces bittersweet chocolate

    1/4 cup sweet, unsalted butter

    6 whole eggs, separated

    1 cup sugar

    1/2 cup unsweetened cocoa powder, plus extra for dusting ramekins

TO PREPARE THE GANACHE:

Chop the chocolate into small pieces. Heat the cream and pour it over the chocolate, mixing until the chocolate is melted. Cover with plastic wrap and refrigerate until firm.

TO PREPARE THE CRÈME ANGLAISE:

Heat the milk with the vanilla bean. Scrape the inside of the vanilla bean pod, adding the scrapings to the milk. Return the bean to the milk. Mix the yolks with the sugar. Add a little of the hot milk to the egg mixture to warm the yolks, then add the rest of the milk and mix thoroughly. Return the mixture to the saucepan and cook over low heat for about 10 minutes, or until it thickens. Remove from the heat and strain into a stainless steel bowl. Set the bowl over a bowl of ice to cool, stirring until cold. Refrigerate until ready to use. Crème anglaise can be stored for up to 2 days.

TO PREPARE THE CAKES:

Preheat the oven to 400°. Melt the chocolate and butter in the top of a double boiler over simmering water. Beat the yolks with 1/2 cup of the sugar until light and fluffy. Fold into the chocolate mixture, then fold in the 1/2 cup cocoa powder. Whip the egg whites until stiff. Add the remaining 1/2 cup sugar and whip until the sugar is incorporated. Fold into the chocolate mixture.

Butter 8 small cake molds or 4-ounce ramekins, then dust each with the extra cocoa powder. Form the ganache into 8 small balls. Fill the molds half full of cake batter. Place a ball of ganache in the center and fill to the top with cake batter. Bake for 12 to 15 minutes. The tops will be crusted and a little cracked. Unmold while hot onto plates and serve with the crème anglaise.

MAKES 8 CAKES

173

RASPBERRY–WHITE CHOCOLATE CHARLOTTE with Raspberry Zinfandel Sauce

A charlotte can be formed in a round springform pan or in the classic, slightly slope-sided charlotte mold, either of which makes a very attractive presentation. It might be lined with cookies or a cake baked for the occasion or one left over from the previous day. Although charlottes are often composed with cooked fruit purées and baked, for this recipe the mold is simply lined with homemade or purchased ladyfingers and filled with a tender white chocolate mousse. Use a young, inexpensive Zinfandel and the large, sweet raspberries of late summer.

LADYFINGERS
10 eggs, separated
1/2 teaspoon vanilla extract
1 cup sugar
3/4 cup plus 2 tablespoons sifted all-purpose flour
Sifted powdered sugar for dusting

WHITE CHOCOLATE MOUSSE
1/4 cup plus 1/3 cup water
1 tablespoon powdered gelatin
1 tablespoon freshly squeezed lemon juice
5 egg yolks
1/3 cup water
1/3 cup sugar
5 ounces white chocolate
1 1/2 cups heavy whipping cream, whipped until stiff

RASPBERRY ZINFANDEL SAUCE
2 cups good Zinfandel
3/4 cup sugar
3 half-pint fresh, plump raspberries

TO PREPARE THE LADYFINGERS:

Line a baking sheet with parchment. Preheat the oven to 350°. Beat the yolks, vanilla, and 1/2 cup of the sugar until light and fluffy. Fold in the flour and mix well. Whip the whites until stiff. Fold the whites into the yolk mixture. Beat in the remaining 1/2 cup sugar until well combined. Place in a piping bag fitted with a plain tip and pipe the batter into 2-inch-long sticks about 1/8 inch apart. When all the sticks are piped, dust the entire sheet with powdered sugar and bake for 12 to 15 minutes, or until light golden brown. Let cool and remove from the parchment. Cut one of the tips off each of the ladyfingers. Line the sides of a parchment-lined 10-inch springform pan with the ladyfingers, placing them upright with the cut edge down. Place the remaining ladyfingers on the bottom of the pan in one layer.

TO PREPARE THE MOUSSE:

Place 1/4 cup water in a small stainless steel bowl and sprinkle the gelatin over it. Let it absorb the water. Add the lemon juice. In a large stainless steel bowl, combine the yolks,

1/3 cup water, and sugar. Place over a pot of boiling water and whip the yolk mixture until doubled in size. Set over a bowl of ice and continue to beat until the mixture is about body temperature. Set the gelatin mixture over the hot water and stir until it melts. Add to the egg mixture, mixing well.

Melt the chocolate in the top of a double boiler over low heat. Fold the melted chocolate into the egg mixture. This will cause the eggs to deflate, but don't be alarmed. Fold in the whipped cream and pour the mixture into the pan containing the ladyfingers. Refrigerate until firm, about 1 hour.

TO PREPARE THE SAUCE:

Mix together the wine and sugar. Add 1/2 cup of the raspberries and crush them into sauce, using the back of a large spoon. Let this mixture sit for 15 to 20 minutes. Strain it through a fine strainer and discard the raspberry pulp. Coat the remaining berries with the sauce. Let marinate for 10 to 15 minutes.

TO SERVE:

Remove the rim from the charlotte if using a springform pan; invert, if using a charlotte pan. Spoon the marinated berries on top of the set mousse. Reserve some of the berry liquid to sauce each slice when served.

SERVES 12

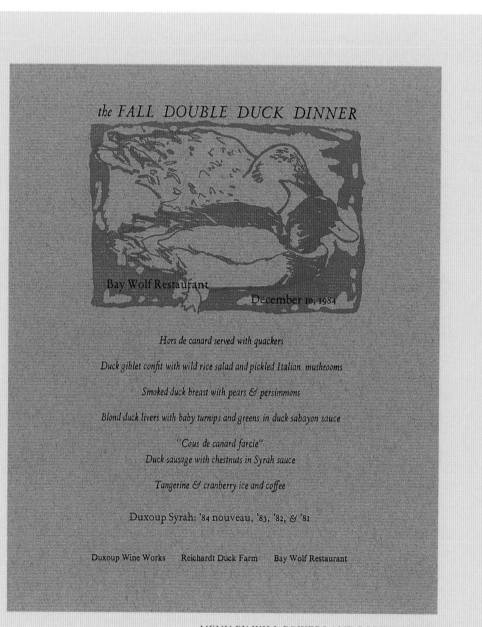

MENU BY WILL POWERS AND ROBIN CHERIN

Gizzards and Grapes

October

I know of no two foods in a more advanced state of ideal empathy than gizzards and grapes. The word "felicitous" comes to mind. Marrying the voluptuousness, the richness of a duck gizzard confit, its depth of flavor, the richly burnished look of it with the perfect foil of tart, crisp, wet green grapes is the embodiment of two of my fiercest admonitions: that the whole is greater than the sum of its parts and that no part of an animal, specifically a duck, should ever be wasted.

We transform the gizzards from the ducks we receive into confit or, as in France, shave them thinly and spread them around little walnut-laced salads in the style of Perigord. Duck gizzard confit is ancient in look and taste. When gizzards are cooked slowly in flavored duck fat, they fulfill their destiny as the essence of the duck, the often-unloved organ through which all of the duck's life passes. This combination finds its way onto appetizer plates that might easily include duck rillettes or flan on crisp toasts with chopped cornichons and capers and a delicate fan of cured, house-smoked duck breast.

Ducks lend themselves so readily to many and varied uses. Duck eggs are finer in texture than chicken eggs and are beloved by pastry cooks for producing finer-textured doughs. Duck egg custards are unsurpassably velvety. Duck fat is the most delectable medium in which to fry potatoes or sauté vegetables. We use enormous quantities of duck fat, rendering a couple of gallons a week on average.

We've used every part of the bird: feet, skin, neck, carcass, every last morsel and mouthful, all transformed into something delicate and edible. We made turkey testicle tempura once and decided that weird and good aren't necessarily interchangeable terms in the kitchen, but a duck neck used as a sausage casing, stuffed with a forcemeat and poached in a red-wine reduction sauce, combines frugality with delectability.

In the fall, the grape harvest provides us with access to real and wonderful grapes. I seek out slightly underripe Chardonnays or Rieslings, ones that are big enough and, ideally, seedless. Red Flames possess the requisite sweetness.

Another superb and unexpected combination is peaches with green almonds from that time of the year when the almonds haven't quite hardened inside the shell and you can extract and eat them. A toasted almond with any sherry that happens to be in your mouth is more complex than if you eat just the almond: they have an incredible affinity for each other, and the whole thing takes off in your mouth.

I've watched people cleaning spinach and discarding the stems, and I think, "You can eat that. In France, they'd make a tart with it." Everything that's grown for our table is labor-intensive and has to be planted, watered, weeded, and harvested, often by hand. No sprig of thyme deserves to end its life as a discarded stick of decoration. If you can't eat it, it doesn't belong on the plate.

Lauren has entered into my fanatical aversion to waste. October is the month in which she rescues olives from the neighbors' gardens and takes them home to cure. She forages in the East Bay hills for chanterelles, often with her coworkers in tow. She writes informed, amusing, vital menu notes to the staff. They aren't strict recipes; they are simple sentences, with context and ingredient proportions and a lot of conversation between one human being and another. She can communicate her passion, her knowledge, her voice, her soul. The soul of a restaurant is held in trust by a committed staff. She can inspire and enhance that commitment.

GIZZARDS AND GRAPES

This is not a salad. It is not exactly a dish. It is a small but beloved component of our "worship duck in all of its forms" appetizer platter (see the photo on page 160). While we were in the final planning stages of one of the annual Pinot Noir dinners, I was looking around the walk-in, searching for something felicitous to accompany duck gizzard. Thinking, "gizzards and what?" Red Flame seedless grapes caught my eye and my fancy: gizzards and grapes it will be. It's delicious.

8 ounces duck gizzard confit, or whatever you have from making duck confit (page 160)

8 ounces Red Flame seedless grapes, halved

Salt and freshly ground black pepper

A few drops of sherry vinegar

A few drops of warm duck fat from the confit

1 teaspoon finely chopped Italian parsley

Trim the gizzards of any tough, silvery skin, then slice them across the grain as thinly as possible. Toss with the grapes. Season with salt and pepper. Splash a little vinegar, fat, and parsley over the mixture and serve.

SERVES 8 TO 10

A high-minded spirit informs the essentials and the details of BayWolf: the delicious, assured food; the congenial, honest service; the art-driven décor. Longtime patrons, many of whom live nearby, take obvious pleasure in having such a superb neighborhood spot. That's what BayWolf reminds me of — a charming, little chef-run place that happens to seat more than a hundred and has been open for two and a half decades.

— PATRICIA UNTERMAN

TUSCAN MINESTRONE
with Black Kale and Chickpeas

Soup should be salted as you go along. Salting only at the end is like salting only the outside of the soup. Layering and salting gradually produces a multidimensional dish. That is what we're looking for. This soup is best if it is made at least one day in advance. It takes a while to cook and will be drastically compromised if you try to make it quickly.

3 tablespoons olive oil

1/2 cup diced pancetta

2 onions, diced

1 carrot, peeled and diced

2 celery stalks, diced

1 small fennel bulb, diced

1 bunch purple kale, chopped

1 bay leaf

An herb bundle containing thyme, savory, and oregano

2 salt-packed anchovies, filleted, rinsed, and chopped

2 to 3 tablespoons chopped garlic

1 tablespoon tomato paste

10 cups poultry stock, heated

1 cup cooked chickpeas

3 dried porcini mushrooms

1/4 teaspoon ground cinnamon

Sherry vinegar to taste

2 tablespoons chopped Italian parsley

Shaved Parmesan cheese

Heat the oil with the pancetta in a large, heavy-bottomed pot over medium-high heat. Cook gently until the pancetta is light brown but not crispy. Add the onions and cook over medium heat for about 15 minutes, or until lightly browned. During this cooking time, scrape the bottom of the pan for the caramelized bits. These bits are what will make your soup really good. Don't burn them. Add the carrot and cook for 10 minutes more, scraping occasionally, then cook the celery for 10 minutes, then the fennel for 10 minutes. The vegetables will shrink down quite a bit. Add the kale, bay leaf, and herbs, and cook until the kale has wilted. Add the anchovies and garlic and sweat some more. Add the tomato paste and half the stock. Bring to a boil, then reduce to a simmer.

Purée the chickpeas with the remaining stock, and then add to the soup. Boil the dried mushrooms with some of the soup in a separate pot until tender. Purée thoroughly and add back to the soup. Simmer for 20 minutes. Add the cinnamon, then simmer for another 20 minutes. Adjust the seasoning and finish with vinegar. Remove the herb bundle.

Just before serving, stir in the parsley. Garnish each bowl with shaved Parmesan.

SERVES 8 TO 10

LITTLE MUSHROOM TARTS

Prepare these tarts as part of an appetizer platter. They reheat well the same day they are prepared, but not beyond that. If you need a million of them, assemble them the day before, then bake them the day you need them.

MUSHROOM FILLING

4 ounces shiitake mushrooms, diced

8 ounces domestic mushrooms, diced

3 tablespoons butter

2 tablespoons olive oil

Salt and freshly ground black pepper

1 small onion, minced

2 garlic cloves, minced

Sherry vinegar to taste

2 teaspoons chopped Italian parsley

SAVORY TART DOUGH

6 tablespoons butter

1 cup all-purpose flour

Pinch of salt

1/4 cup plus 1 to 2 tablespoons cold water

Egg wash of 1 egg and pinch of salt

TO PREPARE THE FILLING:

Cook the mushrooms separately in a mixture of a scant spoonful each of butter and olive oil. Cook the shiitakes over medium-high heat until just browned, and then remove from the heat. Start the domestic mushrooms over high heat so they will release and reabsorb their juices, then lower the heat and cook slowly until they are dark brown and intense. Season the mushrooms well. Cool briefly. Chop finely. In one of the mushroom pans, caramelize the onion in 1 tablespoon of the butter. Just before removing the pan from the heat, add the garlic and deglaze the pan with the vinegar. Add the parsley and mix in the mushrooms. Adjust the seasoning; the mushrooms should be slightly salty and acidic so that they will be able to stand up to the pastry. Refrigerate. The tarts are much simpler to assemble if the filling is cold.

TO PREPARE THE DOUGH:

Place the flour on a cutting board. Dice the butter into cubes and sprinkle it over the flour with the salt. Chop finely with a knife, as you would parsley, but make sure that the butter is not completely obliterated. We want little chunks here and there. Pour some of the water over it and gently push the dough with the heel of your hand. Use just enough water to bring the dough together, then wrap tightly in plastic and refrigerate for 15 to 20 minutes.

TO ASSEMBLE THE TARTS:

Roll the dough out thinly on a floured surface to a 1/4- to 1/8-inch thickness. Brush half the dough with egg wash. Form the mushroom filling into 12 little balls, and line them up 1 inch apart on the egg-washed side of the dough, as though you were assembling ravioli. Fold the vacant side of the dough over the rows of filling, and gently press down around each mushroom mound. Make sure there is a good seal. Use a round or scalloped cookie cutter to cut out the tarts. The tarts can be prepared ahead to this point and refrigerated, covered with plastic wrap.

Bake in a preheated 375° to 400° oven for 15 to 20 minutes. The last 5 minutes of cooking, brush again with egg wash. The tops of the tarts should be golden brown. Serve warm.

MAKES 12 TARTS

CELERY ROOT SALAD

This salad is all about texture. It is very important that you cut the roots carefully so that they are uniform in size. Think angel hair while cutting. This salad is also delicious with a little thinly sliced and julienned prosciutto.

2 large celery roots
Juice of 1 lemon
Salt
Crème fraîche (page 65)
Thinly sliced chives
Ground white pepper

Peel the celery roots with a knife, being sure to remove all of the brown and fibrous parts. Using a mandoline or a very sharp knife, cut the roots into very thin julienne. Put the celery root in a bowl and squeeze the lemon juice over it. Season with salt and let sit for 30 minutes, squeezing it hard every once in a while. Drain off the excess lemon juice and taste. If you find the celery root excessively acidic, give it a quick rinse. Squeeze out all of the excess liquid from the roots, then add a couple of spoonfuls of crème fraîche and some tiny chive rounds. Adjust the seasoning with salt and white pepper.

SERVES 6

FENNEL SALAD

This lightly pickled salad provides a fresh, crunchy contrast to an antipasto platter composed of smoked mussels, fried arancini, *and olive or fava bean toasts.*

3 fennel bulbs
Juice of 2 lemons, Eureka or Meyer, strained
Salt
Pinch of sugar
Julienned mint leaves (optional)

With a mandoline or sharp knife, cut the fennel crosswise paper-thin. Put it in a bowl with the juice, salt, and sugar. Squeeze the fennel with your hand. then let it sit for 20 minutes. Pour off any excess lemon juice and adjust the salt. If the fennel is too acidic due to particularly juicy lemons, give it a quick rinse in cold water. If you like, julienne a few mint leaves and toss into the fennel.

SERVES 6 TO 8

185

ARANCINI

Traditionally, this is a little snack made from leftover risotto. Arancini is Italian for "little oranges," which is what these little saffron rice balls closely resemble. They are tiny balls stuffed with a nugget of cheese and rolled in breadcrumbs before frying. If you are preparing huge quantities for a party, you can fry them an hour or so ahead of time, then pop them back into a hot oven a few minutes before serving. Never allow yourself to be in the midst of a massive frying project during a party.

2 tablespoons butter

1 tablespoon olive oil

1/2 onion, minced

1 cup Arborio rice

1/4 cup dry white wine

Salt and freshly ground black pepper

4 cups chicken stock, heated

1/4 cup freshly grated Parmesan cheese

1/2 cup finely diced fontina cheese

1/2 cup all-purpose flour

2 eggs, lightly beaten

1 cup dried breadcrumbs

Peanut oil 3 inches deep for frying

Lemon wedges

Aioli (page 48)

Heat the butter in a pot with the olive oil. Sweat the onion until it is translucent, then add the rice. Fry the rice for a minute, stirring constantly. Add the white wine and lower the heat. Season the rice with salt and pepper, and add 1 cup of the chicken stock, stirring occasionally. When the rice has absorbed almost all of the stock, add another cup. Continue in this fashion until all of the stock is incorporated and the rice is tender. If you run out of stock, use a little hot water. Stir in the Parmesan cheese and cool. Check the seasoning, then form the mixture into balls, using 2 to 3 tablespoons of the mixture for each ball. Stuff a square of fontina into the center of each ball. Assemble all of the balls and refrigerate.

Place the flour, whisked eggs, and breadcrumbs in three separate, shallow dishes. Roll the balls first in the flour, then in the egg, and then in the breadcrumbs. Put them on a baking sheet and refrigerate until ready to fry. The arancini will fry up best if they are chilled for a few hours. Fry the balls in 3 inches of peanut oil at 365° until golden. Serve with lemon wedges and aioli.

MAKES 15 ARANCINI

FENNEL AND MUSHROOM SALAD

Serve this salad on its own as an appetizer with a few shavings of Parmesan cheese or as a component of an antipasto platter. We usually use portobello mushrooms, but you can use any kind of wild or cultivated mushroom.

2 small fennel bulbs

2 lemons

Salt and freshly ground black pepper

Pinch of sugar

2 tablespoons olive oil

1 large portobello mushroom, whole, stem removed

Virgin olive oil

1 handful Italian parsley leaves

White truffle oil for drizzling

TO PREPARE THE FENNEL:

With a sharp knife or mandoline, cut the fennel crosswise into almost paper-thin strips. Put it in a bowl and add the juice of 1 of the lemons. Season with salt, pepper, and sugar. Squeeze the fennel a bit to help it absorb the lemon juice. Let it sit for 25 minutes to pickle lightly.

TO PREPARE THE MUSHROOMS:

Preheat the oven to 350°. Heat the olive oil in a small ovenproof sauté pan over medium-high heat. Add the mushroom cap and brown on both sides. Season with salt and pepper. Do not pour off any liquid that is released; it is the good stuff. Put the pan in the oven and cook for another 15 minutes, or until the mushroom has softened and shrunk quite a bit. Cool and cut the mushroom in half, then cut each half into slivers as thin as you can. Put in a bowl and squeeze the juice of the remaining lemon over it. Drizzle with a little virgin olive oil. Taste and adjust seasoning.

TO SERVE:

Right before serving, squeeze off any excess liquid from the fennel and toss with the mushroom and parsley. Toss gently. If the mushrooms are excessively wet, they will tint the fennel brown. Arrange on plates and drizzle with a little white truffle oil.

SERVES 4 TO 6

187

BUCKWHEAT FETTUCCINE
with Beets and Their Greens, Walnuts, and Crème Fraîche

This is a dish in which all of the ingredients resonate without any one predominating. Each of the flavors and textures remains just below the surface: the refined delicacy of the buckwheat, the mild astringency of the beets, the crunch of the walnuts, the slightly elastic softness of the fettuccine, the richness and faint sourness of the crème fraîche binding it all together. It has color and absolute clarity. The flavors are all lined up next to one another and look and taste as if they've always belonged together.

BUCKWHEAT FETTUCCINE

1 1/3 cups all-purpose flour

2/3 cup buckwheat flour

2 eggs

Salt

1 teaspoon olive oil

Semolina flour for dusting

SAUCE

4 medium beets and their greens, preferably Chioggias of different colors

1 tablespoon olive oil

1/2 red onion, julienned

Salt and freshly ground black pepper

2 teaspoons minced garlic

2 teaspoons filleted, rinsed, and minced salt-packed anchovies

Splash of sherry vinegar

1/2 cup crème fraîche (page 65)

1 cup walnuts, toasted and roughly chopped

Finely chopped zest of 2 lemons

1/2 teaspoon chopped rosemary leaves

1 cup Italian parsley leaves

1/4 cup fine dried breadcrumbs, toasted and mixed with a little olive oil

TO PREPARE THE PASTA:

Mix the flours on a table, gather into a mound, and form a well in the center. Crack the eggs into the well, and add a pinch of salt and olive oil. Have a small cup of water on hand to moisten the dough if necessary. Mix the eggs in the well with a fork and slowly incorporate the flour. Have a pastry scraper on hand in case the eggs get away. Add a little water if the dough seems excessively dry. Knead the dough until it is elastic, put it in a plastic bag, and let it rest for at least 25 minutes. If your dough seems a bit dry, the time in the bag should help make it moist again. Roll the dough in a pasta machine until it is thin, but not paper-thin, and cut into fettuccine noodles. If you won't be cooking your pasta for a while, dust it with semolina flour; this will keep the noodles from sticking together and you from performing hara-kiri.

TO PREPARE THE BEETS:

Preheat the oven to 375°. Cut the greens from the beets, and place the beets in a small pan with 1/2 inch of water; cover. Roast in the oven, checking after 45 minutes. The flesh should be easily pierced with a paring knife and the skins loose to the touch. When cool enough to handle, peel and cut into thin rounds. Wash the beet greens thoroughly and remove their stems. Tear the greens into pieces. Unless the beets are very young and tender, the greens will require longer cooking than the remaining pasta ingredients. If this is the case, blanch them until they are tender and set aside.

TO ASSEMBLE THE PASTA:

Boil the pasta in a large quantity of boiling salted water, testing after 60 seconds. Meanwhile, heat the oil in a large sauté pan over a hot fire. Add the onion and cook until soft, translucent, and just beginning to brown. Season with salt and pepper. Add the garlic, anchovy, vinegar, and the beets (if you are using red beets exclusively, toss them into the pasta carefully; otherwise, they will tint the pasta bubble-gum pink) and their greens with any juices that have accumulated. If there is a lot of liquid in the pan (there shouldn't be) reduce it down further. Turn off the heat. Add the just-drained noodles (don't rinse them), crème fraîche, walnuts, zest, rosemary, and parsley and toss together. Check the seasoning and acid. Arrange on plates and sprinkle with breadcrumbs.

SERVES 4 TO 6

TWENTY-THIRD ANNIVERSARY BAY WOLF

DOUBLE DUCK DINNER

DUCK plate
  with smoked DUCK breast, DUCK liver crostini, DUCK confit and quackers

Little DUCK lasagna

Roast DUCK leg
  with double corn flan

Poached quince galette
  with Riesling (DUCK egg) sabayon

✳WINES: BAY WOLF BIANCO AND ATAVISTIC THRILL

$55   *chef: Lauren Lyle   dessert chef: G. Earl Darny   October 1998*

MENU BY CHRISTINE TAYLOR

189

PAPPARDELLE
with Rabbit, Pancetta, and Red Wine

The time of year I most like to prepare rabbits is in the fall. They're nice and fat because they've been eating nuts and shoring themselves up for the winter. Whole rabbits can be tedious to eat, but flavorfully braised bits of rabbit prepared with something rich and spicy and salty (like Hobbs prosciutto) and tossed with pappardelle can be an ideal autumn entrée. Rabbit meat is extremely lean, and can be unforgiving if it is even slightly overcooked. No braise should ever cook at a temperature above 350°, but for rabbit I take it even lower, to 325°. Pasta always has to be hot: the bowl, the plate, everything. In Italy you learn how to do it right: hot hot hot.

PAPPARDELLE

2 cups all-purpose flour

2 whole eggs

2 egg yolks

Salt

Virgin olive oil

BRAISED RABBIT

1 rabbit

Salt and freshly ground pepper

2 tablespoons olive oil

4 ounces pancetta, diced

1 carrot, peeled and diced

2 small celery stalks, diced

1 yellow onion, diced

1 tablespoon butter

3 garlic cloves, chopped

2 bay leaves

2 juniper berries

5 thyme sprigs

1 bottle dry red wine, heated

1 cup rich duck or chicken stock, heated

1 onion, diced

1 tablespoon olive oil

Sherry vinegar to taste

1 tablespoon chopped Italian parsley

1/4 to 1/2 cup freshly grated Parmesan cheese

1 tablespoon butter

TO PREPARE THE PAPPARDELLE:

Prepare the pasta dough according to the directions for fettuccine on page 188. Let the dough rest in a plastic bag for at least 30 minutes. Roll the dough in a pasta machine until it is thin, but not paper-thin, and cut into wide pappardelle noodles. The noodles should not be too thin, or they will be texturally overpowered by the rabbit.

TO BRAISE THE RABBIT:

Preheat the oven to 325°. Cut the rabbit into three parts to separate the loin from the legs and forelegs. Split the back legs in half, but leave all bones attached. Season the meat well with salt and pepper. Brown in 1 tablespoon of the olive oil and set aside. In an ovenproof 9-inch sauté pan, sauté the pancetta, carrot, celery, and onion in the butter and remaining tablespoon of olive oil. Season well and brown lightly. Add the garlic and then remove from the heat. Wrap the bay leaves, juniper berries, and thyme in cheesecloth and add to the veg-

etables. Arrange the 4 rabbit legs on top of the vegetables, then pour the wine and stock over them. Cover with parchment and foil or a tight-fitting lid. Braise until the meat is tender, checking after 45 minutes. Remove the legs, add the loin meat to the pot, cover, and return to the oven for 10 minutes, or until just cooked. Remove the loin meat and reduce the braising liquid by half. Remove the herb bundle. When the meats are cool enough to handle, shred by hand. Do not chop with a knife. Put the meat back into the braising liquid.

TO ASSEMBLE THE PASTA:

Boil the pasta in a large quantity of boiling salted water, testing after 60 seconds. Meanwhile, in a large pan, lightly brown the onion in the oil. Add the rabbit, all of the braising liquid, a splash of vinegar, and the parsley. Toss in the cooked noodles, Parmesan, and butter. Let sit for just a minute so the noodles can absorb the liquid. Divide the pasta among heated plates and serve.

SERVES 4

BRAISED CHICKEN with Spicy Greens

Beautifully braised chicken is one of those defining dishes that reinforce Brillat-Savarin's dictum that "poultry is for the cook what canvas is for a painter." This dish is a staple on our menu. It is never remotely mundane. Leaving the skin exposed to dry heat gives the chicken the desirable crispy skin of a roasted bird. To achieve this effect, cook the chicken on the top rack of your oven. Mashed potatoes play counterpoint.

BRAISED CHICKEN

4 chicken legs and thighs
Salt and freshly ground black pepper
1 carrot, peeled and diced
1 celery stalk, diced
1 onion, diced
1 tablespoon butter
1 tablespoon olive oil
Splash of brandy
2 bay leaves, crumbled
4 garlic cloves, chopped
A few black peppercorns
3 cups chicken stock, heated
1 tablespoon chopped Italian parsley

GREENS

1 onion, diced
1 tablespoon olive oil
1 tablespoon butter
1 bunch rapini or broccoli rabe
1 salt-packed anchovy, filleted, rinsed, and finely minced
2 garlic cloves, finely chopped
Salt and freshly ground black pepper
Ground cayenne pepper
Freshly squeezed lemon juice

TO PREPARE THE CHICKEN:

The day before serving, season the chicken legs well with salt and pepper. Refrigerate overnight.

The next day, preheat the oven to 350°. Sauté the carrot, celery, and onion in the butter and oil. Caramelize lightly, then deglaze the pan with the brandy. Transfer to the bottom of an ovenproof pan that will just hold the chicken legs. Arrange the legs skin side up. Add the bay leaves, garlic, peppercorns, and chicken stock. The bottom half of the meat should be immersed in the liquid, but the skin should be exposed. Braise on the top rack of the oven, checking after 45 minutes, until the meat is tender and the skin crispy.

Before serving, pour off some of the braising liquid with the vegetables. Degrease the liquid and reduce by a third. Taste as it is reducing to ensure that the salt doesn't intensify too much. If it is too salty, add a little plain reduced stock. Finish with the parsley.

TO PREPARE THE GREENS:

Lightly brown the onion in the oil and butter. Chop the greens into manageable pieces and sauté slowly until wilted. Add a little water to prevent sticking if necessary. When the greens are cooked through, add the anchovy and garlic and cook a minute more. Turn off the heat and season with salt, pepper, cayenne, and lemon juice.

Serve the braised chicken with the greens.

SERVES 4

193

CONCORD GRAPE, CORN, AND PECAN TART with Vanilla Ice Cream and Grape Compote

This is one of my great favorites. It is something of a cross between a sweet and a savory, making it ideal for odd times of the day (including a late breakfast or a midnight snack). Concord grapes are one of the few grape varieties indigenous to the United States, and they are an object of particular fondness to those of us in California who have lived with, valued, and been stained by them every fall of our lives. The use of fresh corn in the dough may seem strange at first glance, but its sweetness is a counterpoint to the slight bitterness of the nuts and the juicy tartness of the grapes.

CORN TART DOUGH

1/2 cup boiling water

3/4 cup fine cornmeal

1/2 cup fresh corn kernels

1/4 cup sour cream

1 cup all-purpose flour

1/4 teaspoon baking soda

1/2 cup sweet, unsalted butter, at room temperature

2 tablespoons sugar

1 egg

TOPPING

1/2 cup sweet, unsalted butter

3/4 cup sugar

2 egg yolks

1/4 cup all-purpose flour

1 1/4 cups pecans, finely ground

1/8 teaspoon ground nutmeg

1 pound firm, or red or green seedless grapes, or Concord grapes (seeds removed)

GRAPE COMPOTE

3/4 cup water

3/4 cup sugar

3 cups halved seedless grapes

1/2 cup sweet, unsalted butter, at room temperature

2 tablespoons grappa or brandy

___

Ice cream (page 54), omitting the strawberry purée

TO PREPARE THE DOUGH:

Pour the boiling water over the cornmeal and corn, mixing well. Add the sour cream. Mix well and let cool. Sift the flour with the baking soda. Cream the butter with the sugar. Add the egg and mix well. Beat in the corn mixture, and then add the flour mixture. The dough will be very sticky. Wrap in plastic wrap and refrigerate for 1 hour. Roll out on a floured surface into a 12- to 14-inch round. Place on a parchment-lined baking sheet. Refrigerate while you prepare the topping.

TO PREPARE THE TOPPING:

Beat the butter with the sugar until light and fluffy. Beat in the egg yolks, then the flour, pecans, and nutmeg. Spread over the disk of corn dough, leaving ½ inch around the edge. Stud the top of the tart with grapes, covering it to the edges. Refrigerate until firm.

Preheat the oven to 400°. Bake for 15 minutes, or until light golden brown. Let cool slightly before serving.

TO PREPARE THE COMPOTE:

Bring the water and sugar to a boil in a large saucepan. Add the grapes and return to a boil. Add the butter in little chunks, stirring to incorporate. When all of the butter is incorporated, remove from the heat and add the grappa. The compote can be prepared ahead and reheated gently just before serving.

TO SERVE:

Slice the tart and serve topped with the ice cream and warm compote.

MAKES ONE 12- TO 14-INCH TART

RUSTIC APPLE TART

The sheer abundance, the quality, and the variety of apples that become available in the fall never fails to amaze me. Beginning in September, I receive samples of at least twenty locally grown varieties. This is thrilling. Each apple imparts a different taste and texture to whatever I'm creating. I enjoy mixing different varieties for different and ever-changing effects. Similar apple desserts are seldom the same on consecutive nights. This is a very simple and delicious tart that can be whipped up, like all good rustic tarts, on a few moments' notice.

³/₄ cup sugar

1 tablespoon all-purpose flour

¹/₄ teaspoon ground cinnamon

¹/₈ teaspoon ground allspice

2 tablespoons brandy

2 pounds apples, peeled, cored, and thinly sliced

Tart dough (page 39)

Egg wash of 1 egg, pinch of salt, and splash of cream

Sugar for sprinkling

Whipped cream or ice cream

Roll the tart dough out into two 12-inch rounds.

Mix the sugar, flour, and spices. Pour the brandy over the apples and mix well. Toss the apples gently with the dry ingredients. Roll the tart dough out into two 12-inch rounds. Place 1 round of dough on a parchment-lined baking sheet and brush with the egg wash.

Pile the apples in the center of the dough and spread them out evenly, leaving a 1 inch edge all the way around. Lay the other round of dough on top of the apples and press the edges together. Roll the edges toward the center to form a rolled edge. Brush the entire tart with egg wash and sprinkle with sugar. Cut some steam holes in the top and refrigerate until the dough is firm.

Preheat the oven to 425°. Bake for 15 minutes, or until the dough takes on some color. Reduce the heat to 375° and continue to bake for about 30 minutes more. There should be some firmness to the apples when you insert a knife into the tart; they should be a little soft but not mushy. Let cool and serve with whipped cream.

MAKES ONE 10-INCH TART

SEMOLINA WALNUT CAKE
with Fresh Figs and Vin Santo Sabayon

This rustic cake derives its appealing, nutty coarseness from the use of semolina flour. Semolina flour is made from a very hard durum wheat that is harvested in the winter and most familiarly used in the making of pasta and gnocchi, for thickening soups, and in various milk puddings. Partnered with figs, it will transport you to whatever place in your soul aspires to an idyll in the Valle d'Aosta.

4 eggs, separated

1¼ cups sugar

1 teaspoon vanilla extract

½ cup plus 2 tablespoons semolina flour

½ cup all-purpose flour

½ cup plus 1 tablespoon walnuts, ground finely with a little sugar to absorb some of the oil

½ cup sweet, unsalted butter, melted

Quartered figs

Champagne Sabayon (page 57), substituting vin santo for the champagne

Butter and flour a 2-quart Bundt or angel food cake pan. Preheat the oven to 350°. In an electric mixer fitted with a paddle attachment, beat the egg yolks with 1 cup of the sugar and the vanilla until light and fluffy. Mix together the flours and walnuts. Fold into the yolk mixture. Fold in the butter. In a clean bowl, whip the egg whites until stiff and add the remaining ¼ cup sugar, beating until the sugar is well mixed. Fold into the yolk mixture. Pour the batter into the pan. Bake for 1 hour, or until a toothpick inserted into the center comes out clean. Cool in the pan on a cake rack. The cake can be prepared ahead.

Slice into serving portions and serve topped with figs and a generous dollop of sabayon.

MAKES ONE 9-INCH TUBE CAKE

MELON SORBET
with Concord Grape Ice

In the fall, the last of the summer melons come in from the fields so full of flavor and sugar that they are like big slices of candy. The slightly tannic edge of the Concord grape ice provides a nice balance to the melon's heady sweetness.

MELON SORBET

>   8 cups cubed sweet melon, such as canary, cantaloupe, or Crenshaw hybrid
>
>   1/2 cup sugar
>
>   1/2 cup water
>
>   1 tablespoon Midori liqueur

CONCORD GRAPE ICE

>   4 cups Concord grapes
>
>   1/2 cup sugar
>
>   2 cups water

TO PREPARE THE MELON SORBET:

Purée the melon in a blender with the sugar and water. Strain through a fine strainer and add the Midori. Freeze in an ice cream freezer according to the manufacturer's instructions.

TO PREPARE THE CONCORD GRAPE ICE:

Since Concord grapes have a great deal of natural yeast and mold on them, wash them under hot running water to remove some of these parasites. Place grapes, sugar, and 1 cup of the water in a saucepan and bring to a boil. Reduce the heat and cook for about 20 minutes, or until the grapes have burst and the liquid is dark purple in color. Strain the liquid, discarding the skins, and add the remaining 1 cup water. Place over a bowl of ice to chill. When the liquid is cold, pour it into a nonreactive pan and place in the freezer for 30 to 45 minutes. When frozen, chop into fine chips with a blunt pastry scraper.

TO SERVE:

Place some of the chipped ice in a dish, and top with 2 scoops of the melon sorbet.

**MAKES 2 QUARTS SORBET
AND ABOUT 2 CUPS ICE**

Piemonte on Piedmont Avenue

My mother taught me how to cook, how to avoid wasting anything, how to work with the ingredients available to make something wholesome and delectable. My father taught me to eat. He loved going to restaurants, he knew how to order, he knew what he liked, and he enjoyed reacquainting himself with dishes he remembered from his peripatetic youth traveling around Europe in the 1930s. I remember being delighted when he'd order something as exotic as San Pellegrino water in a Los Angeles restaurant. It was so cool, so worldly.

When I was sixteen I had what I think of as my pasta epiphany in a Roman rooftop restaurant with my father. We started, as had become our habit, with prosciutto and melon. My first course was a simple pasta with butter, garlic, and olive oil. The Italians have an innate sense of which pastas perform best with which sauces and embellishments. It was the simplest food and yet I was overwhelmed by it. I followed it with a veal sauté and then had another plate of pasta for dessert. Perfection ravishes you. I was coming into an awareness of the power of the most basic ingredients to move you to tears: butter, garlic, olive oil. Now it feels like a mantra; then it was a miracle of vividness, simplicity, and pungency.

Years ago I found myself in Asti with my beloved traveling companion, Tomas, and young son, Avram, looking for the perfect place in which to imbibe some old Barbera d'Asti and ingest as much as practicable of the local specialties. The majestic signore presiding over a classic oak-paneled, high-ceilinged wine bar directed us to a graciously appointed but seemingly deserted establishment. Repressing our anxiety, we studied the menu with the proprietor. The food started to come. A bottle of an old, good, unlabeled Barbera arrived. The first plate was stunning: a platter of pale green and white figs surrounded by pale pink, locally cured, and wonderfully varied meats. The restaurant filled, the food kept coming. The next platter was agnolotti. Our host, magician that he was, reached into the pocket of his linen jacket to produce an enormous white truffle inside a large white handkerchief. Would we like some? Playing with Avram, he proceeded to slice redolent bits of truffle generously over our gentle agnolotti. Truffles are, not unlike mushrooms, a miracle of taste and essence. The instant they touch something warm, the perfume rises and enchants. The meal was perfect in itself and perfect because it was exactly what we envisioned when we set out on our quest. It consisted of the essential and unquantifiable ingredients that memorable meals are made of: expertise, generosity, and joie de vivre.

For me the Piemonte is to Italy what Burgundy is to France: beautiful, bucolic, pastoral, friendly, populated by local wineries (not big factory productions), a place where wine and food are taken seriously and soulfully. You eat simply or exotically of the local cheeses and fruits, the wild boar with the hair still on it, the ox filet mignon, stewed deer ladled over polenta. We have little access to boar and ox here, but we value our regional wines and revere our local mushrooms.

At BayWolf, as in Piemonte, we can wallow in mushrooms in November. I love mushrooms in omelets, as a topping for crostini, sautéed and served unaccompanied and unadorned or partnered with steak or braised in pasta sauces. We serve porcini as headliners for rustic tossed salads. I like to stuff shiitakes with goat cheese and then bake them and use them as edible polka dots of garnish for meat. I love mushroom soups and potato and mushroom gratins and the fried breaded slices of northern Italy. My favorites are porcini, no question. They have the simplest, finest, and most profound flavor of all.

FUYU PERSIMMON AND ARUGULA SALAD

with Pecans, Pomegranate, and Goat Cheese

The two varieties of persimmons that are most commonly available are the Fuyu and the Hachiya. Fuyus are firm when ripe and are usually eaten fresh and uncooked. Hachiyas are ripened until very soft and almost translucent; they are the persimmons for cookies and cakes and steamed winter puddings. Hachiyas cannot be used in this recipe. If Fuyus are unavailable, substitute another fruit altogether, such as a ripe, crisp pear or apple.

1 shallot, minced

2 tablespoons white wine vinegar or freshly squeezed lemon juice

1 thyme sprig

1/2 cup virgin olive oil

Salt and freshly ground black pepper

1 cup pecans

2 tablespoons sugar

Ground cayenne pepper

3 Fuyu persimmons, peeled with a knife and sliced

2 small handfuls arugula

2 small handfuls red oak leaf lettuce

Seeds of 1 pomegranate

8 ounces fresh goat cheese

Soak the shallot in the vinegar with the thyme for 25 minutes, and then whisk in the olive oil. Season well with salt and pepper. Preheat the oven to 375°. Blanch the pecans in boiling water for 5 minutes, then drain and toss with the sugar and cayenne. Spread on a baking sheet and toast in the oven for about 10 minutes, or until crunchy. Cool the nuts and chop coarsely.

Toss the persimmons and pecans in a bowl with some of the vinaigrette, salt, and pepper. Add the lettuces and gently toss again, adding more vinaigrette if necessary. Arrange on plates and sprinkle with pomegranate seeds and crumbled goat cheese.

SERVES 4

STUFFED MUSSELS

I like eating mussels any way I can get them. It struck me as bizarre that I'd never seen my mother eat a mussel until she moved to Monterey a decade ago. She'd had this love she'd never been able to indulge throughout the years we lived in Los Angeles. Now it's a wonderful sight to see her approaching a nice deep dish of steaming mollusks. My smallest son continues the family affinity: he's known how to suck them out of their shells since he was two. The secret to success with these mussels is to start preparing them several hours before you plan to serve them. If the filling and the béchamel are not refrigerator cold and hard when you put the mussels in the fryer, they will fall apart.

BÉCHAMEL
6 tablespoons unsalted butter

¼ cup all-purpose flour

2 cups whole milk, heated and steeped with a little onion, 1 whole clove, 1 bay leaf, and 1 thyme sprig, then strained

Salt and ground white pepper

Pinch of ground nutmeg

Pinch of saffron threads

20 mussels

2 cups dry white wine

1 thyme sprig

2 tablespoons olive oil

1 yellow onion, minced

1 small fennel bulb, minced

4 ounces pancetta, minced

3 garlic cloves, minced

¼ cup freshly grated Parmesan cheese

1 tablespoon chopped Italian parsley

2 teaspoons chopped tarragon

Freshly squeezed lemon juice

2 cups all-purpose flour

4 eggs, beaten

2 cups fresh breadcrumbs

Peanut oil 2 inches deep for frying

TO PREPARE THE BÉCHAMEL:

The day before serving, melt the butter in a saucepan over medium heat. Add the flour and stir vigorously with a wooden spoon. Lower the heat and gradually whisk in the strained milk. Season with salt, pepper, and nutmeg. Stir in saffron and simmer gently for 20 minutes. Adjust the seasoning. Transfer to a bowl and refrigerate overnight.

TO PREPARE THE MUSSELS:

The next day, wash and debeard the mussels, then steam them open in the white wine and thyme. Cool. Remove the meats from the shells. Save the cooking liquid, strain, and reserve the shells. Chop the mussel meats and set aside. Heat the oil in a sauté pan and lightly brown the onion and fennel over medium-high heat. Add the pancetta and cook until just done. Add the garlic and the mussel cooking liquid. Reduce the liquid to a tablespoon, and then transfer the vegetables to a bowl. Add the Parmesan, parsley, tarragon, chopped mussel meat, and a little lemon juice. Mix everything together and adjust the seasoning. Cool and refrigerate.

TO ASSEMBLE AND FRY THE MUSSELS:

Fill the shells with the mussel filling. Use a tablespoon to smear and seal the top with the béchamel. Dust the mussels with flour, then roll in egg, and then in breadcrumbs. Refrigerate them until it is time to fry. Fry in at least 2 inches of peanut oil until golden. Serve hot.

MAKES 30 TO 35 MUSSELS

GREEN BEAN, WALNUT, AND RED ONION SALAD

This fine combination is a perfect component for an antipasto platter. Walnut oil provides incomparable depth of flavor and a toasty fragrance.

1/2 red onion, julienned

3 tablespoons sherry vinegar or freshly squeezed lemon juice

8 ounces French green beans

3/4 cup walnuts

2 tablespoons sugar

1/4 cup walnut oil

Salt and freshly ground black pepper

Soak the onion in the vinegar or lemon juice for 20 minutes. Boil the green beans in well-salted water until just cooked, then drain and put the beans in a bowl with the onion and vinegar.

Preheat the oven to 375°. Blanch the walnuts for 1 minute, then toss them in the sugar while still hot. Transfer to a baking sheet and toast in the oven until crispy but not at all burned. Cool and roughly chop. Add the walnuts and walnut oil to the beans, and season well with salt and pepper. Serve at room temperature.

SERVES 6

M*y wife and I have been eating at the Wolf for many years. The food is always fresh and tasty. The wines are exceptional. The service and ambience, like the foods, are equally pleasurable. I usually begin each visit with a soup, which has been consistently extraordinary, and end with a sorbet, which has been invariably sensational. I had always fantasized about having a favorite hometown restaurant where I could feel both genuinely comfortable and truly enjoy fine food and wine. The BayWolf restaurant is it.*

—RUPERT GARCIA, *artist*

SAUTÉED SWORDFISH *with*

Red Wine—Anchovy Vinaigrette and Purple Broccoli

This is a perfect illustration of the whole being larger than the sum of its parts. The anchovies function as a salt to provide great depth of flavor. Slightly bitter vegetables like broccoli rabe and radicchio are tamed by the salty anchovies and the acidity of vinegar: it straightens them right out; they become suddenly sweet. The sea factor inherent in the anchovies pumps up the mildness of the swordfish. Fishiness is not a quality that's totally desirable, but there is something innate in swordfish that anchovies can pick up, heighten, and enhance. The recipe makes about 1 cup vinaigrette, which should give you enough leftover for another use, such as to dress steamed or boiled vegetables, another salad, or bitter greens. Serve with French lentils or roasted potatoes.

RED WINE–ANCHOVY VINAIGRETTE

1/4 cup minced red onion

1 cup dry red wine

1/4 cup red wine vinegar

1 garlic clove, smashed

1 thyme sprig

2 salt-packed anchovies, filleted, rinsed, and minced

2/3 cup virgin olive oil

Salt and freshly ground black pepper

Chopped rosemary (optional)

1 1/2 pounds swordfish

1 pound purple broccoli

Olive oil

Salt and freshly ground black pepper

TO PREPARE THE VINAIGRETTE:

Put the onion, wine, vinegar, garlic, and thyme in a small saucepan and reduce until only 1/3 cup remains. Remove the garlic and thyme. Pour the red wine mixture into a bowl, add the anchovies, and cool. Be sure to add the anchovies to the mixture right after it comes off the heat so that they can cook a little bit. Finish with the oil, salt, and pepper. This vinaigrette is also delicious with a subtle addition of rosemary.

TO PREPARE THE FISH:

Lightly oil the fish and season with salt and pepper. Heat a saucepan over medium-high heat and cook fish for 4 to 5 minutes per side, or until cooked through.

TO PREPARE THE BROCCOLI:

Trim the stems and cut the broccoli into florets. Toss it in olive oil, salt, and pepper. Spread the florets on a baking sheet and roast in a 425° oven for about 25 minutes, or until they are just starting to get some color.

TO SERVE:

Place the fish on individual plates or a serving platter. Spoon the vinaigrette over the fish. Place the broccoli alongside the fish.

SERVES 4

MIXED GRILL
with Quail, Sausage, and Mushrooms

This is a great dish for meat eaters. They can nibble on a crispy little bird in one hand and fork in a flavorful little sausage with the other. Pork sausage and any kind of fowl were made for each other and, as all carnivores know, the taste of grilled meat is a thing unto itself. Make grilled or soft polenta to serve as a bed for the meats.

QUAIL

6 quail, halved

Salt and freshly ground black pepper

3 bay leaves, crumbled

2 teaspoons dried thyme

2 cups dry red wine, reduced to 1/2 cup

SAUSAGE

1 1/2 pounds pork butt

8 ounces pork fatback

1 tablespoon fennel seed, toasted and ground

1 teaspoon dried red chile flakes

2 large garlic cloves, minced

2 tablespoons chopped Italian parsley

Salt and freshly ground black pepper

3 feet hog casings, rinsed

SAUCE

1 tablespoon olive oil

1 shallot, minced

1 thyme sprig

4 dried mushooms

8 cups poultry stock, heated

SAUTÉED MUSHROOMS

1 pound fresh domestic mushrooms, quartered

2 tablespoons butter

TO MARINATE THE QUAIL:

The day before serving, season the quail with salt, pepper, crumbled bay leaf, and thyme. Place in a shallow dish and pour the reduced red wine over them. Marinate overnight, turning the birds several times.

TO MAKE PREPARE SAUSAGE:

The day before serving, grind the pork butt and fatback through the big holes of your meat grinder. Mix with the fennel, chile flakes, garlic, and parsley. Season well with salt and pepper. Fry up a little patty, taste, and adjust the seasoning if necessary. Stuff into the casings, tie off into 4- to 5-inch lengths, and hang overnight in the refrigerator.

TO PREPARE THE SAUCE:

Heat the olive oil in a small saucepan. When sizzling, add the shallot and brown lightly. Add the thyme, dried mushrooms, and 2 cups of the stock. Reduce the sauce by half, and then add another 2 cups of stock. Skim the scum frequently. Continue until all of the stock has been added. Reduce the sauce to a spoon-coating consistency, and then strain through a fine strainer. Keep warm until ready to serve.

TO ASSEMBLE AND SERVE:

Light a fire in the grill. Sauté the mushrooms in the butter until lightly browned. Poach the sausages for 7 minutes in gently simmering water. Right before serving, drain the quail and place them, skin side down first, over a hot grill. Mark the birds well on the grill before turning. Put the poached sausages on the fire. Grill the meats for about 5 minutes, or until just done. Serve with the sautéed mushrooms and the sauce.

SERVES 6

QUINCE TART
with Apple Cider Sabayon

Quince is an underappreciated and under-utilized fruit. It is rarely eaten raw but has a pleasing perfume on the tree and an attractive honeylike flavor when cooked. It is excellent in jams, either alone or as an improving thickener to strawberry jams or apple jellies. Equally popular in savory preparations, many recipes exist attesting to its use in Persian and Turkish meat- and fruit-stews. Quinces can be found at farmer's markets and upscale produce stores. The quinces in this tart are first poached, and then half of them are reduced into a paste used to line the tart shell. The poached fruits are very soft and fragrant.

6 large, ripe quinces (quince is ripe when it is yellow and very fragrant)

4 quarts dry white wine

3 cups sugar

5 white peppercorns

Zest of 2 lemons, removed in strips

1 cup honey

Tart dough (page 39), rolled out and fitted into a 9-inch tart pan, unbaked

Sugar for dusting

Champagne Sabayon (page 57), substituting French hard cider for the champagne

TO PREPARE THE QUINCES:

Peel the quinces, cut them half, and scoop out the seeds and inner core with a melon baller. The quinces will be hard. Heat the wine with the sugar, peppercorns, zest, and honey. Do not let it boil. Place the quinces in the liquid. Cover with a piece of cheesecloth or a cloth napkin and weight with a bowl or plate to keep the quinces submerged in the liquid. Cook over low heat for about 3 hours, or until the quinces are slightly pink and soft. Remove from the heat and let cool. Remove the zest and peppercorns.

TO PREPARE THE TART:

Purée half of the quinces with some of the cooking liquid. Transfer the purée to a heavy-bottomed pot and cook over a low flame until very thick. Transfer to a bowl and let cool. Roll half of the tart dough out into a 10-inch round and fit it into a 9-inch tart pan. Spread a layer of purée in the bottom of the tart shell. Slice the remaining quince into 1/4-inch slices and arrange in a nice pattern over the purée. Dust with sugar and refrigerate until the dough is firm.

Preheat the oven to 400° and bake for 20 to 30 minutes.

The top of the tart should appear glossy and the crust will be golden brown. Serve with the sabayon.

MAKES ONE 9-INCH TART

PUMPKIN CHEESECAKE
with Caramel Sauce and Candied Pumpkin Seeds

This a wonderful way of proving, if proof were needed, that pumpkin deserves its revered place on our holiday tables. Mellower than pumpkin pie and spicier than your average cheesecake, this cake is the best of both dessert worlds and gives the desirable illusion of being light as air and soft as silk. We roast our own pumpkin, but canned is a venerable substitute. In a perfect world, home-baked gingersnaps would form the perfect crust. This dessert is so popular with the staff and our purveyors that swapping cakes for fish and other services is not at all unusual.

CRUST

3 cups ground gingersnap crumbs

1/2 cup sweet, unsalted butter, melted

FILLING

8 ounces nonstabilized cream cheese (cream cheese without gelatin), at room temperature

4 ounces mascarpone cheese

3/4 cup sugar

1 egg

1/4 teaspoon ground cinnamon

1/4 teaspoon ground ginger

1/8 teaspoon ground mace

1 teaspoon freshly squeezed lemon juice

1 teaspoon vanilla extract

1/2 cup fresh or canned pumpkin purée

CANDIED PUMPKIN SEEDS

1/2 cup sugar

1/4 teaspoon ground cinnamon

Pinch of freshly ground black pepper

1/4 teaspoon ground ginger

2 cups shelled green (raw) pumpkin seeds (also known as pepitas)

3 tablespoons water

CARAMEL SAUCE

1/4 cup water

2 cups sugar

3/4 cup heavy whipping cream

TO PREPARE THE CRUST:

Mix together the gingersnap crumbs and butter. Press into the bottom of a 10-inch springform pan and set aside.

TO PREPARE THE FILLING:

Preheat the oven to 325°. Beat the cream cheese in the bowl of an electric mixer fitted with the paddle attachment. Add the mascarpone and mix well. Add the sugar and egg and mix well. Add the spices, lemon juice, and vanilla. Be sure to scrape the bottom of the mixing bowl to combine thoroughly. Beat in the pumpkin and pour the mixture into the prepared pan. Bake for 30 minutes. The cake should rise a little around the edge and in the center. Let cool in the pan on a rack, and then refrigerate for 1 to 2 hours, or until firm.

TO CANDY THE PUMPKIN SEEDS:

Preheat the oven to 350°. Mix the sugar and spices. Wet the seeds with the water. Add the sugar and spices and mix well. Pour onto a parchment-lined baking sheet and bake for 15 to 20 minutes. The sugar will stick to the seeds and the seeds will puff a little. Let cool.

TO PREPARE THE SAUCE:

Combine the water and sugar in a heavy-bottomed saucepan. Bring to a boil over high heat and continue cooking for 15 to 20 minutes, or until the sugar darkens to the color of dark tea. Remove from the heat and mix in the cream, a little at a time. Be extremely careful not to burn yourself with the hot sugar. Set aside.

TO SERVE:

Slice the cake and top with the candied pumpkin seeds and caramel sauce.

MAKES ONE 10-INCH CAKE

PEPPERMINT PATTIES

These superior (to everything you believe a peppermint to be) mints are a revered part of Earl's Sweet Treats, a delicate composition of candies, cookies, tartlets, and diminutive cakes that varies with the seasons and Earl's fancy. When Earl first asked me to order peppermint oil, I was reluctant—peppermint isn't one of my favorite flavors or scents. These converted me.

PATTIES

1 tablespoon sweet, unsalted butter

1/8 teaspoon peppermint oil

2 tablespoons light corn syrup

2 cups powdered sugar

CHOCOLATE COATING

4 ounces bittersweet chocolate

2 tablespoons peanut oil

Unsweetened cocoa powder for dusting

TO PREPARE THE PATTIES:

Place the butter, oil, corn syrup, and sugar in the bowl of an electric mixed fitted with the paddle attachment and beat until light and fluffy. It will take some time, so be patient. Place the mixture in a piping bag with a small pastry tip and pipe into small buttons on a parchment-lined baking sheet. Refrigerate until firm.

TO FINISH THE PATTIES:

Melt the chocolate with the peanut oil in the top of a double boiler. The peanut oil will help the chocolate to stay liquid even in a cool state. Let the chocolate cool to 86° before dipping the mints. Place 1 mint patty on top of the tines of a fork and submerge it in the chocolate, then slide it off the fork and onto the parchment paper. When all of the mints have been dipped, chill in the refrigerator once again. When firm, dust with cocoa powder and store in an airtight container.

MAKES 12 PATTIES

GRAPEFRUIT AND BASIL SORBET

You might think grapefruit and basil a bizarre combination, but you'd be wrong. I started making this a decade ago, and our intrepid customers keep coming back for more. Ruby Red and Indian River grapefruit have a high sugar content that makes them ideal for this delight.

2 cups basil leaves

4 cups freshly squeezed pink grapefruit juice, strained

1 cup sugar

Combine 1 cup of the basil with the juice in a saucepan over low heat. Do not let it boil. Remove from the heat. Discard the basil and add the remaining cup of basil. Let the mixture steep for 1 hour. When cool, remove the basil and discard. Add the sugar and mix until it is well dissolved. Freeze in an ice cream freezer according to the manufacturer's instructions.

MAKES 1 QUART

I was surprised when we pulled up to the front door. It looked like a house, not a restaurant. Tables were scattered among several small rooms. The food was like being invited to the home of a gifted French cook. It was simple, rustic, and delicious.

My visit to the BayWolf in the fall of 1977 was the first of many more. The menu changed daily and I ate there often for normal occasions and for special nights out. By my second visit, I knew the names of all four owners (that was easy since three were named Michael). And they welcomed me. They knew my appetite was big and I was always asked if I needed more. To this day, I have never left hungry or unsatisfied. For me, the BayWolf is not just a restaurant, but a welcoming home where good food and warm hospitality always await.

—BRUCE AIDELLS, *founder of Aidells Sausage Company*

Chef's Holiday

The holidays are a wild time for the restaurant. The weeks between Thanksgiving and Christmas are celebratory for our customers and challenging for us. The restaurant is filled with small and large parties throughout the month. What I most enjoy doing is a few encore presentations of some of my favorite dishes from the year: the things we've done the best or that I've enjoyed the most, a small celebration and recapitulation of our greatest hits—at least, of the ones that fit in seasonally. There's no denying the allure and the charm of dishes made with pumpkin or nougat or the holiday-adjusted largesse implicit in a composed salad of several varieties of pristine and well-dressed shellfish.

We've celebrated New Year's Eve at the restaurant from the very beginning, but we didn't always serve dinners on Christmas Eve. We were hesitant to suggest it to the staff. Gradually it evolved that people wanted to work and customers wanted to come, to have an elegant, home-style meal in a home away from home. The ultimate seasonal specialty would have to be prime rib roast. Christmas Eve is the only night of the year that we make it, but it seems perfectly apt: strange and rare and so essentially Christmas.

Though it's insanely busy, we try to keep it light and lively and festive and still reserve a little time for ourselves and out families and friends. The holidays are also a time for chefs to entertain at home. Many of my most memorable meals have been in the homes of restaurant chefs. At home a chef can bring all of his or her skill and generosity to the task and present it on a smaller and more refined scale.

One of the things that gives shape to what I do and determines how I cook at home is that I categorically want to be finished with all the preparation when my family and friends arrive. I want to sit down and not work while they're there, beyond bringing food to them and performing a little theatrical slicing and serving. Other chefs handle this differently. When I eat at Paul Bertolli's, he follows the same plan—everything is done and we sit, talk, drink, eat. In David Tanis's house, David is cooking and serving an endless stream of delicious little things, talking, drinking. Nancy Oakes is a great restaurant cook who stretches out at home. She feeds you what she wants you to eat. She loves to entertain. Alice Waters's meals are simple and delicious; Nancy's are sometimes more complicated and delicious. We start with rustic Italian bread spread 1/4-inch thick with Normandy butter and slathered with an enormous mound of caviar. For Nancy, caviar isn't something you dribble a few beads of onto tiny toasts. You dive into it, you get your fill, and you have what she aptly calls "a caviar moment." From my first meal of crispy little fish with aioli to the most recent dinner of Moroccan chicken with preserved lemons, whether it's her home-cured olives or her refrigerator pasta, whatever Lauren serves is embellished with her characteristic passion.

I leave each of these meals with each of these friends believing it was the best meal I've ever enjoyed. This is the ineffable sense of shared pleasure and well-being we aspire to inspire in our patrons. We have five or six skilled professionals in the kitchen, at their self-organized workstations, sautéing, searing, braising, glazing, plating, and serving—and yet the principles of a superb meal at a restaurant are essentially indistinguishable from those of a great meal in your home dining room. In both settings, the joy of eating isn't a competitive quest for the rarest or most expensive ingredient, a pilgrimage to the isolated cottage in the forest that boasts the finest plover eggs or the tiniest peas. The ideal meal is a seat in a comfortable space, with willing and able companions, enjoying food prepared and served with affection and exuberance.

MENU BY CHRISTINE TAYLOR

2000 NEW YEAR'S EVE DINNER 2001

AMUSE BOUCHE

○

DOUBLE DUCK SOUP WITH PEEKABOO BUNDLES

○

FOIE GRAS AND MUSHROOM RAVIOLI WITH BABY GREENS
OR
BUCKWHEAT BLINI WITH SMOKED STURGEON AND SALMON CAVIAR

○

LOBSTER AND SCALLOP BOUILLABAISSE WITH SHRIMP ROUILLE
OR
RACK OF LAMB WITH TRUFFLED POTATOES

○

CHOCOLATE HEAVEN
OR
LEMON TART WITH CHAMPAGNE ZABAGLIONE

BAY WOLF RESTAURANT
CHEF: LOUIS LE GASSIC
SWEETS: EARL DARNY

SMOKED DUCK SALAD
with Endive, Hazelnuts, and Apple Vinaigrette

For this dish, we caramelize apples for the vinaigrette and then toss raw Fuji apples into the main salad. I like the freshness and the crunch that raw apples provide, but this salad can also be prepared entirely with caramelized apples if you prefer a slightly deeper, sweeter salad.

VINAIGRETTE

1 tablespoon butter

2 apples, unpeeled, sliced 3/4 inch thick

2 teaspoons sugar

1/2 cup pure unsweetened apple juice

1 thyme sprig

1/2 cup white wine vinegar

1/4 cup virgin olive oil

1/3 cup plain duck sauce (page 164)

Salt and freshly ground black pepper

Freshly squeezed lemon juice

SALAD

1 whole smoked duck breast (page 162)

2 Fuji apples

2 heads Belgian endive

1 small head red oak leaf lettuce

3/4 cup hazelnuts, toasted and chopped

TO PREPARE THE VINAIGRETTE:

Heat the butter in a sauté pan, add the sliced apples, and sprinkle with the sugar. Caramelize over medium heat. When deep gold, add the apple juice, thyme, and vinegar. Simmer for a few minutes, then remove the thyme and transfer the apples and liquid to a blender and purée. Transfer to a bowl and finish with the olive oil, duck sauce, salt, and pepper. If the vinaigrette needs more acidity, add some lemon juice.

TO PREPARE THE SALAD:

Right before serving, slice the duck breast very thinly against the grain. Put in a bowl and dress with some of the vinaigrette. Slice the Fuji apples and add to the bowl with the endive, lettuce, and hazelnuts. Add a little more vinaigrette and gently toss again. Arrange on plates and serve immediately.

SERVES 4

SMOKED TROUT AND GRAPEFRUIT SALAD

We prefer to smoke trout ourselves because it's easy and the delicacy of home-smoked trout cannot be matched by anything available commercially. Do not use lighter fluid or briquettes that contain it. They will affect the flavor.

SMOKED TROUT

1/2 cup salt

1/4 cup sugar

2 garlic cloves

1 bay leaf

1 tarragon sprig

A few black peppercorns

1 lemon zest strip

2 whole trout

4 cups cold water

4 cups ice-cold water

SALAD

5 grapefruits

3 tablespoons sugar

1/2 cup extra virgin olive oil

3 tablespoons crème fraîche (page 65)

Freshly squeezed lemon juice

Salt and freshly ground black pepper

2 pinches of chopped tarragon

4 thin levain or sourdough baguette slices

1 tablespoon butter, melted

1 head Belgian endive, julienned

4 small handfuls various red lettuces

About 1/2 cup crème fraîche (page 65) for topping

TO SMOKE THE TROUT:

Prepare a brine by bringing the salt, sugar, garlic, bay leaf, tarragon, peppercorns, and lemon zest to a boil in the cold water. Simmer for 10 minutes, and then pour into a cool container with the ice water. Cool thoroughly before adding the trout. Put the trout in the brine, cover, and refrigerate for 4 hours.

Rinse, pat dry, and oil the trout skin. Build a small charcoal fire in the bottom of the smoker. Soak the applewood chips in water for half an hour. When the coals are gray, add some drained chips to the fire. Put the fish on the top rack of the grill, skin side down, and smoke slowly until they are just done. The slower your fire is, the smokier the fish will become without being overcooked. Remove the fish carefully with a long metal spatula. Cool and remove the skin and heads from the flesh.

TO PREPARE THE DRESSING:

Finely chop the zest of 3 of the grapefruits, then juice them. Mix the zest and juice in a small saucepan with the sugar and reduce to a couple of tablespoons over medium heat. Transfer to a bowl and cool. Whisk in the oil and crème fraîche. If the dressing needs more acid, squeeze in a little lemon juice. If it is too acidic, add a bit more olive oil or crème fraîche. Finish with salt, pepper, and tarragon.

TO ASSEMBLE THE SALAD:

Peel the remaining 2 grapefruits with a knife, then cut out the sections. Cut each bread slice in 3 triangles, brush with melted butter, and toast in the oven to make croutons. Toss the grapefruit sections, endive, and red lettuces in some of the vinaigrette. Arrange on plates. Top each salad with 3 croutons, a spoonful of crème fraîche, and some smoked trout.

SERVES 4

217

LOBSTER SALAD
with Mango and Basil

As I generally prefer to cook solo, it was a major event to prepare this salad alongside Lauren for a lively holiday party. The conjoining of the luxurious lobster with the paradisiacal mango is a most memorable marriage.

3 live lobsters

2 mangoes

Salt and freshly ground black pepper

Zest and juice of 2 Meyer lemons

1 small shallot, minced

1 thyme sprig

3/4 cup virgin olive oil

12 basil leaves, torn

Bring a huge pot of water to a boil with some salt, then put the lobsters in the pot and cook for 8 to 10 minutes, or until just done. Remove the lobsters and let cool, or transfer them to a bowl of ice water. Remove the meat from the tail and claws, cut it into thin rounds, and set aside. Peel the mangoes with a knife, cut the flesh from the pit, then cut the flesh into thin slices. Arrange the lobster and mango on a platter or individual plates. Sprinkle with salt and pepper.

Chop the lemon zest superfine and add it to the lemon juice with the shallot and thyme. Let these ingredients macerate for 20 minutes, then whisk in the olive oil and season with salt and pepper. Drizzle some of the vinaigrette over the lobster and mango. Garnish with the basil leaves and serve.

SERVES 4 TO 6

1997 New Year's Eve 1998 Dinner

Amuse-bouches

Double duck consommé
smoked duck ravioli and old sherry (Solera 1918)

Foie gras terrine
grilled Acme bread
{or}
Smoked salmon
potato cakes and salmon caviar

Swordfish and spot prawns
French lentils, pink grapefruit, and champagne sabayon
{or}
Roast beef fillet
truffled potato purée and wild mushrooms

Warm petite chocolate cake {or} Iced pear soufflé

CHEF: LAUREN LYLE
DESSERTS: KAREN NIELSEN

BAY WOLF RESTAURANT

MENU BY CHRISTINE TAYLOR

OYSTERS ON THE HALF SHELL
with Little Pork Sausages

This a very extravagant contrast: cold, briny oysters and hot little sausages. It is a ubiquitous appetizer in Bordeaux, home of some of the greatest of the French oyster beds, and a welcome and wonderful thing to do in the wintertime when the oysters are at their best. There are many comforting hot and cold combinations, but this is one of the most perfect. Oysters and meat are clearly made for each other. I find Kumamoto oysters appropriate to pair with tiny sausages because they are small and delicate.

SAUSAGES

2 pounds pork butt, cut into thin strips

1/4 pound pork fatback, cut into thin strips

Salt and freshly ground black pepper

Pinch of ground nutmeg

Pinch of ground bay leaf

2 shallots, minced

1/2 cup dry champagne or white wine

Olive oil

5 feet lamb casings, rinsed

Rendered pork fat or olive oil for browning sausages

---

4 to 6 oysters per person, preferably Kumamoto, shucked and on the half shell

MIGNONETTE SAUCE

1 shallot, minced

1/4 cup champagne

1/4 cup champagne vinegar

A few crushed black peppercorns

Lemon wedges (optional, substitute for Mignonette Sauce)

TO PREPARE THE SAUSAGES:

Two days before serving, season the pork and fatback with the salt, pepper, nutmeg, and bay. Refrigerate overnight.

The day before serving, soak the shallots in the wine for 15 minutes. Grind all the pork on the finest holes of a meat grinder. The meat will pass through the grinder most easily if it is cold, cold, cold. Mix the ground pork with the shallots and wine, kneading thoroughly with your hands. Fry up a little piece and taste to check the seasoning. Add more salt if necessary. Wrap the meat in plastic wrap and refrigerate overnight.

The next day, stuff the pork mixture into the casings, twisting it off into 4-inch lengths. Twist the first sausage away from yourself, the next toward yourself, the next away from yourself. Bring the two ends of the length of sausage together, then grab the middle of this length. Tie here with some string and hang in the refrigerator. I attach paper clips to the string and then to a rack in the refrigerator.

TO PREPARE THE SAUCE:

Stir together the shallot, champagne, champagne vinegar, and peppercorns.

TO SERVE:

Poach the sausages gently in a pot of water for 5 minutes. Drain and brown in the fat or oil. Serve the sausages with the oysters and Mignonette Sauce or lemon wedges.

SERVES 6 TO 8

219

BEEF TENDERLOIN
with Pommes Anna and Béarnaise Sauce

Nothing could be as estimable for entertaining as a beautiful tenderloin of beef. It is simple, elegant, and unsurpassably rich, yet delicate and undeniably celebratory. I well remember my first big chateaubriand and my first taste of sauce béarnaise: the indescribable taste of butter and tarragon-flavored beef. To this day, I can't wait to have steak with béarnaise as soon as possible after arriving in France. This isn't an everyday preparation; it's for those special, super-duper, calorie-rich feasts, one of which is often Christmas Eve at my house. Always let your beef rest after roasting (tented with foil). Trust me, it needs it.

BEEF TENDERLOIN

3-pound beef tenderloin

Salt and freshly ground black pepper

1 tablespoon olive oil

POMMES ANNA

4 russet potatoes

Salt and freshly ground black pepper

1½ cups butter, clarified

BÉARNAISE SAUCE

½ cup white wine vinegar

½ cup dry white wine

1 shallot, minced

3 big tarragon sprigs

3 egg yolks

1 tablespoon water

Salt

Ground white pepper

1 bunch watercress

TO PREPARE THE BEEF:

Season the beef generously with salt and pepper. If you can season it overnight, so much the better. Preheat the oven to 375°. Brown the beef thoroughly in the olive oil, then roast until cooked to your taste (allow 15 to 20 for rare to medium-rare). Allow the meat to rest for at least 20 minutes before cutting into it.

TO PREPARE THE POTATOES:

Preheat the oven to 375°. Line a baking sheet with a piece of parchment paper. Slice 1 potato almost paper-thin with a mandoline or sharp knife. Toss it in a bowl with salt and pepper and 2 to 3 tablespoons of hot clarified butter. Arrange the slices in a spiral circle on the parchment. The outer diameter of the circle should be about 4 inches. Make 4 to 6 layers. Continue like this with the rest of the potatoes. This works best if you slice only 1 potato at a time because the butter might congeal and make the slices soft and sticky. Reserve the remaining butter for the sauce. Bake for 45 minutes, or until the potatoes are totally crispy on the outside. They should be gold, not white. The idea is to have a crispy outside and a soft inside. If there are not enough layers, the pommes Anna will turn out more like potato chips. These can be made several hours ahead and reheated and crisped in a hot oven.

TO PREPARE THE SAUCE:

Reduce the vinegar, wine, shallots, and 2 sprigs of tarragon to 2 tablespoons. Strain. Bring a pot of water to a boil, and then lower the heat to medium. Right before serving, put the egg yolks in a stainless steel bowl that will sit comfortably over the pot of water. Whisk the yolks over the heat with the water until thick and lemon colored. This will take a couple of minutes. Be careful not to scramble your eggs. You must whisk as fast as you can. Turn the heat off and immediately whisk in the remaining hot clarified butter (you should have $^3/_4$ to 1 cup) in a thin stream. Whisk and lift, whisk and lift to beat some air into your sauce. When the butter is incorporated, whisk in the reduction and season with salt and white pepper. Finely chop the remaining tarragon and add to the sauce to your taste. If the sauce is particularly thick, you can whisk in a little hot water to thin it.

TO SERVE:

As you slice the tented beef, recrisp the pommes Anna in the hot oven. Serve with some béarnaise over the beef and the potatoes on the side. Garnish with watercress.

SERVES 6

SLOW-COOKED LAMB SHANKS
with Olives, Roasted Fennel, and Celery Root Purée

I love serving whole lamb shanks at the restaurant. They are big, delicious, primal pieces of meat on the bone. Lamb on the bone is always more to my taste than lamb in any other incarnation. Lamb cooked off the bone, with the possible exception of a perfect braise, is insipid, missing the ineffable essence that makes lamb so richly succulent and so very popular all year around at the restaurant.

Vegetable purées are most frequently prepared by boiling the vegetables, draining, and then puréeing them. When celery root, with its innate capacity to absorb an inordinate amount of water, is prepared in the usual fashion, it inevitably is loose and unappealing. Steaming prevents it from becoming waterlogged and simplifies the preparation.

BRAISED LAMB SHANKS

4 lamb shanks

Salt and freshly ground black pepper

1 carrot, peeled and diced

1 onion, diced

8 garlic cloves

1 orange, halved

5 parsley stems

1 bay leaf

4 thyme sprigs

1 teaspoon black peppercorns

2 allspice berries

1 juniper berry

1 teaspoon fennel seed, toasted

1 rosemary sprig

6 olives

6 cups lamb stock, heated

SAUCE

1 tablespoon olive oil

1 shallot, minced

1 thyme sprig

3 olives, roughly chopped

8 cups lamb stock, heated (or use some of the strained braising liquid)

FENNEL

2 fennel bulbs

Salt and freshly ground black pepper

Pinch of sugar

2 tablespoons butter, melted

1 tablespoon olive oil

CELERY ROOT PURÉE

4 large or 6 small celery roots

1/4 cup butter, at room temperature

Salt

Ground white pepper

1/2 cup heavy whipping cream

Freshly squeezed lemon juice

TO BRAISE THE LAMB:

The day before serving, season the lamb shanks with salt and pepper and refrigerate overnight.

The next day, preheat the oven to 500°. Put the remaining braise ingredients except the stock into a deep, ovenproof pot that will hold the shanks in a single layer. Arrange the seasoned shanks over the vegetables. Roast in the oven until the shanks are nicely browned, 25 to 30 minutes. Pour the stock over the shanks and lower the heat to 350°. Put a piece of parchment over the shanks, then cover with a tight-fitting lid or some foil. Cook for another hour or two, or until the meat is just wanting to fall from the bone. If you wait a couple of days to serve the shanks, cool and then store them in their braising liquid.

TO PREPARE THE SAUCE:

Heat the oil in a small saucepan, then add the shallot and brown lightly. Add the thyme, olives, and 2 cups of the heated stock. (Don't add the olives to your sauce if you use any braising liquid.) Simmer gently until reduced by half then add another 2 cups of stock. Skim any scum that rises to the top. Continue adding and reducing stock and skimming until the sauce is a spoon-coating consistency. If you use strained braising liquid in the sauce, taste to be certain it isn't becoming too salty. Strain through a chinois or fine strainer. Warm just before serving.

TO PREPARE THE FENNEL:

Preheat the oven to 375°. Cut the fennel into wedges and season well with salt, pepper, and a pinch of sugar. Toss in the butter and olive oil. Spread over a baking sheet and roast in the oven until golden on the underside. Turn the fennel and continue to cook until both sides are caramelized.

TO PREPARE THE CELERY ROOT:

Peel the rough skin of the celery roots with a knife. Cut the roots in 1/4-inch slices and arrange in the top of a steamer. It may be necessary to cook them in batches. The celery root will steam more quickly if the steamer is not overcrowded. When tender, 5 to 10 minutes, transfer to the bowl of a food processor. Add the butter and purée for 3 minutes until completely smooth. Season with salt and pepper, then add the cream. Pulse to blend. Add a few drops of lemon juice and pulse again. Pass the purée through a fine strainer. You can also use a food mill, blender, or mortar and pestle to purée the celery roots. The purée should be served hot, so don't waste any time putting the plates together.

TO SERVE:

Arrange the lamb shanks on plates with some celery root purée, the fennel, and the sauce. You may also serve this with a little sautéed spinach.

SERVES 4

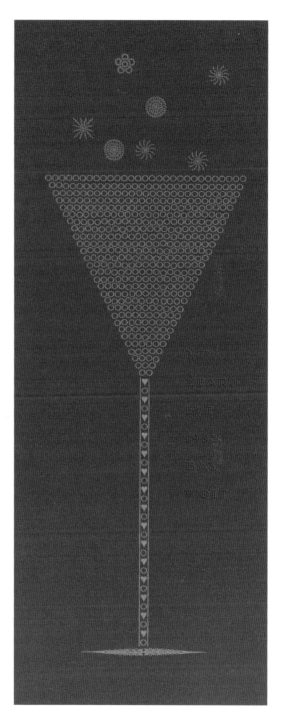

MENU BY WILL POWERS

223

BOUDIN BLANC
with Cabbage, Pommes Sautées, and Mustard Sauce

This sausage has a wonderfully ethereal texture, a little bite from the skin, a richly voluptuous interior of cream and bread and pork fat. It's ideal in itself and sublime partnered with pommes sautées. Pommes sautées aren't practical for us to cook to order in the restaurant, but they're simple enough to prepare at home. I could happily eat them every day of my life.

BOUDIN

2 pounds boneless, skinless chicken breast meat, cut into strips

10 ounces pork fatback, cut into strips

6 ounces salt pork, well rinsed and cut into strips

1 1/2 cups diced onion

Ground nutmeg

Pinch of ground cloves

Ground bay leaf

Salt

Ground white pepper

2 to 3 cups heavy whipping cream

1 cup fresh white breadcrumbs

4 eggs

10 feet hog casings, well rinsed

1/4 cup duck fat or olive oil for browning

MUSTARD SAUCE

2 tablespoons rendered duck fat (page 6)

2 shallots, minced

Small chunk of pancetta, diced

1 thyme sprig

8 cups duck or chicken stock, heated

2 tablespoons whole-grain mustard

1/4 to 1/2 cup heavy whipping cream

CABBAGE

2 tablespoons rendered duck fat (page 6)

1 onion, julienned

2 small heads savoy cabbage, julienned

Salt and freshly ground black pepper

2 garlic cloves, chopped

White wine vinegar

POMMES SAUTÉES

1 pound Yukon gold potatoes, peeled and cubed

Olive oil

Butter

Salt and freshly ground black pepper

Sliced cornichons

TO PREPARE THE SAUSAGES:

Put the meat and fats through the finest holes of a meat grinder. Be sure to remove the sinew from the chicken tenderloins so that it doesn't jam up the grinder. Chill thoroughly, then grind again with the onion. Season frugally with the spices, starting with 1/4 teaspoon of each. Heat the cream and pour it over the breadcrumbs. Cool and add to the meat with the eggs. Mix well, then fry up a small patty and taste to check the seasoning. Take note that this recipe uses salt pork, which can vary dramatically in terms of saltiness. Sometimes the salt pork is enough to salt the entire batch of sausage.

The next day, stuff the pork mixture into the casings, twisting it off into 4-inch lengths. Twist the first sausage away from yourself, the next toward yourself, the next away from yourself. Bring the two ends of the length of sausage together, then grab the middle of this length. Tie here with some string and hang in the refrigerator. I attach paper clips to the string and then to a rack in the refrigerator.

(continued)

225

To cook, poach very gently for 10 minutes, then brown in fat or oil. Handle the sausages carefully; they are very delicate.

TO PREPARE THE SAUCE:

Heat the fat in a small sauté pan and brown the shallots with the pancetta. Add the thyme and 2 cups of the duck stock. Reduce by half, and then add more stock. Continue in this fashion until all of the stock has been added. Skim the scum constantly. Reduce the sauce to a spoon-coating consistency, then strain through a fine strainer. Right before serving, whisk in the mustard and a little cream.

TO PREPARE THE CABBAGE:

Heat the fat in a heavy-bottomed pan and sauté the onion until it is just beginning to color. Add the cabbage and brown over medium heat. Cook until the cabbage is tender but not soft. Season well with salt and pepper. Add the garlic and a few shots of vinegar.

TO PREPARE THE POMMES SAUTÉES:

The nicest and easiest way to prepare them is to cube them, steam them, and then finish in a nonstick pan in a little olive oil or a tiny bit of butter until they are crispy all over. Season with salt and pepper to taste.

TO SERVE:

Serve the sausage with the cabbage, the mustard sauce, and some pommes sautées. Garnish with cornichons.

SERVES 10

BAY WOLF RESTAURANT

Crostini : Asti Spumanti

Smoked duck salad with baby greens, mushrooms, and aged goat cheese
'85 Volpe Pasini, "Zuc di Volpe"

Seafood risotto with champagne, prawns, scallops, and crab

Roast veal loin with wild mushrooms and Barolo sauce
'82 Barolo, "La Serra di la Morra," Voerzio

Frozen hazelnut mousse & Kate's lace cookies

NEW YEAR'S EVE ★ 1986

MENU BY WILL POWERS

PEAR AND HAZELNUT TART

There are several thousand varieties of pears, but my choice for this tart are ripe Winter Nelis, Bartlett, Anjou, or French butter pears. Winter Nelis is small and rough and slightly spicy. Bartlett and Anjou are European varieties cultivated in America since colonial times and justly popular for their flesh, their musk, and their distinct flavors. You can prepare this tart early in the day and rewarm it just before serving.

Sweet tart dough (page 53)

PUDDING

1/2 cup hazelnuts

1/2 cup sugar

1/2 cup sweet, unsalted butter, at room temperature

3 eggs

1 teaspoon vanilla extract

1 tablespoon amaretto liqueur

1/2 cup all-purpose flour

1/2 teaspoon baking powder

2 or 3 medium-ripe pears, peeled, sliced, and sprinkled with freshly squeezed lemon juice and sugar

Sugar for sprinkling

Whipped cream

Roll the tart dough out 1/4 inch thick and line a 9-inch tart shell. Refrigerate.

Preheat the oven to 350°. Toast the hazelnuts on a baking sheet for 10 to 15 minutes, stirring occasionally until lightly browned. Cool thoroughly before grinding. Grind the toasted hazelnuts with 2 tablespoons of the sugar to a fine meal. The sugar will absorb some of the oil from the hazelnuts. Set aside.

Preheat the oven to 350°. In the bowl of an electric mixer fitted with the paddle attachment, beat the butter with the remaining 6 tablespoons sugar until light and fluffy. Beat in the eggs, vanilla, and amaretto. Beat in the ground hazelnuts. Sift the flour with the baking powder, and then mix it into the nut mixture until well blended. Spread the filling into the tart shell. Arrange the pear slices, closely spaced, filling the shell to the top. Sprinkle with more sugar and bake for 40 to 45 minutes, or until the filling is cakelike and fluffy. Let cool and serve with whipped cream.

MAKES ONE 9-INCH TART

227

PERSIMMON STEAMED PUDDING

Steamed puddings are ancient. Before refrigeration and sophisticated chemicals, they were a device for creating something sweet and dense and long-keeping in the summer that could be warmed and served in the winter. Persimmons are highly decorative on the tree and turn sweet and soft with the first frost. The sight of the first ripe persimmons is exciting: I know it's time to make this personal favorite dessert. Steamed pudding molds are available from cookware stores, or seek them out in antique or secondhand stores. They are molds with tightly fitting lids, often with little clamps to hold them in place. You will need very ripe persimmons for this pudding. I start by ripening persimmons in late October and then puréeing and freezing the purée for use during December.

PUDDING

1¹/₂ cups all-purpose flour

¹/₂ teaspoon ground cinnamon

¹/₄ teaspoon ground nutmeg

1 tablespoon baking soda

2 cups persimmon purée

2 tablespoons freshly squeezed lemon juice

2 tablespoons good brandy

2 tablespoons vanilla extract

1 cup sweet, unsalted butter

1¹/₂ cups sugar

2 eggs

1 cup lightly toasted sliced almonds

1 cup dried currants

HARD SAUCE

¹/₂ cup sweet, unsalted butter, at room temperature

1 pound powdered sugar

2 teaspoons freshly squeezed lemon juice

¹/₄ cup brandy

TO PREPARE THE PUDDING:

Sift the flour with the spices and baking soda. Set aside. Mix the persimmon purée with the lemon juice, brandy, and vanilla. In the bowl of an electric mixer fitted with the paddle attachment, beat the butter with the sugar until light and fluffy. Beat in the eggs, one at a time, scraping the sides and bottom of the bowl after each addition to incorporate the eggs completely. Alternately mix in the flour and persimmon mixtures. Mix in the nuts and currants. Pour into a well-oiled 6- or 8-inch mold.

TO STEAM THE PUDDING:

You will need a large pot with a tight-fitting lid. The pot needs to be tall and wide enough for there to be ample space around the mold and space between the lid and the top of the mold. You will need some type of ring (such as a well-washed tuna can with both ends cut out or a cookie cutter) to set the mold on while it is steaming to keep it above the water. Let the pudding steam, checking every 15 minutes to see if the pot needs water and adding more hot water as needed. Do not let the pot boil dry. Steam the pudding for about 2 hours in all. It is done when a knife inserted into the center comes out clean. Unmold the pudding while it is still warm.

TO PREPARE THE HARD SAUCE:

Beat the butter with the powdered sugar until light and fluffy. Add the lemon juice and brandy and mix well. Do not refrigerate, or the sauce will firm up and not be a sauce.

TO SERVE:

Slice the pudding and serve it warm with the hard sauce.

SERVES 12

229

CHOCOLATE MASCARPONE TORTE

When life requires, as it sometimes will, a gratifying chocolate fix, this is the answer. The combination of creamy mascarpone and bitter chocolate is heavenly. This cake bakes up slightly soft, so be very careful not to overbake it. Mascarpone is a soft Italian cream cheese that has been elevated to cult status by the introduction and popularity of tiramisù. It is available in many specialty food stores.

2 ounces unsweetened chocolate

1/4 cup sweet, unsalted butter

2 whole eggs

1 cup sugar

Pinch of salt

3/4 cup all-purpose flour

1/4 teaspoon salt

2 egg yolks

1 cup mascarpone cheese

2 teaspoons vanilla extract

Whipped cream or ice cream

Preheat the oven to 350°. In the top of a double boiler, melt the chocolate with the butter over simmering water. Beat the whole eggs with 3/4 cup of the sugar and the salt until light and fluffy. Fold in the chocolate, and then fold in the flour. Pour into a buttered 10-inch springform pan.

Mix the yolks with the mascarpone, vanilla, and the remaining 1/4 cup sugar. Pour this mixture over the chocolate. With a blunt knife, swirl the two together. Bake for 45 minutes. The top should be crusty but the batter still soft. Let cool on a rack. Run a knife around the edge before releasing the rim. Remove the sides of the pan and place the cake on a serving plate. Serve with whipped cream.

MAKES ONE 10-INCH CAKE

I remember no New Year's Eve so remarkable. BayWolf was not over-elaborate, merely perfect, elegant, deliquescent. That amazing combination of real and faux white and silver lilies at the entrance made it seem as though all flowers are handmade. Michael catered with extraordinary graciousness to [my companion] David's unusual food preferences. The food was superb, the evening merry and blissful. The staff was amused and attentive. The champagne was exactly the required effervescence. It was exactly the right pitch of exquisitely unreal. It was a dream to be there, in our own private restaurant, with just these people.

Each of us had watched some moment of Millennium cover-

GRAPEFRUIT CAMPARI SORBET

Campari is an Italian bitters with a pungent flavor distilled from a blend of herbs and spirits, its exact ingredients a closely guarded secret. Its role in this sorbet is to sharpen and enhance the flavor of the grapefruit and add its own distinct edge to the mix.

4 cups freshly squeezed grapefruit juice, strained

3/4 cup sugar

1 cup Campari

Mix well and freeze in an ice cream maker according to the manufacturer's instructions.

MAKES 2 QUARTS

age and described it with something like awe—the fireworks everywhere, the first sunrise in New Zealand, the sense of camaraderie and calm. I remember no similar degree of merriment (even in this crowd of lusty decadents). It remains vivid and, shall we say, a peak experience.

I realize I brought a very large subtext to it—I loved the idea of the turn of the century, I felt amazed and revitalized by it, I felt as if we all had that moment you're supposed to have when you're dying where your whole life flashes before you except that, in this event, the century was doing the flashing and, beyond it, the Millennium. Weird milestones move me and I was moved to mark this one in just this way.

I love that BayWolf allows itself to be an extension of little bands of revelers such as ours and allows the celebrants to believe that "we few, we happy few, we band of brothers" encompasses not just these beloved friends (with whom we've enjoyed many hours of excess over the years) but everyone present: Jacinta or Jessica or a Michael at the door, every individual on the wait staff, and all the heroes in the kitchen.

—ADELE CRADY, *Twenty-five-year patron and coauthor*

231

INDEX

BayWolf

September 18, 19, 20, and 21, 2000

Appetizers

September tomato soup with little meatballs, shell beans, and basil

Jambon persillé: ham in aspic with grilled bread, housemade mustard, and pickles

Gizzards and grapes: double duck plate with duck confit, smoked duck breast, and duck liver crostini

Shrimp-stuffed calamari with saffron beurre blanc

Green and red Caesar salad

Entrées

Duck confit ravioli with porcini mushrooms, arugula, and Reggiano cheese

Crispy halibut with roasted potatoes and salsa verde

Coq au vin: chicken braised in red wine with chanterelles, bacon, and turnips

Liberty Ranch duck with Pinot Noir sauce, berries, and double corn cake

Grilled lamb chops with cabbage bundle and spicy greens

Desserts

Summer's end fresh berry pudding

Chocolate in a cloud with crème anglaise and cocoa sauce

Last Chance peach galette with champagne sabayon

Black raspberry sorbet with almond macaroon

Wines   Au Bon Climat Bay Wolf 25th Anniversary Pinot Noir,
Qupé Anniversary Blend Mourvèdre-Syrah, Billecart-Salmon Birthday Champagne
Special thanks to Jim Clendenen, Bob Lindquist, Alan Sobczak

CHEF DE CUISINE: Louis Le Gassic
DESSERTS: Earl Darny
Also in the kitchen: Lauren Lyle and Nathan Peterson

Since 1975

January: The Wolf at the Door

February: Venice and Mardi Gras

March: Spring in Lyon

April: In Paris

May: When Northern Italy Took Hold

June: Wine Matters